I GOT MINE

Also by John Nichols

Fiction

The Sterile Cuckoo
The Wizard of Loneliness
The Milagro Beanfield War
The Magic Journey
A Ghost in the Music
The Nirvana Blues
American Blood
Conjugal Bliss
An Elegy for September
The Voice of the Butterfly
The Empanada Brotherhood
On Top of Spoon Mountain
The Annual Big Arsenic Fishing Contest!

Nonfiction

If Mountains Die (with William Davis)
The Last Beautiful Days of Autumn
On the Mesa
A Fragile Beauty
The Sky's the Limit
Keep It Simple
Dancing on the Stones
An American Child Supreme
My Heart Belongs to Nature
Goodbye, Monique

I GOT MINE

Confessions of a Midlist Writer

JOHN NICHOLS

HIGH ROAD BOOKS | ALBUQUERQUE

HIGH
ROAD

High Road Books is an imprint of the University of New Mexico Press

ISBN 978-0-8263-6379-4 (cloth)
ISBN 978-0-8263-6380-0 (electronic)

Library of Congress Catalog-in-Publication data is on file with the Library of Congress

Founded in 1889, the University of New Mexico sits on the traditional homelands of the Pueblo of Sandia. The original peoples of New Mexico—Pueblo, Navajo, and Apache—since time immemorial have deep connections to the land and have made significant contributions to the broader community statewide. We honor the land itself and those who remain stewards of this land throughout the generations and also acknowledge our committed relationship to Indigenous peoples. We gratefully recognize our history.

Cover illustration courtesy of John Nichols
Designed by Felicia Cedillos
Composed in Adobe Caslon Pro 10/14.25

To John Randall and Beth Silbergleit for all the love and
help they have given to me and many other writers over the years.
Mil gracias, también, to Dennis Trujillo.
And let's not forget Em Hall and Jim Bensfield: they saved my life.

I went to a crap game the other night,
It certainly was against my will.
I lost all the money I had
Except a greenback dollar bill.
A forty-dollar bet was lyin' on the floor
And my buddy's point was nine;
Then the police broke down the door—
But I got mine.

Yeah, I got mine, brother, I got mine.
I grabbed all the money, put it into my pocket,
And out the back door I went flyin'.
Ever since that big crap game
I've been dining on chicken and wine.
I'm a leader in high society, boys—
Ever since I got mine.

—VERSION INSPIRED BY PINK ANDERSON, "I GOT MINE"

Yours truly in Barcelona, Spain, displaying my James Dean persona. Photographer unknown. Courtesy of John Nichols.

PART I

1

WHEN I GRADUATED from Hamilton College in June 1962 and was declared 4-F by the army because of my torn ACLs from playing varsity ice hockey, I headed overseas to live in Barcelona with my French grandmother, Maggie Robert Le Braz (you pronounce Robert, "Row-bear"). All my French family and relatives called her "Mamita." A large and imperious woman with tinted blue hair, she was often referred to as the "Elsa Maxwell of Barcelona." Maxwell was a gossip columnist and a high-society party animal who arranged big shindigs for the rich and famous. My plan was to teach English as a second language at the American Institute, learn Spanish and French myself, and hopefully write a novel that could be published and launch me on a career that would make Hemingway groupies jealous.

In Mamita's apartment guest room I worked every night until dawn on my novel, *The Sterile Cuckoo*. For me, the free room and board for twelve months was precious.

But I was twenty-two, Mamita was sixty-nine, and we had very different agendas. Too, we scarcely knew each other because my stepmother, Brownie Gleason, who was deeply jealous of Monique and my French roots, had angrily discouraged Mamita's visits when she came to America during my childhood. Monique, my birth mother, died at age twenty-seven when I was only two, on August 4, 1942. She and Pop were married for just four years. When Brownie took me over at age five she successfully erased Monique from my life. Dad divorced Brownie when I was fifteen.

Despite my Loomis prep school and Hamilton College educations I was determined *not* to become a doctor, a lawyer, a stock broker, an ad man, an investment banker, a realtor, a millionaire, or a pipe-smoking Harvard professor with leather patches on the elbows of his sport coats. I wanted to be either a novelist, a cartoonist (like Chester Gould who drew *Dick Tracy*), or a rock 'n' roller (like Little Richard). And it was clear to me I'd better get cracking if I hoped to escape a boring middle-class life of being trapped by a successful dead-end job when I returned to America.

But obviously the clock was ticking.

Things turned out painfully for Mamita and me. She yearned to civilize yours truly by hosting cocktail parties and petite dinners for me, soirées during which she insisted I speak my limited Spanish or French with the distinguished guests. Little Lord Fauntleroy. Too bad I hated chatting up marquesas, ambassadors, fops, and rich dilettantes in any language. That said, Mamita "encouraged" me to attend an entire season of operas at Barcelona's famous Liceo, where I was obliged to wear a tuxedo and sip champagne *delicias* during the intermissions with all her aristocratic cronies who had no problem with Generalísimo Franco, the fascist dictator of Spain. Mamita's desire to make me a social butterfly was aggravating to the max. In turn she was hard-pressed to deal with my American proletariat vulgarity. I was her Eliza Doolittle and she my Henry Higgins. The only difference is, I wouldn't budge an inch. And I never fell in love with her.

Mamita insisted we dine together each evening in her Barcelona apartment. It was a price I had to pay, yet those meals were excruciating ordeals. The small circular table in her dining area sported candles, wine goblets, and a large silvery globe centerpiece that reflected our weirdly oval faces with Gargantuan bulbous noses. The conscientious maid, Saluita, waited on us, hovering in the kitchen, eager to come offer more food from a serving dish whenever Mamita rang her little bell. I ate shriveled over, embarrassed, suicidal. I couldn't stand having a servant instead of doing things myself. I abhorred being aware of Saluita waiting nearby on pins and needles for the bell to tinkle while I choked down my delicious victuals and spoke baby-talk French with Mamita. I felt like a pampered moron trapped in a Luis Buñuel film like *The Discreet Charm of the Bourgeoisie* (which would not be released for another decade).

To make matters worse that year, I made my own bed, thus insulting Saluita. I polished my own shoes, further demeaning her. I fetched milk from the refrigerator and created my own sandwiches, thereby affronting the cook, Iréné. This was scandalous behavior but I didn't care. Instinctively, I despised being a member of the upper class and proved it by offending everyone around me who was locked into the caste system. Though I wasn't overtly "political," I hated being waited upon; it felt so *wrong*. I was a young, slim, good-looking American boy, but when I confronted myself in the mirror all I could see was a fat capitalist pig smoking a cigar and cackling sadistically while crushing tiny third-world people like hapless bedbugs under his thumb.

2

FOR TEN MONTHS, like a man possessed, I chain-smoked cheap
Spanish black-tobacco cigarettes called *Celtas* from midnight to
7:00 a.m. and listened to three LP records, repeatedly, every night, all night
long. One featured Pablo Casals, another the Brandenburg Concertos, a third
Chopin piano preludes. Who knows why a philistine like me enjoyed those
three. Too, I drank champagne. Mamita always kept a half dozen bottles on ice,
so I helped myself and some nights typed on my novel snockered to the gills.

Parts of the story were sketched out even before I graduated college. My
imaginative and self-destructive heroine, Pookie Adams, narrated the saga of
her royally fucked-up life. Every sentence she spoke was outrageously clever
and sardonically funny. I was mixing *Catcher in the Rye* with Damon Runyon's
gangsters from *Guys and Dolls* and hefty swaths of Max Shulman's novels *Barefoot Boy with Cheek* and *Rally Round the Flag, Boys!* You can look them up.
Pookie's Indiana childhood was bizarre, her parents total nudniks. Her college
romance with a nerd called Jerry Payne had been ridiculous, boring, paralyzing.
After college she moved to New York City, indulged in several whacky affairs,
then died dramatically of early-onset breast cancer, awash in dyspeptic soliloquies.

Throughout another version Pookie occupied a New York barstool getting
drunk and telling her sad tale to a cat squatting on the polished surface beside
her lineup of empty whiskey sour glasses and a half-consumed screwdriver. She
used witty spoonerisms and couldn't stand not being cute, outrageous, sarcastic,
overbearing, and melodramatic, a farcical Queen Lear in pigtails using invented
words like "bigluvulating" and writing nonsense poetry à la Lewis Carroll's
Jabberwocky.

Poor Mamita. Poor Johnny. For years Mamita had dreamed of teaching me
her world and Monique's, the sophisticated culture of Europe. Good luck with
that. I was not at all what she'd yearned for and envisioned during our two
decades apart following Monique's death. I was a surly American cretin, enam-
ored of Fats Domino and Chuck Berry, who crouched like a deformed

troglodyte in her house and typed all night, crashed at dawn, slept most of the day, then went to work teaching ESL, came home for our grim supper ritual, and evaporated into his writing cave again.

I doubt my domineering and bewildered grandmother had an inkling of how scared I was of the persona she wanted me to adopt.

———

At the end of May 1963 I was just as glad to escape Barcelona as Mamita was happy to see me go. We had said almost nothing about Monique. I don't know why Mamita did not open that conversation, nor did she ever mention her other daughter, Ninon, dead at age thirty, or her husband, Marius Robert, who succumbed to TB at fifty-one. Nor do I recall any photographs of my mom or Ninon or Marius on the walls of her apartment, although it's true I never once entered Mamita's bedroom. And possibly I was simply oblivious, blinded as a kid by my jealous stepmother's impossible-to-overcome brainwashing.

A 1989 letter to me from Dad said, "I did not overcome my deep attachment and affection for Monique, which created enormous jealousy on the part of Brownie. . . . a jealousy which was taken out on you, the son of my true love."

And years later Pop wrote that during the time he and Brownie were married he didn't know "whether to commit suicide or murder her."

But I'm not gonna go there with this memoir.

3

IN NEW YORK I found a five-floor walk-up apartment for $42.50 a month on the corner of West Broadway and Prince Street a block south of Houston, an Italian neighborhood in lower Manhattan. There I became a one-man writing factory, working on five novels at once. *The Wind Heart* (my North Shore, Long Island Gold Coast, Scott Fitzgerald tragedy); *"Hey!" and "Boo!" and "Bang!"* (about the final week of a homeless Bowery bum who collects cardboard in a rusty shopping cart); *The Wizard of Loneliness* (in which a bitter, orphaned boy spends the last year of World War II with his grandparents in upstate Vermont); *Autumn Beige* (a novel where the narrator accidentally shoots his brother while duck hunting); and *The Sterile Cuckoo*. Most advanced (*I* felt) was *The Sterile Cuckoo*. After failing to get an agent, I decided, "So what, I'll sell it myself." And I began making rounds.

The odds against me were a million to one, but so what?

Carrying the manuscript uptown, I laid it on the front desk at Random House. Then a bus carried me upstate to my best pal Alan Howard's Hamilton graduation. During my visit an English professor friend, George Nesbitt, asked for a copy of the *Cuckoo* manuscript. I gave him one, returned to New York, received my rejection from Random House, and switched the novel to Viking. In three weeks *they* rejected it. So I moved Pookie Adams over to Knopf, where she was shot down immediately. Next stop? Farrar, Straus and Giroux.

The thing is, back in 1963 publishers hired young lackeys who actually scanned the slush piles. Sometimes those interns even wrote comments on the SASE postcards I included asking them to get in touch so I could personally retrieve my opus. COD repatriation of the novel would have busted me. I could not afford a telephone. My tub was in the kitchen. There weren't any sheets on the bed, only a grungy sleeping bag. And the radiators didn't work, or else they hissed so loudly I couldn't sleep.

Naturally, free at last, I'd never been happier.

———

After each rejection I rewrote the book, often in a week, staying awake for thirty hours typing madly on my little Hermes Rocket, the original pea-green disposable typewriter. Forty bucks a pop. I had more energy than thirty pounds of cocaine. For recreation I played my guitar or pitched a tennis ball against a loading dock on the east side of West Broadway when the storage lofts shut down after 5:00 p.m. On occasion I earned a few bucks at a nearby labor pool unloading trucks. Or I performed folksong gigs at coffee houses on Bleecker and MacDougal. The Café Wha? The Id. The Café Why Not? A few times I teamed up with Phil Ochs, exchanging sets. We dragged on the sidewalk, soliciting crowds while the other guy performed inside. Phil had talent, was political, became famous, then hung himself at age thirty-five.

I offered Spanish songs like "Malagueña Salerosa," "Clavelitos," and "El Preso Numero Nueve." Also blues tunes: "Hollywood Bed," "She Changed the Lock on her Door," and "Strange Fruit." Then "Frankie and Johnny," "Tom Dooley," and "Downtown Strutters Ball." I was a big fan of Oscar Brand's bawdy songs, especially "Seven Old Ladies Locked in a Lavatory," and the satirical rants of Tom Lehrer, most notably "Be Prepared" and "The Old Dope Peddler." Brand and Lehrer were "right up my alley." They spoke to my "soul." I loved violating "good taste."

We passed a basket after each set, but I never scored more than two bucks if I was lucky. Those days Bob Dylan, Dave Van Ronk, and Peter, Paul, and Mary were finding their sea legs, opening the doors to stardom. Myself, I lasted four months in the game, the most cutthroat scam on earth. My farewell song was "Goodnight, Irene," then I bolted in another direction after crossing "rock 'n' roll musician" off my list.

Instead, I preferred hanging out at a tiny empanada stand on MacDougal Street between the Hip Bagel and Figaro's Café, almost at the intersection of MacDougal and Bleecker streets. The chubby kiosk owner, Áureo Roldán, became a good friend. I loved talking Spanish with him and Latin hangers-on like Horacio Porta, who was obtaining a math PhD at NYU; handsome Gino, who sometimes ran the joint for Roldán; a bubbly Chilean named Andrés Rieloff; and a slew of flirtatious señoritas who materialized whenever Gino held court. I had no money for restaurants or bars. Roldán played Carlos Gardel tangos on a little phonograph. Three people could fit inside the kiosk at a standup counter. Otherwise, we mingled on the sidewalk or sat on the fenders of parked cars drinking coffee or mate and, if we were flush, noshing on a delicious empanada. You bit off one end and shook in the tabasco sauce. Ambrosia!

For two years my connection to Spanish-speaking culture made me feel happy and alive. Those people were my friends and my social life when I was broke and writing my ass off around the clock on five different novels. They made me laugh. I was their pet gringo.

4

MY HAMILTON ENGLISH prof, George Nesbitt, pulled a fast one. He never read *The Sterile Cuckoo*, instead giving the manuscript to Max Wylie, a Hamilton grad, novelist, and ad executive who would soon create *The Flying Nun*, a show that propelled Sally Field into her movie career. During the summer of 1963 Max sent me a telegram, calling me up to his midtown Manhattan office where he handed over a typed, four-page critique of *The Sterile Cuckoo* that changed my life.

Max had nothing positive to say about the novel. It was a mess. "Book has no plan and no order, so criticism of same cannot have much." I was clueless about a woman's perspective, therefore nothing Pookie said rang true. I'd have more luck making Jerry Payne the narrator. My story had no plot and no control; it was a random hodgepodge of witty babble, hence the reader had no sense of what I might be trying to do. I employed embarrassing cleverness simply for the sake of calling attention to my precocious (puerile) imagination. "What kind of story are you going after? You, as author, have not resolved this. So there cannot be any resolution for reader either and no satisfaction, for him, in his exploration of the girl."

Yet everything Max said indicated *he* had taken the manuscript seriously enough to give it an honest criticism. His *professional* opinion. Which I realized instantly was a gold mine capable of guiding me to the land of fame, fortune, and a glamor girl on my arm. I was flattered that he'd taken the time.

My novel turned on a dime. So long Pookie Adams as narrator, welcome Jerry Payne. That was a start. And perhaps five drafts later the publisher David McKay expressed interest in *The Sterile Cuckoo*. By then it was a novella, which they wouldn't publish unless I doubled the length. Could I do that? Are you kidding? It took me about forty-eight hours. In those days I was an F5 literary tornado. A young editor at McKay, Phyllis Grann, helped with a list of suggestions.

Then suddenly they *bought* my book. It had been sold "over the transom," without an agent, which even back then was rare. And get this: I had been starving in a cold-water New York garret for only *eight months* before I hit pay dirt! I was twenty-three years old, still a virgin, and barely had to shave.

McKay drew up a check for five hundred dollars. Phyllis Grann led me downstairs to obtain cash at their bank because I did not have my own account, being still so poor I operated on a cash-only basis. I stared at the five hundred bucks a teller handed over until Phyllis snapped her fingers in front of my nose, waking me up.

———

Max Wylie's generosity in 1963 enabled me to keep rewriting *The Sterile Cuckoo* and another novel, *The Wizard of Loneliness*, eventually publishing them both. I owe Max deeply for the start of my career. Later that year this generous man's twenty-one-year-old daughter, Janice, was horribly murdered in her uptown apartment along with her roommate, Emily Hoffert. Those were called "The Career Girl Murders." Five years later Max's wife, Isabel, died of cancer, and two years after that his other daughter, Pamela, succumbed to the Asian flu. On September 22, 1975, Max shot himself in a Fredricksburg, Virginia, motel room. He was seventy-one years old.

I remember him with more gratitude than you could possibly imagine.

5

WHEN DAVID MCKAY coughed up their five-hundred-dollar *Cuckoo* advance, I jumped on a bus for Guatemala City to visit my friend, Alan Howard. He was on a Fulbright studying third-world illiteracy. His friendship and political ideology would change my life. In the spring of 1964 there were many drunken Quiche Maya men on market day in Chichicastenango. I was staying a few days with Alan's friend, Diana Oughton, a VISA program volunteer for the Quakers. Diana and I drove around in a large car rented by her visiting parents. Hitchhiking Indians flagged us down for rides, then tried to hand Diana payment for the lift. She said, "No, no, no," and their insistence made her cry. They were so *poor*. These people had filarial worms in their eyeballs, no teeth, bare feet. Some deliberately maimed themselves to beg. The dictatorship, first installed with United States CIA help in 1954, was committing genocide against its own population. American corporations owned much of the country: the railroads, telecommunications, half the arable land. Our government paid death squads to halt union organizing on United Fruit's banana plantations. Don't mess with "the Octopus." The American embassy had high walls topped by broken glass and surrounded by barbed wire. I think I even remember a machine-gun nest. Things were immeasurably worse here than in Franco's Spain.

Hours were spent rewriting my second novel, *The Wizard of Loneliness*. Smoke rose from volcanoes north of Guatemala City. Assault-weapon bullets smashed the windows and some bottles behind the bar of our favorite cantina near Alan's apartment. Two federal judges at a bus stop on the corner died in that fusillade from the FAR. Fuerzas Armadas Rebeldes. Three rebel leaders stood out in the country: Yon Sosa, Luis Turcios Lima, and César Montes. Incredibly, Montes is still alive.

After cheering for Marlon Brando in *One-Eyed Jacks* I pranced merrily across Guatemala City, deserted because it was after curfew. On every corner stood a soldier with a rifle, but nobody shot me. I guess I was just another Yankee tourist and they would've caught hell from US embassy personnel who were

Diana Oughton and me in Chichicastenango, Guatemala, spring 1964. Photo by Tim Weld. Courtesy of John Nichols.

supporting the new government (dictatorship!) of Enrique Peralta Azurdia, our current puppet. After all, 77 percent of Guatemalan exports went to the United States.

My ignorance was astounding.

———

Who knows why I read Émile Zola's novel *Germinal* while visiting Guatemala. Did I select it from Alan Howard's library? Or bring it with me from New York? On the sunny roof of my friend's apartment building I lolled for hours absorbing the book. My romantic Latin American vacation was veering astray. *Germinal* is a big novel about the class struggle between crucified French coal miners and the vicious bourgeoisie who run their "pit." Eventually there's a strike, and the enraged miners march on their oppressors who've hired Belgian soldiers to put down the rebellion. When the cursing proles start pelting the soldiers with bricks, the Belgians open fire, slaughtering many workers. That ends the insurrection. Afterward, defeated miners sabotage their mine, which collapses in a symbolic catastrophe, filling the pit with water and killing a few more hapless drones. Though *Germinal* is about as funny as terminal cancer, reading it at age twenty-three made a huge impression. The author's harrowing descriptions of hopeless poverty were exhausting. A similar poverty surrounded me in Guatemala.

Alan and I talked about that a lot. His insights were far deeper than mine. Though my year in Spain should have warned me, Guatemala was a whole different ball of wax.

———

One night in Guatemala City I picked up a hooker at a café and returned to the apartment, where we drank half a bottle of Indita and smoked a doobie. My girl led me into the bedroom. She was chubby and very cheerful. I was so drunk I don't even recall having an orgasm. That's when I finally "lost my virginity" at age twenty-three. After we showered together, she left. All the quetzals had been stolen from my wallet, and I returned to New York with crabs.

Around the corner from Alan's apartment was a red-light street where you could pay women fifty cents and fuck them on a cot in what amounted to a horse stall. I tried that just once, came up impotent, and stumbled out ashamed after accidentally kicking over a bucket of douche water. When cognition finally pierced my ivory dome I realized: *How oblivious am I?* Maybe *Germinal* had taken a hammer to my contradictions. Certainly the misery of Guatemala's downtrodden had touched my conscience more than Spain's inequalities had. There were no *Brandenburg Concertos* or champagne bottles in a refrigerator. Upon leaving the country I felt guilty for my behavior, and for belonging to a nation, a culture, and a people who had created and now controlled that enslaved Central American satrapy.

My life was about to change. A book-length essay I published in 2001 discusses that process. It's called *An American Child Supreme*. When, in 1964, I boarded a bus in Guatemala City headed for San Diego, in *many* different ways I was no longer a virgin. Not to be overly melodramatic, but it's as if I had glimpsed a picture of Dorian Gray rotting in the American attic.

About to joyously publish my first novel, I was actually cruising for a bruising.

———

Six months later I performed my first anti–Vietnam War political action. On election day of 1964 I was a poll watcher in a barber shop for Mel Dubin, a Coney Island peace candidate. Elderly mafioso types kept leading little old ladies and little old men into the voting booths and pulling the levers for them. When I protested to an obese gendarme about the blatant electioneering, he ordered me to go sit in a fucking chair and shut the fuck up or he'd clap on the iron cufflinks and fucking arrest me. Point taken. I went and sat down and kept my fucking mouth shut, starting to realize that the rest of my fucking life was *not* going to be a fucking cakewalk.

6

ON FRIDAY, JANUARY 15, 1965, *The Sterile Cuckoo* was officially published. The *New York Times* flattered me that day, publishing a review by their distinguished literary critic, Eliot Fremont-Smith.

On Thursday night I gathered to celebrate with pals at the empanada kiosk. We waited for trucks to drop off bundles of tomorrow's *Times* at a Sixth Avenue newsstand. I rushed back with the newspaper, overcome with excitement. Áureo Roldán opened a bottle of champagne and passed around little *dulce de leche* paper cups filled with bubbly. I began reading and translating the review to my eager Argentine brethren who gathered around like shiny kids eager to welcome my success into their world.

That enthusiasm lasted for twenty seconds.

Fremont-Smith began by calling *The Sterile Cuckoo* "a novel of unlikely adolescent jabbering." He mocked almost every word out of Pookie Adams' mouth. "At times she does play a kind of nutty Franny to Jerry's Holden Caulfield—the influence of J. D. Salinger is everywhere apparent (though one could also say she plays a grown-up Lucy to Jerry's Charlie Brown)—and if this intrigues, one may overlook the more psychotic aspects of her speech and life. But to get around the dullness is something else."

Attempting to translate this bloodletting for my expectant friends was difficult. I did not have the Spanish skills to describe the sophisticated venom ripping my novel to shreds. In the end, everybody signed the champagne bottle label—*Felicidades, Juanito!*—after which, devastated, I glumly trundled home and spent the rest of the night typing a poison-pen letter to Eliot Fremont-Smith, which I had the smarts never to send. (Instinctively I must have understood: "Never burn your bridges, Johnny, you might need them later on.") My rant was in fable form and titled, "Hunting the *New York Times* Book Critic." At the end I brought my foot down upon the "conscience" of Fremont-Smith, "grinding the small weaselly thing into the turf from whence it came."

So began my professional career. And reactions to it haven't changed all that much over the last fifty-five years.

At a 1965 bash in Frank Taylor's Manhattan apartment I shook hands with Ralph Ellison and chatted with Muriel Spark. Eliot Fremont-Smith was attending and warmly congratulated me on my success, though he did not elaborate. Frank Taylor, also a Hamilton graduate, was the head of Avon paperbacks, which had paid $37,500 for reprint rights to *The Sterile Cuckoo*. Half that sum was mine, minus the agent's 10 percent and taxes. A serious killing, and still the most money ever paid to me for reprint rights. Five years earlier, Frank had produced a troubled movie, *The Misfits*, starring Clark Gable, Marilyn Monroe, and Montgomery Clift. Written by Marilyn's hubby, Arthur Miller, it was the last movie for both Marilyn and Clark Gable.

When the paperback *Cuckoo* came out in 1966 I ventured one glimpse at the cover and fell over backward. Never had I been so caught by surprise and offended. In big, boldface, sans serif letters, the top third of the cover yelled: **When the All-American boy meets the New-American girl—ZOW—and then some!** Under that was my name, and, in red: **THE STERILE CUCKOO**.

Beneath the title was a sleazy, amateur painting of a gloomy, skinny, and naked girl covered with Band-Aids, including one barely hiding the nipple of her left breast. Behind her was a naked, blond-haired, lasciviously-grinning jock with a muscular arm reaching around the girl's shoulder, his big hand almost clutching her tit.

Yes, I'm a wanton guy, and Philip Roth, Henry Miller, and Eric Jong give me sexual thrills and make me laugh. But this was the creepiest thing I'd ever seen. How could my novel be sold like such a sordid piece of whale shit? I wrote a one-sentence enraged letter to Peter Mayer, who was either the head of production or the new publisher at Avon, to that effect. Peter apologized, and Avon's next edition had a respectable cover. But from that moment on I've insisted on cover (and often design) approval in every contract I signed with publishers. Over the years this has resulted in a few bitter conflicts, but I usually stick to my guns. And, occasionally, I've avoided more cover disasters—for example: Voluptuous naked women riding bareback on big white horses. Or openly racist stereotypes gracing the front jackets of novels featuring a host of Hispanic characters.

That first *Sterile Cuckoo* cover alerted me to what the consequences could be for such a generous purchase price of the reprint rights to a novel. When you

Avon Paperbacks first edition of *The Sterile Cuckoo* that really knocked me for a loop. Courtesy of John Nichols.

AVON / V2143 / 75¢

When the All-American boy meets the New-American girl ZOW—and then some!

John Nichols'
The Sterile Cuckoo

cash the checks, horns immediately sprout on your head and your feet transform themselves into tiny little hooves. From then on there's a perky miniature angel on your right shoulder and an aggressive little devil on your left shoulder, both of them chattering incessantly about how you should flaunt your integrity like a Goody Two-Shoes, or tie a small mirror onto your sneaker-laces in order to peep up the skirts of sexy women on Fifth Avenue gazing at the display windows of Bonwit Teller or Tiffany's.

7

1965 IS THE year I went from rags to riches, earning thirty-five thousand dollars before taxes. A lot of money. The *New Yorker* had said I was "clearly a comic writer with a natural and original gift." The *Denver Post* had dubbed my book "one of the best undergraduate novels to come along since F. Scott Fitzgerald wrote about Princeton." H. Allen Smith opined, "This 24-year-old lad will likely become the best comic-novel writer of his time." Good (and bad) reviews poured in from all over the country. Folks running the business explained that oodles of *ink* is all that really matters. They quoted Oscar Wilde: "The only thing worse than being talked about, is not being talked about." Today I reflect on all the nasty gossip, scandals, hooker hush money, pussy groping, and serial bankruptcies that won Donald Trump the White House.

Literary agents immediately dropped from the sky promising me the moon. The first one that landed at my feet, Perry Knowlton of Curtis Brown, shook my hand and we were off to the races. I opened a bank account. It was full of money. I owned a checkbook I could wield like Paladin's Colt Dragoon cavalry pistol. "*Have Moola—Will Spend.*"

I wanted so much to bask in the glory. I had yearned to be a "real writer" all my life, inspired since age five by Uncle Wiggly stories, the Palmer Cox brownies, the Oz books by L. Frank Baum, Howard Pease tramp steamer mystery novels starring Todd Moran, Booth Tarkington's mischievous *Penrod, Penrod and Sam,* and *Penrod Jashber* (with chapter illustrations by Gordon Grant). Pop had typed out for me my first "official" story at age eleven, *Case of the Unsolved Mystery.* My Loomis school notebooks from age fourteen to eighteen were crammed with hundreds of short stories, obnoxious poems, one-act plays, reams of random dialogue, sarcastic creations spoofing prep-school misadventures, and myriad cartoons of weird boys and girls almost always illegally smoking cigarettes. I still have access to those notebooks, although they are now housed by the Center for Southwest Research at the University of New Mexico's Zimmerman Library in Albuquerque. Some paragraphs are total nonsense. I copied the style of Damon Runyon stories like "Johnny One-Eye," "Little Miss

Marker," "The Brain Goes Home," and "The Snatching of Bookie Bob." Beginning sardonic diaries at age fifteen, I have kept them off and on throughout my lifetime. I wrote for the Loomis and Hamilton newspapers, published stuff in their literary magazines, and began writing novels, not for grades but for fun, when I hit seventeen. My Hamilton notebooks are a chaotic fanfaronade of prose bits and pieces that are filthy, stupid, sentimental, sensational, weird, maudlin, hilarious, or serious. Some had a social conscience, condemning Jim Crow in the South and the murder of Emmett Till. I wrote about an alcoholic semipro hockey player and about an old man and a boy in a penitentiary. Influences were Hemingway, Fitzgerald, Carson McCullers, *Look Homeward, Angel*, Dorothy Parker, Truman Capote. I hated George Eliot, Jane Austen, William Faulkner, Shakespeare. Fuck Henry James. Reading *The Old Man and the Sea* in *Life Magazine* at age twelve gave me an orgasm. Though I was a bad and unsophisticated writer, god how I *loved* it. Loved words, loved making stuff up, loved dialogue (especially irreverent slang), loved reading books, watching movies, drawing cartoons, *being an artist*.

And here I was, abruptly realizing my dream after Guatemala at age twenty-five and about to hit a wall that would almost destroy it.

———

In 1965 I married the initial, and enduring, great love of my life, Ruth "Ruby" Harding, who was still attending New York University on Washington Square three blocks north of us. We had moved to a slightly bigger apartment on Sullivan and Prince Streets, two blocks west of my previous West Broadway digs at double the rent. Ruby's major dental and orthodontist surgery cost a fortune but didn't make a dent. My friend Alan Howard, back from Guatemala, occupied my old apartment, and I gave him a hundred dollars a month while he worked on a novel. Then my ex-stepmother, Brownie, was nearly incarcerated for tax evasion, so I paid the IRS three grand to keep her free of the hoosegow. Practically the next day Brownie's older brother Fritz Gleason's wife, Aunt Stubby, pleaded with me to refund three thousand dollars she had fronted Brownie to cover my stepmother's "kited checks." *My* check was in the mail to Aunt Stubby immediately. Meanwhile, Dad and Brownie were at war because she hadn't used his alimony and child-support payments to cover my half-brothers Tim and Dave's school bills at Saint Albans prep in Washington,

DC. No problem. I ponied up the dough, which angered Pop, who claimed I was enabling Brownie to be an irresponsible spendthrift. No shit, Dick Tracy. However, I ordered Dad to go fly a fucking kite because he didn't know his financial ass from a hole in the ground, either. I was sick of my family's dysfunction. Notwithstanding, I forked over three thousand dollars for my brother Dave's first year at Dartmouth. Pop's mom, Cornelia Floyd Nichols (a.k.a. "Grammie"), reimbursed me twelve months later of her own volition. Why did I tolerate Brownie? Because I loved my little brothers—*her* kids—and did not want to lose them.

———

While these payouts were going down, my new agent, Perry Knowlton at Curtis Brown, switched my second novel, *The Wizard of Loneliness*, from David McKay to G. P. Putnam's Sons because Putnam's was offering a prize worth $210,000 to an "exceptional novel," and *The Wizard of Loneliness*, according to Putnam's, was sure to be "it." Despite personal misgivings I allowed Perry to desert McKay for Putnam's. I knew nothing about the publishing world, and he was "looking after me." Better follow his advice. Perry explained, "It's just business. McKay will wish you Godspeed." Prize money would come from Joseph E. Levine, a film producer; Fawcett's paperback reprint rights; *McCall's* magazine serial money; and the publisher itself.

The little devil on my left shoulder said, "Go for it! You're sure to win! You're gonna *be* somebody!"

The angel on my right shoulder was drowned out when Putnam's senior editor, Bill Targ, suggested I hire a lawyer to handle all the prize money. A *lawyer*? *Me*? I asked my rich uncle, David Weld, about that, and he hooked me up with his attorney, Edward Handelman. Who probably charged three hundred bucks an hour—I never dared ask. He garnered a small fortune to fill out my tax return . . . on which I owed the Feds a bundle of cash. I had not learned the habit of saving "business receipts," balancing a checkbook, or knowing when to say "when."

Lord help this babe in the woods. Uncle David was a millionaire investment banker for White, Weld & Company on Wall Street, married to my dad's sister, Mollie. One of my Weld first cousins, Bill, would become governor of Massachusetts. After Monique died I had lived with the Welds for three years until

Dad married Brownie and she took me up to her hometown of Montpelier, Vermont. Hiring Uncle David's mouthpiece was like engaging Aristotle Onassis' yacht for a journey between Manhattan and Staten Island! Dumbfounded at how fast all my money was disappearing, I shivered. Was I becoming Lemuel Pitkin, the rosy-cheeked, optimistic schlemiel in Nathaniel West's novel *A Cool Million*, just begging to be drawn, quartered, blinded, and bifurcated by cruel sadists in charge of the insane asylum?

The first (and last) ad for *The Wizard of Loneliness* in the *New York Times Book Review* in early 1966. The Photo of me, in Guatemala, is by my cousin Tim Weld.

PART II

8

ALMOST IMMEDIATELY A film producer, Alan Pakula, wanted to take an option on *The Sterile Cuckoo*. Curtis Brown—a literary agency—did not have a film division, so Perry Knowlton hooked me up with a West Coast agency, Adams, Ray & Rosenberg, who did the deal with Boardwalk Productions, Pakula's company, and returned it to Perry for my approval. My new lawyer, Ed Handelman, asked to review the contract. He made two dozen changes, "protecting my interests" and, coincidentally, demanding more money. I gave the papers to Perry, who said Handelman was off his rocker. But he passed on the changes to Adams, Ray & Rosenberg, who sat down with Boardwalk and Pakula, who rolled their eyes to heaven and made some minor changes that they returned to Perry, who in turn sent me the adjusted legal agreement to humor my lawyer. When I passed the deal on to Handelman, he ripped the whole thing asunder again. After I'd returned those changes to Perry he explained to me, as if teaching a retarded infant how to suck on a pacifier, that Handelman didn't know bananas about entertainment law, and Pakula would dump the project if I encouraged Perry to mail this new travesty on to Boardwalk Productions.

Totally befuddled, I called off Ed Handelman, and Perry completed the negotiation. Lee Rosenberg, my new Hollywood rep, told me that in movies aggravating delays were par for the course. "So don't sweat the small stuff."

———

On top of everything else, *The Sterile Cuckoo* was a Literary Guild Alternate. Its new film producer, Alan Pakula, had recently scored big with *To Kill a Mockingbird*. Alan hired me to write a screenplay, and next thing you know I was flying first class on United's "red carpet flight" to Los Angeles with stewardesses sheathed in colorful floor-length Hawaiian muumuus serving me champagne cocktails with orchids floating on top. I spent several days spit-balling with Alan and his director, Robert Mulligan, then returned to New York and began writing. To teach me the form, Alan suggested I buy Horton Foote's published screenplay of *To Kill a Mockingbird*, which I did. That was my only lesson ever on how to write for movies. I was like a Chihuahua puppy going into battle with a Yellowstone wolf pack.

My first day in Hollywood I met Natalie Wood and Robert Redford and received a jaywalking ticket for crossing Sunset Boulevard against the light. I threatened to tear up the ticket, but Pakula cried, "No, no, we'll pay it! Otherwise they'll put out a warrant for your arrest." I protested, "In New York nobody gives a damn about how, where, or when you cross the street. It's your life, good luck." Alan offered me a trenchant piece of advice: "You're not in Kansas anymore, Dorothy."

———

Pakula was among the nicest people I ever met. His intense interest in *The Sterile Cuckoo* was unnerving. We had widely rambling discussions on childhood, first love, families, and the complexity of Pookie Adams' personality. Alan, then in his late thirties, remembered his awkwardness with teenage heartthrobs. I talked about my puppy loves, my first sweethearts. It seemed Alan, Bob Mulligan, and I were conducting relativity sessions about searching for young love, childhood abuse, and alienation at school. Alan encouraged me to reminisce for long stretches while he took notes. I confessed I'd never had sex in college. Pookie Adams and her boyfriend, Jerry Payne, were two aspects of my own split personality. The outgoing, energetic, inventive, and comic self versus my repressed side, very shy and terrified of confrontation stemming from my fear of my stepmother, Brownie. *The Sterile Cuckoo* was a wholly invented story.

Alan asked, "What does the title mean?" Nobody understood it. I explained that European cuckoos are "brood parasites," laying their eggs in other bird's nests, having no part in raising their young. Occasionally American cuckoos act similarly (I hoped!). A "sterile cuckoo" would be a bird whose eggs don't hatch, or, if they do, their creator doesn't care for them. Pookie Adams goes out of her way to ingratiate herself, but she can't take responsibility for what follows. Despite her aggressive behavior, she kills the things she wants, running away from them.

Something like that. I was vague. You might say I had no idea what I was talking about.

As Alan and I palavered, Natalie Wood and Redford were making a film at Warner's that Alan produced and Mulligan directed: *Inside Daisy Clover*. It was Redford's first movie, and it bombed like Lyndon Johnson over North Vietnam. I met other actors on the picture, Ruth Gordon and Roddy McDowall. I think Natalie was having an affair with David Lange, the little brother of Hope Lange, who was married to Pakula. Nominated for a Supporting Actress Oscar in the 1957 film *Peyton Place*, Hope would also garner a couple of Grammies for her work in the 1968–1970 sitcom *The Ghost and Mrs. Muir*.

After I had dinner at Hope and Alan's house in Brentwood, Alan accompanied me on our walk down the gated-community drive flanked by palm trees to the security station where a taxi awaited. On our ramble I complained to Alan that my life was—abruptly—too complicated. At age twenty-six I had just walked the aisle, Ruby was pregnant, my first novel was popular, my second book might win the Putnam's Prize, New York publishing politics were very cynical, and I hated the Vietnam War, racism, Lyndon Johnson and Robert McNamara, and our exploitation of Guatemala, Nicaragua, Haiti. I was blowing my mind becoming politicized by reading books like *The Autobiography of Malcolm X*, Senator Fulbright's *The Arrogance of Power*, Seymour Melman's *Our Depleted Society*, William Appleman Williams' *The Tragedy of American Diplomacy*, and James Baldwin's *The Fire Next Time*. My pal Alan Howard had gifted me a copy of *The Rise of American Civilization* by Charles and Mary Beard. To boot, my extended family's finances were so fucked up I had to bail everyone out and was almost broke. And now he'd hired me (for peanuts!) to write a screenplay. Life had been simple. But these days I was a fish out of water, riddled with contradictions. It was too confusing.

Alan put his arm around my shoulders and advised me gently, "Get used to it, John, because that's the way the rest of your life will be."

9

I BEGAN TO truly understand the writing on the wall after the *Sterile Cuckoo* money vanished. Yes, Perry Knowlton had sold my second novel, *The Wizard of Loneliness*, to G. P. Putnam's Sons for $15,000 while the Putnam's Prize of $210,000 remained "in abeyance." Turns out a tough operative at McCall's, Geraldine Rhoads, didn't feel *Wizard* was "major" enough "to win the big money." But nobody ever told me that.

It's late 1967. My screenplay for *The Sterile Cuckoo* is sucking wind. I recall sitting at the Oyster Bar of the Plaza Hotel while Perry Knowlton and Putnam's editor, Bill Targ, faced each other doing a deal at our table. I think Perry was selling the memoirs of Svetlana Alliluyeva, Stalin's daughter. Maybe Bill was haggling for the book (*Twenty Letters to a Friend*) for Putnam's. I forget. Svetlana had recently defected to the United States. Targ and Perry were talking millions. Harpers eventually published the book, and I don't know if Perry was the guy who sold it to them. I suspect he and Targ were just blowing smoke at each other.

A couple of years earlier, when Bill had said I was going to win the $210,000 Putnam's Prize with *Wizard of Loneliness*, he was jerking me off so much I wouldn't have had to get laid for a year. In the end, *nobody* won the prize. It had been a ruse enticing authors from other publishers to head for Putnam's, who'd published *Wizard* in 1966 and instantly abandoned it about the same time Avon Books brought out *The Sterile Cuckoo* with its naked waif and leering blond groper on the cover.

Ostensibly, Perry and I were also at the Plaza's Oyster Bar to discuss, with Targ, Putnam's option to buy my small novel, *Autumn Beige*. Which I knew Putnam's would reject because of the large advance for my next book's option decreed in *The Wizard of Loneliness* contract. I wanted out of any further obligation to Putnam's. Bill Targ readily acquiesced, glad to see me vanish. I did not publish *Autumn Beige* elsewhere. Frankly, I was already sick of publishing.

I also let go Edward Handelman and never again hired another lawyer to handle money or my literary rights.

After the Putnam's Prize was exposed as a scam, *Esquire Magazine* had published a long article in February 1967, written by Saul Braun, titled, "I Mean, My God, If You Can't Produce *A Great American Novel For Two Hundred Thou, Pre-Sold To The Flicks, What The Hell Hope Is There For American Literature?*" I came across as a witless patsy in Braun's article, which exposed New York publishing as the most inept, cynical, fucked up, comically corrupt business on the planet.

I almost fired Perry Knowlton too. We agreed instead to tear up my contract with Curtis Brown and operate on a book-to-book basis, with me free to operate on my own if I desired. For my part I determined to grow up, read every contract carefully, discuss in detail each deal, and be sure to make clear *my* opinions and decisions. My career needed a *plan*. It needed an attitude. It needed *integrity*. Too bad it also needed somebody a lot more skilled than me in the art of the deal—the commie version.

I did exchange a few letters with Lee Rosenberg in LA because producer Norman Lear held a brief option on *The Wizard of Loneliness* (before he became famous for *All in the Family*). Then a husband-and-wife team, Alan and Judy Seeger, signed on for a year option. But they quickly faded into oblivion like the Pet Rock or Nervous Norvus.

———

Bill Targ and Putnam's (with a big nudge from Guatemala, the Vietnam War, and Ed Handelman) taught me lessons. Ever since I've been scared of "the money." I'm frightened to think how my life might have changed if I'd won that Putnam's Prize. In the real world it's so easy to be co-opted (by yourself) then become strangled by the contradictions. We all have the right to earn a modest living from our labor. But the inequalities on earth are unforgivable. And when the money is blown out of proportion you're up a moral shit creek minus a paddle. If you're learning to hate how global capitalism is destroying the planet, too much money is like the electric chair.

If I wanted to be a writer, I would live poor—whether I earned a hundred grand or just five thousand. Our economic ideology based on planned obsolescence and conspicuous consumption sucked. I would not buy things, or get in debt, or just *consume*. No matter what, I would write what I *wanted* to write, even if I starved to death. Publishers could take it or leave it. I would accept no other jobs, ever. If my wife and kids didn't like that existence they could lump it.

10

MEANWHILE, HERE ARE a few reviews of *The Wizard of Loneliness* (with a trigger warning up front). Some writers read their reviews, others can't be bothered. I've always cared. I was *curious*. Positive or negative reviews held equal weight, and occasionally I gleaned helpful tidbits from them. They were often entertaining, especially those that urged me to be tossed in jail for cutting down trees to make the pulp that created the pages of books filled with my hackneyed prose and nugatory sense of humor. The more scathing the better. They were fun. After *The Sterile Cuckoo* I never bitched at a critic nor toadied up to positive praise. For a couple of decades many newspapers paid attention to my output. I subscribed to Burrelle's Clipping Service Bureau and glued the reviews they sent into a scrapbook. For me, the reviews were like a Greek chorus that followed the release of any novel or memoir I managed to push over the finish line, which I considered to be a Library of Congress Cataloging-in-Publication data notice.

Hence, throughout this memoir I intend to add a Greek chorus of critical opinions that celebrated or decried the publication of whatever I'd been writing about. My UNM Press editor has urged me to keep that chorus down to a dull roar, the sort of cautionary advice that usually eggs me in the opposite direction. You (the reader) may skip over these roundups and motor on, keeping in mind that my self-indulgence is my problem (and the publisher's) but not yours.

So: concerning *The Wizard of Loneliness*, let's have fun by starting with *The New York Times*:

> For the first hundred pages, author John Nichols seems to be soaring on a unique blend of humor and sadness to a new dimension in American fiction. Then he goes haywire. Mr. Nichols is unable to control this melange of insights and problems. Consequently, the novel ravels away in a string of scenes, some brilliant, many repetitious. Finally comes the certain sign of lost control. Mr. Nichols starts to *tell* us what he is driving at. In his climactic (and badly coincidental) scene his grip on his style goes too. For dozens

of pages at a stretch, 'The Wizard of Loneliness' is pure pleasure to read. It is too bad the author did not hang on for another rewrite. He might have made that big bold machine he built in his first 100 pages go all the way.

The New York Herald Tribune:

The tone of his book is unexpectedly, even sentimentally old-fashioned. Perhaps he has written too fast. His descriptions of events beyond his obvious range are often perfunctory and his awareness of mature emotions is sketchy in the extreme.

Yet on the plus side:

Nothing of the tyro, except perhaps his energy, marks this new book: it might have been written by a good novelist of any age who was skilled at transmuting what he has known into what can be known by others and who happened to have a gift for comic invention and a sure feeling for the rhythm of events and discovery.

—*The Washington Post*

Richly comic, abounding in decency (in the largest and finest sense), never reluctant to wear its heart on its sleeve and proclaim its passions straightforwardly, this is a novel to be remembered and cherished.

—*The Cleveland Plain Dealer*

Not so fast, however. The *Boston Pilot* wrote, "This is not a warm nor an intense book." Said the *Bellows Falls* (Vermont) *News Review*, "His conception of life in a small town is unreal and contrived." According to the *Peninsula Herald* of Monterrey, California, "In theme the novel is trite, in treatment dull." And *The Miami News* cut right to the chase: "Mr. Nichols' first novel was 'The Sterile Cuckoo.' This, his second, might very well be called 'The Sterile Humbug.'"

On the other hand, *The Milwaukee Journal* chimed in with: "John Nichols has written a moving story about a boy regaining his childhood before it is irretrievably lost—and about a lot of grownups exploring loneliness and the limits and limitations of love. Read it. You will be very glad you did."

11

GIVEN MY GATHERING radical bent created mainly by growing opposition to the Vietnam War, what was the answer to my future career? As a youngster in my twenties I had limitless energy and wanted so much to be an "American writer." How could I abandon that ship? Momentarily I'll explain *The Empanada Brotherhood*, begun in 1965 and not published until 2007. But first: I commenced another novel when Ruby and I married in April 1965. We honeymooned at a cottage owned by my great aunt Susan Pulsifer near East Harpswell, Maine. Aunt Susan had an adopted son, David Pulsifer, a lobsterman out of Cundy's Harbor. A wild fellow, victim of two nervous breakdowns by age twenty-one, David invited Ruby and me to help him run a boatload of liquor to the dry island of Monhegan. We zigzagged between uninhabited islets to avoid the Coast Guard. Thirsty residents of Monhegan greeted us with open arms, waving fifty-dollar bills. Based on that experience I typed several drafts of a novella, *A Big Diaphanous Wild Man*. David Pulsifer inspired my chief protagonist, Bart Darling. In real life David had a lovely wife and four kids, and they lived in poverty. He drove a big motorcycle and ultimately crashed it, losing a leg. Later on his teenage daughter, Missy, died in a car accident. His wife Nancy split. When the sons took over their father's boat the business failed. Soon after my honeymoon I lost touch with David, but never with Bart Darling. For me he represented the tragedy of America's destructive creative energy. Perry Knowlton almost sold the book to a German publisher. A US publisher rejected it. And although I consigned Bart Darling to my slag heap, I never threw him away.

Even before *The Sterile Cuckoo* or *Wizard of Loneliness* hit bookstores I began an angry novel called *An American Child Supreme*—my first attempt to produce "political" fiction. *American Child* was autobiographical and against the Vietnam War, the sad tale of a gung-ho all-American boy and aspiring writer, Sammy Hauck, as he becomes disillusioned with his country and strives to create art capable of advocating for radical change. An homage to my confusion at the time. Many conversations in the novel between Sammy and his friend Julian

Chutter derived from my long discussions with Alan Howard. I owe him for that education, but it wasn't much fun. Determined to shed one skin, you're leery of adopting a contrary ideology that betrays you. After publishing twice at a young age I was urging myself to reject all the hype (and most of its money) by abandoning (in print, and in my life) its destructive financial (and moral) contradictions. But every day when I put my feet on the floor I was scared stiff of the new obligations.

Come evening Ruby and I watched the war news on TV until, enraged, we turned to Jackie Gleason, Art Carney, Audrey Meadows, and Joyce Randolph in black-and-white reruns of *The Honeymooners*, which caused us both to roll on the floor laughing, a euphoric release. Even today I credit *The Honeymooners* for saving our lives.

———

Though reluctant to sabotage my writing career, I was torn. With the brass ring in hand, I wanted to let go of it. That's counterintuitive when you've latched onto the dream of a lifetime. Yet if I didn't release my grip, how could I live with myself? Over seven years I created thirty-six drafts and section rewrites of *An American Child Supreme* before giving up circa 1971. My files contain quotations from other writers relevant to Sammy Hauck's dilemma. Here's one by Albert Camus:

> The artist of today becomes unreal if he remains in his ivory tower or sterilized if he spends his time galloping around the political arena. Yet between the two lies the arduous way of true art. It seems to me that the writer must be fully aware of the dramas of his time and that he must take sides every time he can or knows how to do so.

To Bernard Malamud, shortly after he published *The Fixer* in 1966, I wrote a letter asking what was the social responsibility of an artist during the indefensible Vietnam War. His generous reply insisted that "in art no compromise with the ideals of art." It was possible to write, teach, and be political simultaneously. "What a writer must say changes as he rids himself of provincialism, fear; yet he must always struggle to make it art."

I was floundering. Almost broke after five minutes of being almost rich. Still working on *The Sterile Cuckoo* screenplay, a possible meal ticket. Should I keep writing books or make my stand on the radical barricades, throwing bricks and Molotov cocktails with a pistol in hand? Being married was difficult as Ruby and I adapted to the chaotic 1960s. We had been raised to exist in a conventional marriage, yet that rug had been pulled out from under our feet, leaving us spinning in mid-air. We weren't hippies, but we were seriously trying to shed our bourgeois politics. We protested the Vietnam War and demonstrated for civil rights and feminist agendas—*equality*.

But whatever on earth had happened to my once-giddy sense of humor?

12

WHEN OUR SON Luke was born at New York Hospital in September 1966 they had to cut a wider episiotomy, because his shoulders were *big*. He emerged in a startling geyser of blood. Ruby and I taxied home, but she hemorrhaged and I raced her back to the hospital. Then found myself alone carrying a two-day-old baby searching the supermarket for Enfamil. I succeeded. Luke devoured two bottles at a time, then burped like Krakatoa barfing all over me.

So Real Life began.

A year later I confronted police horses jamming anti-war demonstrators through plate-glass windows on Forty-Second Street. In one arm I held Luke, in the other hand my Bolex 8mm movie camera was filming the scene. A cop galloped toward me, intent on whacking the camera from my fist with his baton. Another cop drew his revolver, but a nearby sergeant shoved him away ordering the guy to holster the weapon. Demonstrators hollered at the riot police, calling them "pigs!," "murderers!," "faggots!," "morons!," "assholes!," "fascists!," "baby killers!," and "cocksuckers!" They spit at the cops. It was difficult not to yell at my fellow peaceniks: "Back *off* a little you blithering morons!"

When soldiers were battering us on the Pentagon ramp in the fall of 1967, my sister-in-law Pammy grabbed at their rifles, eager to be arrested. I begged her to *stop!* I didn't *want* to be arrested. Ruby had one-year-old Luke somewhere behind us in his stroller. What were we *thinking?* Pammy was crazy. Why didn't we both get shot? By some act of mercy we avoided capture *and* jail time. So Luke lived to enjoy his Pablum and zwieback next morning.

———

I took movies of Luke while cherry blossoms bloomed in the Washington Square kiddie area. One day the women of that playground sicced a cop on me. They thought I was a bum, a voyeur. Luke toddled over and hugged me, proving to the fuzz, "This is my dad." He was just learning to walk. In those days not many "house husbands" ferried their children to play areas where only bleary-eyed moms in curlers and half-open bathrobes monitored their kids while the hubbies were uptown selling their souls to the devil designing ads for Mr. Clean and Coca-Cola.

(That's a cheap shot. I take it back. Nobody likes superior assholes, do they? From now on, after every five hundred words I write, maybe I should apologize.)

But I can't sleep because baby Luke awakens screaming from bad dreams every night. I walk the Manhattan streets at 11:00 p.m. or midnight like Travis Bickle in *Taxi Driver*. First I swing north to the burlesque theater near Union Square and contemplate overripe strippers behind glass display cases flanking the ticket booth. Deteriorating posters on nearby walls depict wailing Vietnamese women and children about to be murdered, or a simple drawing of a coffin beneath the query: "IS YOUR KID IN THIS BOX?" Next, I traipse over to the Purple Onion on Fourth Street near Sixth Avenue and stand at the window with other male insomniacs, watching topless dancers inside. I'm torn apart by anger, lust, bitterness. I want to fuck Brigitte Bardot and Anita Ekberg. Or buy a ticket to Saigon, track down William Westmoreland, and smear his face with pig snot. I am no longer employed by Alan Pakula writing a script for *The Sterile Cuckoo* because I couldn't induce Pookie Adams to shut up enough to make her believable on the Big Screen. If you consider my experience with Avon books and G. P. Putnam's, I'm obviously going off the deep end.

It's still 1967, and wasn't that "the summer of love?" For me it was the summer of escalation in Vietnam (LBJ sending forty-five thousand more troops and bombing Hanoi), Muhammad Ali refusing the draft ("No Vietcong ever called me 'nigger'"), major anti-war marches in New York, the Arab-Israeli six-day conflict, and race riots across America (forty-one killed in Detroit, a city occupied by federal paratroopers). The Kerner Commission would explain poverty and race in our country (where pretty much nothing has been done about these wounds ever since). The "summer of love" ended when Che Guevara was executed in Bolivia, Woody Guthrie died in New York, and I marched on the Pentagon with thousands of demonstrators to halt the overseas massacres. But we didn't stop even one napalm explosion.

———

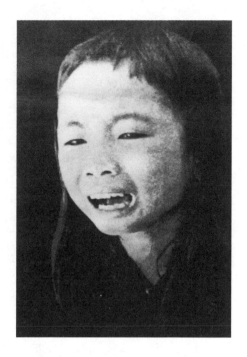

Face of a terrified Vietnamese girl crying, from a large "END THE WAR NOW" poster for a SANE rally in Madison Square Garden, December 1968. Courtesy of John Nichols.

In 1966 I'd written several drafts of a novella titled *The Empanada Brotherhood*, covering my first three years in New York when I hung out with Argentine friends at the kiosk on MacDougal Street. Too bad my current writing wasn't alive. If you haven't guessed by now, I was frazzled by life in New York. My three *Empanada* drafts were too cute to be rewritten with any hopefulness in 1967 or 1968. Had I tried they would have sounded like Charles Bukowski or Hubert Selby Jr.: *Last Exit to Hell on Earth*. So I stashed the manuscripts in a trunk where they remained for thirty years before I peeked at them again.

Instead I churned out a cheerful nightmare called *Medal of Honor*. My hero, Peter Hurlburt, earned that award for bravery in Vietnam. After the US president pins it on his chest, Peter reenters American civilian life and is quickly appalled by all the homegrown violence, crime, racism, ignorance, inequality, class warfare, misogyny, environmental depredations, obscenities, and so forth. Hardly the "freedom" and "democracy" he'd fought for in Vietnam. So he cracks, shoots to death all his friends at a holiday party, then staggers down to the nearby beach and hurls his Medal of Honor into the ocean.

Put *that* in your pipe and smoke it.

13

SHORTLY BEFORE LUKE was born, Ruby and I had moved over to 11 East 7th Street, where we rented a third-floor apartment above McSorley's Old Ale House, directly across from Cooper Union and slightly west of an onion-dome Ukrainian church. We were around the corner from Andy Warhol's "Balloon Farm" on St. Marks Place, just a hop and a step from Gem Spa and its famous "egg creams" on the corner of Second Avenue and St. Marks. A block south, on Second Avenue, stood the Fillmore East.

In that cool neighborhood we met James and Dinky Forman. Once a prime organizer for SNCC (Student Nonviolent Coordinating Committee), Jim supported the Black Panthers and created a "Black Manifesto" demanding reparations from New York's Riverside Church and others for slavery and the racist treatment of Blacks. Dinky, a nurse, was the daughter of Jessica Mitford, a British writer best known for *The American Way of Death*.

Ruby and I knew Jim and Dinky because they lived in our neighborhood and helped a group of us create a storefront child-care center where we shared looking after each other's kids on different weekdays. We had Luke; they had two boys, Chaka and James Jr. They also told us about their friend from SNCC, Elizabeth "Betita" Martínez, who had recently relocated to Española, New Mexico, where she'd started a Chicano Movement newspaper, *El Grito del Norte*.

By then I wanted to escape New York, possibly moving to Taos, a town fifty miles north of Española that I'd visited during the summer of 1957 at age sixteen when I traveled out west. After ten days in Taos, I had then worked for room and board at a museum research station down in Portal, Arizona. By chance I also battled forest fires burning the Chiricahua Mountains surrounding Portal. A magical summer. My book *If Mountains Die* explains that adventure. Should our family head for Taos, Jim and Dinky urged us to connect with Betita Martínez in order to continue political organizing among like-minded cohorts.

This suggestion was providential.

But first, back to Hollywood. After my attempts at a *Sterile Cuckoo* script were discarded, Alan Pakula hired his friend Alvin Sargent to clean up the mess, which he did. I toured New England with David Lange, scouting locations. Using my wind-up Bolex 8mm camera, I shot several four-minute rolls of the Hamilton College campus. Pakula liked them, and the summer of 1968 he began film production at my alma mater in Clinton, New York, near Utica. The first movie Alan ever directed himself, it starred Liza Minelli in *her* first major role.

I'm having dinner at the Hamilton Inn with Alan, David Lange, and Liza (and her husband Peter Allen) on location for *The Sterile Cuckoo*. Liza keeps giggling nervously and flopping her head over into my lap. I can't feel good about the movie because of the Vietnam War, the Tet Offensive, the assassinations of Martin Luther King (in April) and Bobby Kennedy (in June), and the August Days of Rage at Chicago's Democratic convention. (A day after that convention, the US ambassador to Guatemala was killed during a rebel ambush.) In fact, 1968 was the worst year of my life. What was the point of wasting millions to make a trite movie about a silly college romance during all those assassinations and Armageddons? I was creeped out by *The Sterile Cuckoo*'s apolitical irrelevance. Such thoughts I never expressed to Pakula and company. I liked Alan too much. Hence I behaved like a normal, preppie lad with one of those alien creatures from *Men in Black* hiding underneath my phony, tear-away skin.

After only three days on location, I fled. Alan offered to cast me as an extra in a rowdy fraternity house-party scene, but I vigorously demurred. Although only six years had passed since my graduation, I now considered college fraternities the most racist, antisemitic, exclusionary organizations on the planet. Another scene I witnessed had Liza Minelli descending some stairs repeatedly while the cameraman futzed with different angles and lenses and the lighting crew kept changing their aluminum reflectors and colored gelatin sheets covering a window to set the appropriate mood. Hollywood in action imitated the film *Groundhog Day*. Was it Woody Allen who famously said that making motion pictures was like "running the mile in one-foot segments?" Pakula required four hours to shoot fifteen seconds of action. My interest flagged after the first three takes.

Excerpt from a Paramount Pictures publicity sheet for *The Sterile Cuckoo* in 1969. Courtesy of John Nichols.

Liza Minnelli Was Determined To Win Pookie Role In Cuckoo

Long range planning just doesn't seem to be a part of my way of life. I believe in taking things as they come and getting the most out of them while they're happening. That's why the story of my involvement with Pookie Adams surprised many of my friends and most of all, me.

Still #SC3   Mat 1C
Liza Minnelli, in her first star-ring role, appears with new-comer Wendell Burton in THE STERILE CUCKOO, produced and directed by Alan J. Pakula. This Paramount Picture in

Pookie is the strange, lonely college student who appears in John Nichols' novel, "The Sterile Cuckoo." A friend had told me how much she enjoyed the story an when I saw the book in an airport newsstand, I bought it and read straight through that same night. It was a strange feeling, but seemed to know exactly what Pookie was experiencing in her relationship with Jerry Payne. I felt a deep sense of understanding and sympathy for Pookie. I knew that if film was made of "The Sterile Cuckoo" I wanted to play the part even though I had never been a picture at that time.

I checked with the publisher the book and found that Pakula-Mulligan Productions held an option on the story for a motion picture. I went to their office and told them that when they decided to make the film, I was the one to should play Pookie.

Early in 1968, after Alvin Sargent had written a screenplay Alan Pakula had decided to make his debut as a director with "The Sterile Cuckoo," I was called in addition. In the meantime, I had been in a picture called "Charlie Bubbles" with Albert Finney and learned some of the techniques of film acting.

There wasn't any doubt in my mind that I would get the part, it just seemed like that's the way it had to be. Wendell Burton, who played Jerry in the picture, played ... A Good Man

More to the point, my conversations with former professors during those three days were unsettling. I had loved being a student at Hamilton. Yet now my interactions with academic friends and teachers revealed how deeply conservative and reactionary the college was. A safe little repository for white American elitists. I know things have changed now, but that was then. And over my six years since graduation everything I'd believed in had been overturned by a tsunami of experience, and almost total reappraisal of world political history. Cocktails and conversations with former profs made me jittery to extremes.

Cuckoo filming that summer and autumn went well, and the editing occurred without many hassles. The movie was released in 1969, which I'll elaborate on in a moment. It launched Liza into the world of Hollywood acting success, and Pakula proceeded to a distinguished career behind the camera, directing *Klute*, *All the President's Men*, and *Sophie's Choice* among others. He and Hope Lange did not stay married long. And Alan is gone now—he died, perfectly healthy and working on a new film at age seventy, in a freak accident while driving on the Long Island Expressway. A lengthy piece of metal pipe, kicked up by the car ahead, crashed through his windshield and killed him.

That happened on November 19, 1998.

14

AS FOR ME? By 1968 my writing was floundering like a horse in quicksand. Our small Manhattan apartment had no space for a work table. Ruby and I slept on a foldout bed that became a couch during the day. The only door was to the bathroom where I could pass hours on the toilet futzing with a manuscript. Mostly I wrote in nearby cafés, or in study karels at NYU beside Washington Square. The streets were littered with offal because of a garbage strike. Blowing newspaper pages displayed photos of US and Vietcong soldiers killed in Vietnam during the Tet Offensive. On February 8, just before Tet, three Black students in Orangeburg, South Carolina, were shot to death by police during a civil-rights demonstration at South Carolina State University. Twenty-eight other Black students were wounded in the "Orangeburg Massacre." Terrible news from Vietnam buried that story on inner pages of the *Times*. I was losing the thread on *Autumn Beige*, *American Child Supreme*, *The Empanada Brotherhood*, *Diaphanous Wild Man*, and my stridently anti-war novel, *Medal of Honor*. Martin Luther King Jr. was assassinated in April, and race riots ensued. Bobby Kennedy died in June. The civil war between Nigeria and Biafra drove me crazy. I wanted to visit Resurrection City in Washington, DC, but we didn't. Warsaw Pact tanks invaded Czechoslovakia, killing the "Prague Spring." Goodbye to Alexander Dubček and "Socialism with a human face." In Paris, maybe rioters could overthrow *their* stupid government. The colonels of Greece were creating fascist amendments to their constitution. China's Cultural Revolution was a disaster. Mexico City cops had slaughtered protesting students moments before the Olympic Games. George Wallace was going to run for president in November. Jackie Kennedy's true colors blazed when she married Aristotle Onassis. And fuck those stupid astronauts orbiting the moon like Make-A-Wish kids on a merry-go-round.

———

By 1969 our money had dried up. Though Ruby and I were frugal, the bread evaporated anyway. If 1968 had been totally demoralizing, 1969 would replicate the same ordeal. New York was expensive, overcrowded, violent, and no place to raise a kid. Ruby and I hit a wall, desperate to escape, apparently headed toward hell on a handcart. Then in mid-1969 a miracle saved us.

Blame this one on the release of that "bourgeois, apolitical" *Sterile Cuckoo* film. Because of interest spurred by the movie, the Literary Guild sent me eight thousand dollars. I stared at the check in disbelief. Should I tear it up as the ill-gotten gains of yet one more capitalist hoax? Are you out of your *mind?* Suddenly we could abandon the belly of the beast. No more feeling guilty while stepping over homeless derelicts on our way to the grocery store. No more calling ourselves monsters while handing dollar bills to hapless window washers whenever we stopped the car at a red light. Every black lining has a silver cloud.

Capitalism had saved the day!

———

We left New York the morning after Neil Armstrong and Buzz Aldrin walked on the moon. On the night of that historic event our apartment on 11 East 7th Street was empty except for our portable TV set and sleeping bags on the floor waiting to enfold Ruby, Luke, and me. Of course Ruby and I were fascinated, although I considered the moon landing a cynical waste of impoverished tax-payer dollars to promote Cold War propaganda. Apollo 11's basic purpose was to advance Nazi Wernher von Braun's chemical rocketry for nuclear missiles (secretly manufactured by Krupp), which were aimed toward the Soviet Union. It wasn't a "giant leap for mankind" but rather a nihilistic step *backward*, a bla-tant ploy to distract attention from the Vietnam War and the Santa Barbara oil spills, canceling the Smothers Brothers Comedy Hour, the death of Judy Gar-land, and Eldridge Cleaver's escape to Algeria, then to Paris where the former angry Black Panther and celebrated author of *Soul on Ice* created his fashionable codpiece-decorated "Penis Pants" before returning to America where he became a Mormon and a reactionary Republican.

I had become a regular barrel of laughs myself.

Next day, July 22, 1969, we headed west in our VW Bus followed by a U-Haul van. Around the middle of Kansas on day two, Ruby pulled over the Bus, and I veered the U-Haul in behind her. My wife came back to the van bearing a cupcake with a single burning candle stuck through the chocolate frosting. She sang "Happy Birthday" to me. I blew out the candle, we kissed, and our "Little Fur Family" continued westward toward Taos, New Mexico.

I had just turned twenty-nine . . . going on seventy-three. Taos was a real shot in the dark.

15

BUT WAIT A sec: we weren't free yet. "It's never over til it's over
. . ." Not two months later, at a Harlem police station, two
officers played good cop / bad cop with me and Charleen Lane. September
1969. Though I'd never met her before, I had loaned Charleen my VW Bus to
go buy more envelopes for a political mailing a group of us were doing near
Columbia University in upper Manhattan. With the car she hit a five-year-old
girl in the middle of Harlem who was listed as critical at a nearby hospital.
Those cops couldn't understand what this preppy white boy was doing with a
radical black woman, a member of the Black Panthers who had an expired
driver's license and no confirmable address. They held us until ten at night
performing their ritual grilling. After they let us go, for the next five or six years
I had a half-million-dollar civil lawsuit pending against me. By law I was not
allowed to inquire about the little girl. She survived and was released from
hospital eight weeks after being struck, owing a lien of $6,400. I received copies
of that information in February 1971. Two witnesses testified the car was going
slow, and the child had jumped out suddenly from between parked cars. But in
New York State a person five years or younger could not be held liable for an
accident. And the car's owner was responsible no matter who sat behind the
wheel.

Charleen Lane disappeared. We'd met because I had driven east to fetch the
last of our New York possessions—and also to see a sneak preview of *The Sterile
Cuckoo*. My pal Alan Howard had recruited me to help with the mailing
intended to raise money for a rural health clinic in Tierra Amarilla, New Mexico, fifty miles west of Taos. Ruby and I had just put a down payment on a
humble Taos dwelling, the first property, other than our VW Bus, that we'd ever
owned. What did that lawsuit teach me? *There is no such thing as security.*

———

Two days following the accident, in a small theater with fifty other people, I was so stressed during the *Sterile Cuckoo* projection that I nearly wriggled out of my skin. A child was in the ICU, she might die, and I couldn't concentrate on the movie. Everything about it was warped and embarrassing, with color so bad it seemed to have been shot by a Brownie camera in 1948. What sort of reprehensible sellout had written the book spawning such a project? A greedy little prick. My high-and-mighty aspirations for a distinguished literary career were turning into an off-color joke. Afterward I smiled, shook hands, congratulated Alan Pakula and Liza and hugged everyone else, grabbed a handful of chocolate-chip cookies, then ran (spewing tears!) into the heartless city.

———

Liza received an Academy Award nomination for her role in the movie. *The New Yorker* said, "*The Sterile Cuckoo* is a small, delicate tragicomedy, beautifully written (Alvin Sargent did the adaptation of John Nichols' 1965 novel), and directed very simply, but with a remarkable and sustained *tact*, by Alan J. Pakula."

Del Carnes, the *Denver Post* drama editor, wrote, "All that you've heard about Liza Minelli in her first starring movie, 'The Sterile Cuckoo,' is true. She gives us one of the most marvelous and indelible performances of this or any recent year."

And according to *The National Observer*, "She does not play 19-year-old Pookie Adams, she *is* Pookie Adams, and you may mark your Oscar ballots right now."

Two movies later Liza *won* her Oscar playing Sally Bowles in the 1972 musical drama *Cabaret*, directed by Bob Fosse.

———

A year post accident I returned east by Greyhound to stand criminal trial on May 11, 1970, for allowing a person without a valid driver's license to pilot my vehicle in New York State. I think the penalties could have been a year of jail, or a five-thousand-dollar fine, or both. My hired lawyer joined me at Court Street in Manhattan. He charged me a thousand dollars. The courtroom was jammed with shackled black and brown men wearing prison jumpsuits. When the judge arrived he asked, "Does anybody here have a lawyer?" I raised my hand

and he barked, "You first." Yet at the bench he said, "The police officer who covered this accident isn't here, so the case will be continued." My lawyer argued that I had made an extreme effort to be present that day, riding a bus all the way from New Mexico, and a continuation would cause me undue hardship. The judge agreed and threw out the case. In America, that's what being white and paying a lawyer can obtain for you.

———

That year, 1970, was another really tough sell. On March 6 Alan Howard's dear friend from Guatemala, Diana Oughton, by then a member of the Weather Underground, accidentally blew herself up while building a bomb in a West Eleventh Street brownstone near my great-aunt Susan Pulsifer's house. (A reminder: my Aunt Susan, who also owned property in Maine, was the adoptive mother of David Pulsifer, the lobsterman I wished to immortalize with *A Big Diaphanous Wild Man*.) Two men, Ted Gold and Terry Robbins, died with Diana in the dynamite blasts. Cathy Wilkerson and Kathy Boudin escaped from the house unhurt and went into hiding for years. The house had belonged to Cathy's father. She eventually turned herself in and spent only eleven months incarcerated. Kathy Boudin stayed underground, became involved with the Black Liberation Army, and was the getaway driver for a 1981 Brink's truck robbery where one guard and two policemen were killed in a shoot-out. Immediately captured, Kathy served twenty-two years in prison before being paroled in 2003. I had sympathy for Diana because Guatemala, the Vietnam War, the 1965 Marine invasion of the Dominican Republic, and the Civil Rights Movement had deeply affected my life and my political awareness. Diana's death scared me. My friend Alan Howard had seen her just a few days before she died.

Compounding the paranoia was this: My wife Ruby had gone to Cuba in early 1970 with a Venceremos Brigade to cut sugar cane for Fidel Castro. She was there when Diana died. Mississippi's Senator Eastland had accused the brigade volunteers of learning to be terrorists in Cuba, radicals just like the Weathermen who'd blown up that New York townhouse. After Ruby returned from Cuba, the FBI bounced up our potholed Taos driveway a few times, yet they lacked search warrants so we never let them inside our house. I always watched them leave, however, afraid they would throw marijuana seeds out their window into our front field then return months later to bust us for growing pot.

Two months after Diana Oughton's death, on May 4, 1970, four white students at Kent State University in Ohio protesting Richard Nixon's invasion of Cambodia were killed by rifle fire from National Guard troops. Their deaths, unlike those of black students in the Orangeburg Massacre two years earlier, created a huge upsurge in anti-war unrest at universities all over America.

Suddenly "our" angry young generation had become mortal.

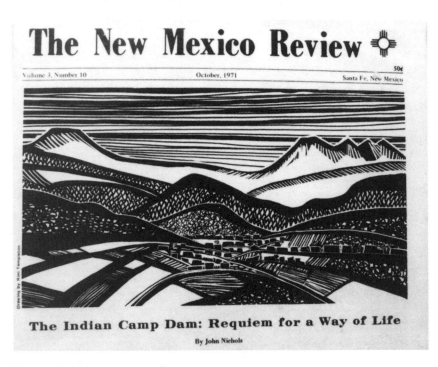

The New Mexico Review ❋

Volume 3, Number 10   October, 1971   50¢   Santa Fe, New Mexico

The Indian Camp Dam: Requiem for a Way of Life

By John Nichols

My first article against the Indian Camp Dam and Taos conservancy district for the October 1971 *New Mexico Review*. Illustration of Taos by Rini Templeton. Courtesy of John Nichols.

PART III

16

TALK ABOUT A change of scene. Our new town was very poor, rich in despair, yet enchanting and powerful. An Indian pueblo had been in Taos for over eight hundred years. The valley was crisscrossed by irrigation acequias built by Spanish and mestizo people who'd arrived four hundred years ago. Sustainable agriculture was important. A renowned art community had existed since the early 1900s. Its paintings idolized colorful hollyhocks against adobe walls, natives from the pueblo, and golden aspen trees in autumn. Mabel Dodge Luhan, D. H. Lawrence, and Georgia O'Keeffe had helped create the "Taos myth." All across the valley sheep grazed, cattle were important, horses seemed everywhere. Instead of parking meters the plaza still had hitching posts. Pickup trucks toting high loads of piñon wood emerged from the mountains—most residents heated with that bounty. Elderly Spanish-speaking men pitched rows of loose hay onto horse-drawn wagons. Rabbit-brush bushes on Indian land displayed sulfur yellow bouquets. Pueblo dances and celebrations took place on September 30, San Geronimo Day. Hispanic women roasted *chicos* made from corncobs in rounded mud *hornos*. Perched on ladders, *enjarradoras* mud-plastered the Ranchos de Taos church. Most pickups had deer rifles on rear-window racks. I listened to the whining of periodical cicadas on Devisadero Trail. Tarantulas crossed the roads. Prolific tarantula hawk wasps were shiny black with bright-orange wings. The stands at Friday or Saturday Taos High football games boasted cheering fans. Overhead, doves flew south trailed by noisy sandhill cranes. The Wednesday drive-in movies featured Tony Aguilar—I parked the family there to learn Spanish and enjoy the music. Lightning streaks lit up the western sky as we pigged out on butter-drenched popcorn. When a projector broke down, patrons beeped horns and blinked their headlights. Suddenly, life could be *fun*.

Yet if I've painted Taos as an almost idyllic place, let me correct that impression. We arrived during a migration of counterculture longhairs to maybe a dozen sketchy communes around Taos, an invasion that had become a Hippie-Chicano war. It was violent and very disruptive. Store windows displayed bullet holes or were boarded up. Newspaper headlines screamed in outrage. Hippies were raped at several hot springs, and angry Chicanos were shot. Pot, LSD, peyote, mescaline, heroin, and cocaine ran down gutters of the few paved streets. Evangelicals on the radio verbally lynched the communist freaks for stealing all the county's food stamps. They weren't communists, but rather disoriented trust-fund babies, or bizarre refugees from Haight Ashbury, or bumbling lost souls covered in mud, high on brown acid, wearing psychedelic T-shirts drenched from swimming in Fillipini Pond at Woodstock. Actor Dennis Hopper had moved to town, purchased the Mabel Dodge Luhan mansion from Mabel's granddaughter, Bonnie Bell, and turned the fabled dwelling into a lunatic free-for-all as he was cutting, chopping, and channeling his disastrous Peruvian picture, *The Last Movie*, while threatening to shoot local gangbangers with an AR-15 screwed to a tripod atop the Mabel Dodge roof, or so I heard. The weapon was allegedly manned by wackos from the Family, a commune run by a cat named Lord Byron.

This editorial appeared in *El Grito del Norte* about the same day Ruby, Luke, and I arrived in Taos:

> Think about the fact that as much as you reject your middle-class Anglo society and its values, you are still seen here as gringos. Anglos. Think about the 120-year-old struggle by chicanos and the even older struggle by Indians to get back millions of acres of land stolen from them by Anglo ranchers with their Anglo lawyer buddies. Think about what it means for a new influx of Anglos—no matter how different their purpose from those others—to come in and buy up land that the local people feel to be theirs and cannot afford to buy themselves. Think about the fact that a real estate agent in Taos reports having sold almost $500,000 worth of land to longhairs. . . . Think about this: the longhair has opted out. Most of the chicanos and Indians have no option—except revolution. People here cannot flee to islands of peace in a nation of horrors, this *is* their nation. It cannot be said too often: there is a long, hard political and economic struggle in these beautiful mountains, a struggle for land and justice. That struggle calls for fighters and supporters, not refugees with their own set of problems. You may see the scenery as relief from an oppressive America: we see a battleground against oppression.

Immediately I got in touch with Betita Martínez at the *El Grito del Norte* newspaper an hour south of Taos in Española. I never wrote articles for the radical paper, but I did sometimes help with mailings and brought armfuls of *El Grito* back north for distribution in Taos, which wasn't easy. Our tourism-oriented storekeepers were gun-shy about *El Grito*'s Chicano Movement politics, especially when the paper grew more overtly feminist and socialist, branching out from northern New Mexico land-grant issues to articles friendly toward North Vietnam and Cuba. Most of my Taos neighbors wouldn't have touched *El Grito* with a ten-foot cottonwood branch. But funky Mondo's Bar accepted almost all the issues and provided free copies with every purchased bottle of MD 20/20 or six-pack of Colt 45.

Through *El Grito* I met Rini Templeton, Enriqueta Vásquez, and Craig Vincent. They connected me to that notorious people's *clinica* in Tierra Amarilla (west of Taos) and activists like María Varela, Chemo Tijerina, and Valentina Valdez. Craig Vincent was an elderly lefty, his wife, Jenny, a marvelous folk singer who knew all the traditional Spanish songs. Craig involved me in the Taos branch of The US-China People's Friendship Committee. We sent local Taoseños to China long before Richard Nixon walked the Wall. Rini Templeton founded the *Taller Grafico* beside the Tierra Amarilla clinic, illustrated *El Grito*, and gave artwork to other publications. Enriqueta Vásquez's *El Grito* columns, *Despierten, Hermanos!*, were later collected in a book published by Arte Público Press. Betita's daughter, Tessa, became a respected actor in the theater. María Varela, a former SNCC organizer and political photographer, began wool and livestock cooperatives in Tierra Amarilla and nearby Los Ojos called *Ganados del Valle* and *Tierra Wools*. After *El Grito* died, Betita ran the Chicano Communications Center in Albuquerque, publishing the massive photo-essay book *450 Years of Chicano History*.

These activists had courage and dedication that helped transform northern New Mexico. Their friendship and politics would educate and enrich my life for years to come. So did their laughter. What I love about the left organizers I've known or worked with is that they have *hope*, along with a remarkably upbeat sense of humor. Emma Goldman said it best when she declared, "If I can't dance, I don't wanna be in the revolution."

17

RUBY DANCED A jig on our tiny lawn wearing her fluffy pink slippers the day before Tania was born. Our daughter arrived at the Embudo Clinic (a half-hour south of Taos) next evening on August 7, 1970. She entered the world blue marbled and completely silent for twenty seconds until she began to cry.

At home I filmed Ruby on our portal holding the baby in one arm and a large zucchini squash from our garden in the other arm. It's a toss-up who's bigger, the squash or Tania. That's when she got her nickname, Tootie, because she was such a "wee, tootie lump."

Next, only nine weeks old, Tania almost died of pneumonia. Her mom and I maintained a vigil at Holy Cross Hospital day and night. During my turn one early morning Tania turned blue; she couldn't breathe, and she barfed if the

Tania ("Tootie") Nichols and her older brother, Luke, in Taos, 1972. Photo by John Nichols.

nurse gave her a bottle. I asked for a doctor. The nurse said, "Don't worry, this is normal." A half-dozen other babies occupied nearby mist tents. Finally I said, "If you don't call the doctor, I'll call the police." They phoned the sawbones, who arrived disheveled and sleepy. He muttered, "This better be good." But listening to Tania's heart he blanched, declaring, "We can't save her, get her to Los Alamos, fast!" They gave us a five-minute course on how to administer oxygen. Then Ruby and I rode a Hanlon Funeral Home hearse driven by a seventy-five-year-old man at 4:00 a.m. down to Los Alamos Hospital sixty miles away, where they pumped our baby full of digitalis and, over the next few days, saved her life.

No ambulance served Taos in 1970. You pretty much had to fly by the seat of your pants.

———

That winter the Pacheco Ditch froze over and flooded the neighbor's front field. Kids from the vicinity came to skate and slide on the ice. A little girl knocked on my kitchen door: "Mister, the dogs are killing your chickens!" I ran outside, grabbed a shovel, and trapped a mongrel still in the coop. Raising my shovel to bash it, I could not strike the blow. The poor mutt squealed, scooting past me out the door expecting a demise that never came. Dead chickens lay everywhere.

Pretty soon we had chickens, turkeys, guinea hens, geese, pigeons, two goats, a couple of ponies, a dog, and multiple cats as well as apple, pear, and plum trees, a big vegetable garden, a huge woodpile, a half-acre back field, a half-acre front field, and two irrigation ditches on our 1.7 acres. The ramshackle adobe house featured a big kitchen and living room and two bedrooms. The flat dirt roof leaked like a sieve, our septic tank didn't work (but we had a decent outhouse), and our gray water flowed through a pipe over the Pacheco Ditch into the front field.

And so the East Coast, college-educated, white, politicized, bourgeois Marxist-Leninists wound up as cliché hillbilly hippies in Spanish-speaking Appalachia. Every day required hard work to keep it all from falling apart. Neighbors showed us how to patch the roof with lapseal cement and strips of tarred felt, correct plumbing problems, collect and chop wood, fix broken fences, prune the fruit trees, irrigate the fields, enrich the vegetable garden, repair the irrigation ditches with our fellow *parciantes*—the headgates, the *desagües*—put up our garden produce for winter, jerry-rig the broken well pump, wash Tania's cloth diapers in an old Maytag roller machine and hang them on the line to dry, rid skunks from under the floorboards, and clean the outhouse using a posthole digger, lifting lime-coated turds up into a garbage-bagged waste can that would be accepted at the town dump.

Difficult work, but rejuvenating, though I cursed it. Seated in the outhouse with the door open mid-summertime I enjoyed watching hummingbirds at the hollyhocks three feet away. Camped there with the door closed during winter blizzards wasn't as much fun. You learned really fast how to shit quick.

Alienation that had overwhelmed me in New York was dissipated overnight by my neighbors in Upper Ranchitos and at the Taos Pueblo. I loved the people, their history, the different cultures, multiple languages, scandals, acequias, sustainable agriculture, and politics surrounded by high-mountain, deep-river, and sagebrush mesa landscapes. A complicated and richly varied small town. It was very poor, tough and resilient, and had suffered much tragedy and social injustice. The scale was intimate and, unlike New York, "knowable." There existed a remarkable range of personalities. Art appreciation, Indigenous music, and zany humor reigned. Everybody had guns. A crazy quilt of potent human variety. Universal humanity in a nutshell, the opposite of homogeneous. Once I gave a speech titled, "Everything I Always Wanted to Know about the West, I Learned in New York City."

But Taos, where pretty quickly you knew everybody *personally*, was a novelist's wet dream.

18

I HAD A glumness hangover after leaving the Big Apple. Our offspring helped cheer me up. What follows is a collage over several years.

Tania was afraid of our biggest gobbler, who attacked her regularly. One day she bit into a turkey turd, mistaking it for candy. Tubby had many puppies that kept licking Tania's face. She was only a year old and hated being slurped on by puppies. Luke ran naked around the front field waving a cheesecloth net chasing butterflies. We searched for monarch eggs under the milkweed leaves along our rutted driveway. In that driveway Luke set up a wooden ramp he'd built from plywood and raced his bike downhill, over the ramp, crashed, and broke his collarbone.

Ruby, Luke, and I spread a blanket beneath a piñon tree, shaking down the nuts. We baked them on cookie tins inside our old combination stove (half wood burning, half propane). With Luke and Tootie I walked through sagebrush searching for horned toads. They wore homemade shin guards to protect against rattlesnakes. We caught *guajalotes* at Bernardin Lake, guarding them in an aquarium on the kitchen table. The newt stage of Tiger Salamanders, they ate countless grasshoppers before being released into the nearby Pueblo River or the Pacheco Ditch.

Luke and Tania donned their Superman costumes and charged across the living room, leaping at me to wrestle on the mattresses. We tumbled, squealed, grunted, and twisted, intermingling arms and legs. I worked hard to keep it pretend/serious and exciting with nobody getting hurt. Tootie was so fierce she practically cracked her head open every time we wrestled. At age three she acted like a linebacker from the NFL trying to sack a quarterback. Think Lawrence Taylor of the New York Giants. She had no boundaries, flying through the air to knock me and Luke askew on arrival. The WWF in miniature. Ergo: many bloody noses! And tears. And triumphal, chest-pounding bragadoccio.

———

On nights when the kids bathed, they splashed water onto the floor. Finally, I'd had enough. I threatened, for the first time ever, to give them ten whacks on their fannies if they did that again. So of course they immediately, deliberately, did that again. I'm surprised the floorboards held up, preventing the tub from crashing into crawl space below.

I said, "Okay, you asked for it."

They stepped out, dried off, went into their room, and each put on eight pairs of underwear. Then they said, "Have at it, Pop." I "spanked" them. Afterward, snarky little Tootie wrinkled up her nose and sneered, "*That* didn't hurt."

19

WHENEVER I DROVE to Santa Fe I mixed myself a tall vodka and coke for the journey. Never wore a seat belt, either. I'm talking about the early 1970s when I wrote for the *New Mexico Review*. Their office was in Santa Fe. Our state had liberal open-container laws (and a high death toll from alcohol-related auto accidents!).

I've written about working for the *Review* in my books, essays, and speeches, most notably in *If Mountains Die*, *A Fragile Beauty*, *Dancing on the Stones*, and *An American Child Supreme*. The paper was started by a fellow named Ed Schwartz as a New Mexico legislative review. He soon turned the rag over to a couple of Harvard "alternative lawyers," Em Hall and Jim Bensfield, who imagined it becoming a kind of southwestern *New Yorker*. However, because they couldn't pay writers for their articles, the *Review* soon became a collective effort supported by volunteer "contributing editors" who pushed the journal leftward into the land of investigative-cum-muckraking journalism. Not quite *Pravda*, yet a far piece from the *New Yorker*. Many fine writers and artists floated the magazine for free on their good will, writing, and artistic skills. Hall and Bensfield hustled grants from well-to-do Santa Fe folks until the *Review* did a Dutch act when donations evaporated in 1972, probably because Nixon had slaughtered McGovern in the presidential election with all his dirty tricks, and the Democratic liberals were shell-shocked.

I first met Em Hall circa 1970 on the Los Alamos ice rink where his Albuquerque squad beat the crap out of my Omega Canyon physicist compadres. Princeton and Harvard Law defeated MIT and Lawrence Livermore every time. Later, Em and I played hockey for a rough-tough Albuquerque league where we had great fun scoring goals together in each game until mild-mannered Em would be thrown out for brawling. If somebody checked him too hard into the Iceland Arena boards plastered against the west-side cement wall, he bounced up raging, "That's money in the bank, you motherfucker! That's money in the bank!"

Off the ice he was a compassionate, even-tempered "angel." Also a great writer.

Em Hall (left) and Jim Bens-field (right) at the top of Lake Fork Peak decades after the *New Mexico Review*, but obviously they're still going strong! Photo by John Nichols.

———

I began publishing long articles in the *Review* May of 1970. Thereafter, many issues had a piece by yours truly about this or that northern New Mexico outrage. These were not flippant commentaries by my alter ego, Pookie Adams; they were *serious*. Not exactly "Up against the wall, honky m—effers, or black power's gonna get your momma," but I oozed a political agenda, planning to become New Mexico's I. F. Stone, Bernard Fall, or Jonathan Schell. My articles were about a worker fired by the molybdenum mine in Questa (north of Taos), a racist school system, police brutality, a history of Los Alamos and modern-day protests against nuclear weapons, a feminist art show in Taos, the protracted hippie-Chicano war in my home county, poverty at the Taos Pueblo and the Indians' struggle to take back their sacred Blue Lake land from the Forest Service, a State Capitol protest by the poor against Welfare cuts, and an Española speech by rabble-rousing land-grant activist Reies Tijerina.

My pièce de résistance was multiple stories about an attempt by the Bureau of Reclamation and the state engineer to impose a conservancy district on Taos County so as to build the Indian Camp Dam to impound twelve thousand acre-feet of San Juan–Chama water diverted from Colorado to New Mexico, yada yada yada. To explain *that* battle, I ultimately wrote a large novel that might be described as a third-rate Tinkertoy cross between *Catch-22* and *Little Big Man*. (Of course I'm disingenuously flattering myself, but *somebody* has to toot my horn because I'm the only guy in my band.)

The conservancy struggle endured for much of the 1970s. I absorbed more information about my town—its history, politics, poverty, and personalities—and Southwest water wars, water law, and government chicanery than I could've ingested at a top-ranked university over thirty years of scholarly research. I covered community meetings and court hearings in Taos and Santa Fe, and attended gatherings where state engineer medicine men tried selling water-rights snake oil to recalcitrant local farmers who didn't trust any legal BS—in English *or* Spanish—issuing from government employees wearing a coat, a tie, and an American flag pin in their lapel buttonholes. A few testy confrontations almost led to blows or threats of gunplay. When I stood up once to shoot my mouth off, two realtors, a banker, and a big-time developer ordered me to sid-down and shut up—Taos didn't need any outsider gringo pinko agitators telling it what to do. A propos New Mexico water history, think of the films *China-town*, *Jaws*, or *Titanic*. Out here water is a complicated muddle of court battles, adjudication suits, acequia politics, and local customs and history versus demands for urban growth (i.e. cutural genocide), deliveries owed to Texas, water on paper but never in the mountains or deep underground, and the ongoing droughts caused by climate change caused by capitalism's planned obsolescence and conspicuous consumption's infinite growth syndrome using finite resources in its expand-or-expire syndrome.

And every legal explanation of our water problems is written in Egyptian hieroglyphics by white-collar criminals infesting minimum-security prisons, on break from making personalized auto license plates.

Bensfield and Hall never paid me a plug nickel for my lefty tracts. This created a silver lining: they felt disempowered to edit me. I had free reign to be dogmatic in reporting "the news." Though I worked hard to tell "the truth," I never pretended to be "neutral." I was proselytizing from the "correct historical side," and don't you forget it. When my bombast once drew threats of a lawsuit,

I told my benefactors not to worry: the *Review* was destitute, and none of us contributors had any land or property worth a hill of beans, anyway.

My bosses appraised me with gimlet eyes.

Then the guy who threatened legal action wound up at the State Pen for embezzling client trust funds from his own law firm.

Above all, though, Jim and Em's greatest gift to my life was this: they *published* my work when nobody else was interested. My so-called writing career remained quasi *alive* thanks to their loyalty. Hall and Bensfield's publication gave me reason to gain a super education on how humanity truly works. I hope they don't flinch (or vomit) when I say this, but, quite honestly, I owe Em and Jim (and their *New Mexico Review*) for the last fifty years of my writing career.

Mwah!

20

PICTURE THIS: IT'S early 1972 and Dennis Hopper (of *Easy Rider* fame) is crawling around on the floor of the Tony House, which is across the road from the Mabel Dodge Luhan mansion that he owns *aquí en Taos*. There's a loaded semiautomatic Colt .45 pistol on the coffee table. Dennis is so fucked-up on drugs he makes John Belushi look like a confused teenager licking wax from a Chapstick tube. My friend Justin Locke and his little boy, Ivan, are playing on the lawn outside. I had brought them with me because I was paranoid somebody might kill me if I showed up alone, unarmed, yet dangerous (given the power of the pen).

Dennis said, "Shhh, don't talk loud, they're listening." I asked, "Who's listening?" He said the undercover cop Ted Drennan, the DA Jim Brandenburg, and his lawyer, John Ramming. "I just had lunch with them. They're over in the Big House with a remote bug pointed at us. I have to report back to them everything we've said after you leave."

Ted Drennan had come to Taos two years earlier spreading rumors that I and other activists in Taos had formed an assassination team ready to kill the top fifty businessmen of Taos. Dennis had been on that list. Apparently our team had purchased a half dozen jeeps mounted with .50 caliber machine guns to take over the town. Drennan also "revealed" that an activist friend I worked with in a Chicano Movement group, Trabajadores de la Raza, had dynamited the Peñasco Forest Service headquarters. More recently, Drennan had participated during an incident when Black Beret activists Tony Córdova and Rito Canales were murdered by Albuquerque police while Tony and Rito were allegedly stealing dynamite at a construction site on the west side of that city.

Some of the evidence suggested that Tony and Rito were killed elsewhere, then transported to the construction site. Dynamite was planted at the Black Beret headquarters in Albuquerque, only it wasn't. By mistake the dynamite appeared at the house of a neighbor who lived nearby. The *New Mexico Review* was writing an in-depth article on the killing of Rito and Tony. My job was only to explain Ted Drennan's background as an agent-provocateur in Taos from 1969 to 1971, before the killing of Rito and Tony. I was checking the facts with Dennis to make sure I had down pat what he'd previously told me about Drennan.

As Dennis read my article his face brightened like a year-old baby's clutching a bowl of Maypo. He said, "This is *great*, man. Can I have a copy to show Drennan and Brandenburg when we meet after you're gone? They think you're writing an article exposing Drennan as a cold-blooded assassin who killed those guys to make the Black Berets look bad, but this is harmless. All it says here is that in Taos a couple of years ago he was an asshole provocateur."

I said, "Sure, why not?" and gave him a copy, then peeled out of there with Justin and Ivan.

Back then, Dennis was a bona fide lunatic. There were more out-of-control substances at the Mabel Dodge house than in Afghanistan poppy fields or Colombian coca plantations. Johnny Winter and Leonard Cohen sang "Subterranean Homesick Blues" in the kitchen for days on end. Dennis bumbled around his studio full of Moviolas with his pal Alejandro Jodorowsky (director of *El Topo*), cutting 35 mm film strips into short tabs that could be used for rolling joints. He was smoking his own *The Last Movie* in more ways than one. Finally he left Taos for rehab, pulled his crazy act together, and became a functioning movie star. Yet in the early 1970s, during a time of much violence and the hippie invasion of northern New Mexico, Dennis was off his rocker and the law had him by the balls. So he was snitching. I later used Ted Drennan loosely as inspiration for Kyril Montana, an undercover cop in my novel *The Milagro Beanfield War*.

Taos was so crowded with people I could translate into fictional characters it was as if, upon leaving New York City, I had landed in the planet's most colorful (and productive) briar patch.

———

When the *New Mexico Review* approached rock bottom the late summer of 1972, my friend Rini Templeton and I volunteered to edit the final three issues. September, October, November. Rini the radical artist taught me about design, formatting, the use of artwork, type styles, headline writing, and how to cut and paste. She lived in a cabin with no running water on the mesa about ten miles south of Taos just before entering the Río Grande Gorge. Rini was very gifted

The New Mexico Review ✲

Volume 4, Number 11 November 1972 50¢ Sante Fe, New Mexico

Every Five Days a Hiroshima Bomb Is Dropped On Vietnam

It was a sunny day at the end of a crisp autumn   bought a one-way bus ticket from Los Angeles to   In the Plaza, after the Teatro, an Indian Veteran

El Teatro Campesino in Albuquerque, October 14, 1972. Photo by John Nichols.

and we became close to each other. Those last three *Review* issues looked great. I was given access to a darkroom, where I developed pictures. My satirical cartoons appeared in the paper (and would shortly be featured for several years in an Albuquerque underground publication, *SEER'S CATALOGUE*). As well, I wrote half the *Review*'s sardonic brief filler articles without a byline. I yearned to keep the journal alive because it was keeping *me* alive.

The front-page story and photograph of our November 1972 issue featured a short, bilingual play, called an *acto*, performed by El Teatro Campesino of Luis Valdez at an anti-war demonstration in Albuquerque's Old Town Plaza. The *acto*, Soldado Razo, is about a barrio Chicano kid who joins the army and is killed in Vietnam. It's fifteen minutes long, maybe twenty, max. My headline under the photo read: "EVERY FIVE DAYS A HYDROGEN BOMB IS DROPPED ON VIETNAM."

I loved El Teatro Campesino (Farmworker's Theatre). Luis Valdez began it in 1965 during the Delano Grape Strike in central California. In 1971 El Teatro had come to Taos and did a night of their hilarious, almost slapstick *actos* on stage at the Old Martínez Hall, a venerable bar and large auditorium in Ranchos de Taos. So many locals attended that we had to put loud speakers and a hundred folding chairs outside in the parking lot so the overflow crowd could at least hear the fiercely combative dialogue.

All the skits were irreverent, angry, in Spanish and English slang, laugh-out-loud funny, and up-against-the-wall political. The message was delivered with tears, compassion, and outrageous laughter. I was soul struck. El Teatro was a wonderful epiphany for me, saying, "You must learn to deliver a social message like *this*."

Fifty years later El Teatro Campesino is still going strong. Not so the *New Mexico Review*, because when both Rini and I were exhausted and broke at the end of 1972 we threw in the towel. And next day I began writing a new novel, which I now refer to as the "albatross around my neck." The first words I ever wrote on that book owed a large part of their heart, attitude, and freedom to the politics and humor of El Teatro Campesino.

Me and my editor Marian Wood in front of the Holt, Rinehart and Winston building, 1992. Photo by Patsy Catlett. Courtesy of John Nichols.

PART IV

21

STORIES AND exaggerated tall tales about *The Milagro Beanfield War* (and the movie made of it) have been beaten to death. Obviously, *Milagro* was inspired by my neighbors, my *Review* articles, and all aspects of local culture and *movidas*—especially everything I learned during the attempt by Taos residents to defeat a conservancy district and the Indian Camp Dam.

I had notebooks crammed with scribbled blow-by-blow accounts of argumentative, often hilarious meetings crowded by speeches, stories, cursing, accusations, praises, and appeals for money to finance appeals for justice. More intimate details of conflicts, personalities, and puzzling tangents occupied my personal daily journals. File-cabinet drawers contained dozens of manila folders crowded with newspaper clippings. I could refer to my own densely annotated amicus curiae brief filed at a district court hearing. State engineer hydrographic survey maps were pinned or taped across the walls of my house, revealing every plot of land with water rights in the Taos Valley.

At least a half-dozen books chock full of water-adjudication suits, land battles, culture, history, and justice in New Mexico and the Southwest had their pertinent facts copiously underlined by me. They occupied my floor-to-ceiling bookshelves. The first one I read on arriving here was a George I. Sánchez work published in 1940: *Forgotten People: A Study of New Mexicans*. The second was by Stan Steiner: *La Raza: The Mexican Americans*. Cleofas Jaramillo penned the third, a delightful 1956 collection of memories and Hispanic mythology called *Shadows of the Past*. I can't accuse myself of unimpeachable accuracy or boundless perspicacity, but I *was* willing to throw in, study, and absorb the entire kitchen sink.

That's what investigative journalism had taught me.

———

Obviously New Mexico's sense of humor, its history and cultures, as well as its

"BASTA YA!" means "ENOUGH, ALREADY!" This picture is an excerpt from a large cartoon I did for the front page of Albuquerque's March 1973 *SEER'S CATALOGUE* underground paper. Courtesy of John Nichols.

poverty and inequalities affected each sentence I crafted. The novel's attitude and style had been with me since childhood. Earlier I mentioned a passel of books that influenced me growing up. I feel that now, speaking of *Milagro*, I should spotlight Giovanni Guareschi, an Italian writer and cartoonist responsible for a half-dozen humorous and touching inventions about a feisty small-town Catholic priest in the Po Valley, Don Camillo, and his archenemy, the communist mayor of that town, Peppone. A third great character is Christ on the crucifix of Don Camillo's church, who constantly reprimands the hotheaded priest for his temper tantrums, patiently explaining how to amicably resolve his numerous conflicts with Peppone.

Underlying Camillo's and the mayor's clashes is the fact that they respect, and probably love, each other. Their colorful Italian village is rich with opinionated, wise, stupid, memorably funny, clumsy, and also tragic characters.

As a 1950s teenager I avidly read *The Little World of Don Camillo*, *Don Camillo and his Flock*, and *Don Camillo's Dilemma*. I also attended a couple of Franco-Italian film ventures starring the French actor Fernandel as Don Camillo and a cool Italian guy, Gino Cervi, who played Peppone. Those movies, like the books, made me laugh, cry, and rejoice even as I sobbed.

Each chapter in Guareshi's books begins with a cute and irreverent cartoon drawn by the author. The belligerent priest is depicted as a little angel with feathery wings (and a Boris Johnson haircut), and the contrary mayor is a miniature devil with horns, bat wings, and a pointed tail. Sometimes they are face-to-face, ready to box each other or commit mayhem with guns or sledgehammers like goofy, obstreperous kids. Those comical drawings affected me as much as the prose.

And while I'm at it there's another book, published in 1966 (and also depicting a small Italian town) that's a legitimate precursor to *The Milagro Beanfield War*. Written by an American, Robert Crichton, the novel spent fifty weeks on the *New York Times* bestseller list, eighteen of them at #1. *The Secret of Santa Vittoria* is a rollicking, laugh-out-loud—but also tragic and deadly serious—story about a village crammed with memorable characters trying to hide a million bottles of fabulous wine (its livelihood) from German occupiers during World War II. The clownish mayor, Bombolini, somehow rises to the occasion against the Nazi captain, von Prum, who's willing to torture his way to the secret hiding place so that his soldiers can abscond with the booze.

Bombolini's small town with its characters and conflicts, and Don Camillo's village cutups and numerous contretemps, are seminal reference points that helped me create my own lively Milagro of northern New Mexico.

My agent, Perry Knowlton, was Robert Crichton's agent. I met him at a party where we had an interesting conversation. *Santa Vittoria* was Crichton's first novel. Although he'd possessed a vision of the story, he couldn't get started. Miserably, he stared at his typewriter for weeks unable to put down a word. Finally he began writing a Dick and Jane children's primer. "Once upon a time there was a little town. It was in Italy. Italy is in Europe. That's across the ocean. The Atlantic Ocean. This was long ago. During World War Two. Different kinds of people lived in the town. Some were poor, a few were rich. They had a stupid mayor. His name was Bombolini. See Bombolini run. The people grew grapes. They picked the grapes and made wine. They put the wine in bottles. That's how they earned a living . . ."

Crichton said he produced thirty or forty pages at this level until, of a sudden, real words and sentences appeared and the novel took off.

A Stanley Kramer film of *Santa Vittoria* starring Anthony Quinn was released in 1969, the same year as *The Sterile Cuckoo*. Although Crichton's novel was an international best seller, the movie thrilled nobody. Crichton himself only published two other books.

One last important footnote: A movie I saw in 1970, thanks to Em Hall and Jim Bensfield, was made in 1953 by a blacklisted Hollywood director, Herbert Biberman, after he was released from prison for refusing to testify before the House Un-American Activities Committee. The story of a New Mexico miners' strike, *Salt of the Earth* was released in 1954. It was considered outright communist propaganda and only shown by twelve United States theaters. Hall and Bensfield tried to present the movie outdoors at night on the Santa Fe Plaza, but were shut down by the mayor's office. So a group of us watched it at Em Hall's adobe hovel in Pecos. Biberman hired only five professional actors; all others were local amateurs, largely Mexican Americans. During the strike most male miners are jailed under the Taft-Hartley Act, so their wives take over the picket lines. *Salt of the Earth* is considered a great feminist film as well as a grueling portrait of class struggle in America.

Suppressed for decades, it's now an honored work. But for sure, as I wrote *Milagro, Salt of the Earth* was always on my mind, along with El Teatro Campesino, Don Camillo, Santa Vittoria, and, of course, all the rest of my untethered imagination and memory overloads.

22

THE NOVEL WAS banged out in desperation to keep my fiction-writing career alive and provide for my family. Ruby and I had separated for a year, she in Albuquerque, me alone in Taos. Soon we would divorce. The kids traveled back and forth from Burque to Taos on a bus. If this book didn't work out after my other failures of the past eight years, what was I gonna do? Wash dishes? Take acid? Commit suicide?

When alone I could slave fifteen hours at a stretch, bag five hours shut-eye, then stay awake for another twenty-four hours. Given my cast of thousands I never quit typing about Joe Mondragón, Ruby Archuleta, Bernabé Montoya, Ladd Devine, the state engineer Nelson Bookman, Amarante Córdova, and Horsethief Shorty Wilson. My recollection is that I continued this frantic pace for five months until I amassed six hundred pages by March or April 1973. Along the way Rini Templeton read and critiqued many chapters. Her comments and political insights were helpful. Her laughter at many scenes buoyed me up. She agreed to illustrate the part headings and jacket cover when I finished. I corrected and edited the raggedy first draft for a couple of weeks (rereading and rewriting each page thirty times!). Next, I spent a month retyping it on my pea-green Hermes Rocket that jumped all over my kitchen table like a frog as I whacked the keys. I attribute much of my enthusiasm to the departure of American troops from Vietnam.

The clean copy went to Perry Knowlton at Curtis Brown in New York, and he promptly sold it to Marian Wood, an editor at Holt, Rinehart and Winston. I owe Perry the sun, moon, and stars for hooking me up with Marian. Holt paid me five thousand dollars (minus the five-hundred-dollar commission for Curtis Brown). The company promised to fork over another five grand on publication day a year later.

Oh my god, how awful. Saved *again* by capitalism! How could I ever come to terms with such hypocrisy?

———

Then I panicked. *Milagro* needed tons of rewriting. It wanted a thousand hours of editing. It required new chapters and deletions of old chapters. How could I find *time* to mold them into a semi-decent novel? Holt said they must print by September 1974. That gave me ten months to accomplish what should've taken three years of rewriting, polishing, and *upgrading* the epic. Could I possibly flesh out Nick Rael, Flossie Devine, one-armed Onofre Martínez, Pacheco's pig, and Herbie Goldfarb, the VISTA Volunteer, so quickly?

Marian Wood knuckled down. We exchanged a hundred letters and phone calls. Her suggestions and criticisms were invaluable. We argued over additions and deletions. Often she thought I was too over-the-top and I ignored her. "That's my style," I said. "Give me liberty or give me death." Among her major quibbles were chapters involving a writer and his wife in the Milagro village. "They seem awkwardly autobiographical." She was spot on. Eliminating the writer and his wife, I allocated their tasks to other characters like the recalcitrant lawyer, Charley Bloom. But I refused to budge on VISTA volunteer Herbie Goldfarb's next-door neighbor, Stella Armijo, throttling her chickens and rabbits for dinner, then blowing away an oversexed mongrel that got his penis stuck while fucking the Armijo's in-heat bitch, Esperanza. My philosophy seemed to be, "If it bleeds, it leads."

Marian mumbled, "Well, it's *your* funeral."

Until *Milagro* entered its final page proofs I was adding corrections, begging for more days, hours, and minutes until they cut me off. What Marian and I had forgotten to omit were the far too many gratuitous obscenities. And the expression, "*Ai, Chihuahua!*" should have been spoken *only once* throughout the entire book instead of on fifty different occasions. Each occasion is still a bullet of shame fired directly through my faltering heart, an example of literary Tourette's syndrome carried to extremes. Kurt Vonnegut got away with it with "So it goes." But after I'm dead there will probably be a few literary gangbangers who'll regularly, sarcastically, spray paint "*Ai, Chihuahua!*" across my crumbling tombstone.

———

Here's how the jacket copy on Milagro's first edition hardcover described the novel:

It was a soft, early spring morning with the mist still clinging to the mountains and the blackbirds just starting to swoop low over the alfalfa fields when Joe Mondragón—thirty-six with not much to show for it, a feisty hustler with a talent for trouble—slammed his battered pickup to a stop, tugged on his gumboots, and marched into the arid patch of ground his father had once cultivated. Carefully, if impulsively (and also illegally), he tapped into the main irrigation channel.

And so began—though few knew it at the time (least of all Joe)—the great Milagro beanfield war.

But like everything else in the dirt-poor town of Milagro, it would be a patchwork war, fought more by tactical retreats than battlefield victories. Gradually, ever so fumblingly, the small farmers and sheepmen began to rally to Joe's beanfield as the symbol of their lost rights and their lost lands. And downstate in the capital, the Anglo water barons and power brokers huddled in urgent conference, intent on destroying that symbol before it destroyed their multimillion-dollar land development schemes.

The tale of Milagro's rising is wildly comic and lovingly tender, a vivid portrayal of a town that, half-stumbling and partly prodded, groped its way toward its own stubborn salvation. It is, in the words of Edward Abbey, "a bellyful of a story—very funny, easy-going and sharp as a taco" and it amply fulfills H. Allen Smith's prophecy that John Nichols "will likely become the best comic novel writer of his time."

———

Holt had great hopes for the book. *Milagro* was going to be my "breakout novel." Champagne, fast cars, fancy women, and a Fender Strat. Rumors were Book-of-the-Month Club would take the novel. Ballantine paperbacks offered twenty-five thousand dollars for reprint rights. Holt rejected Ballantine's offer as insulting. They expected much higher bids from other reprint operations. Film producers wanted to sign an option on *Milagro* even before it reached the age of consent (i.e.: *before* it was published). Myself, I had just turned thirty-four.

One minute later the bottom fell out. Book-of-the-Month Club withdrew. No other paperback companies wanted the book, so Holt informed Ballantine they'd accept their $25,000 offer. Too late. By then Ballantine was hip and only ponied up $7,500. Yes, the novel did go on film option for a few thousand dollars—nothing to brag about or alleviate poverty.

The Putnam's Prize all over again.

When the economic balloon deflated, Holt retreated overnight. Their first edition had been a small printing. Before the bottom dropped out they had produced a modest second edition, then immediately remaindered the book, which became an orphan selling for ninety-nine cents on Marboro discard tables. The party was canceled before even the first guest had arrived.

Cut my legs off and call me "Shorty."

———

Still, many newspapers reviewed *Milagro*. Sometimes good, sometimes bad. On October 27, 1974, the *New York Times* made Eliot Fremont-Smith's savaging of *The Sterile Cuckoo* seem like a genteel tea party in an English country garden. First off, the critic stated that I'd "moved away from the sentimental narrowness of 'The Sterile Cuckoo' and 'The Wizard of Loneliness,' to facing big issues— social justice, the American class system—but failing to rise to the material." The novel was not Joe Mondragón's or *Milagro*'s story, "it is Nichols's story, and he dominates every page, every moment, with his wit. He does not let the characters act or move but that he steps in and *says*. The book is so full of his saying that little else gets done."

The long review ridiculed my creation of the immortal old man, Amarante Córdova, and declared that all the characters "are stereotypes" who "don't exist in and of themselves, and they don't act because of inner necessity." Too: "As for the prose, it is either so slack as to be hastily composed, or so intentionally folksy as to be patronizing to the folk."

Then, after quoting a half-dozen of my boring clichés, the reviewer stated, "I don't think that the common man speaks and acts in clichés only." And he (or she) insisted that I turned "the potentially magical into the stereotyped cardboard cutout," which came across "as an act of literary colonialism, an acquisition of images by the writer for the sake of his own sensibility. A writer's characters deserve more sensibility than he does."

I admit that "literary colonialism" *hurt*.

Members of the home front also gave me guff. The *New Mexico Independent* dubbed *Milagro* "a bomb" and "a shallow insult" to us all. The *Río Grande Sun* accused me of creating a world "utterly without moral subtlety," functioning with a literary design that "is too obvious, too calculated and polemical, and not one character escapes symbolic function to achieve the status of a person you know, let alone care about." Out west the *Los Angeles Times* accused me of being "a second-string sports reporter" and said *Milagro* was "a book that takes hours to read, a moment to forget." The *News-Journal* of Mansfield, Ohio, remarked, "Nichols' ambitious comic novel is often fun, but it is not a book for anyone in a hurry. It has more excess baggage than the circus fat lady."

A brighter note appeared in the *Independent Journal* of San Rafael, California. "'The Milagro Beanfield War' will be enjoyed by all manner of readers on any level of participation, a hallmark of literary achievement shared with works like 'Gulliver's Travels' and 'Don Quixote.'"

I'm being hypocritically lopsided for comical effect. The fact is, some newspapers nationwide *did* praise the book, taking the sting out of the others who cut out my heart and ate it while it was still beating.

Did *Milagro* sell? Does a bear shit in your bathroom toilet and then scrub the bowl with Lysol?

23

TRUE TO FORM, my chef-d'oeuvre sank like an unlucky mobster with cinder blocks wired around his ankles. Though a borderline product, Ballantine kept the novel in print so that years later *Milagro* could be defined as "an underground cult classic." Nowadays, people often approach me assuming the story has been a best seller since its inception (and later reincarnation as a [doomed!] film directed by Robert Redford) and because of that I must be a millionaire. How should I respond—by telling them, "If you'd loan me twenty bucks I'll treat you to a chalupa at the Guadalajara Grill?" Since that would be impolite I usually shrug, call forth my cheery grin, and remark, "No, I hate to disappoint you, but my mansion and the Lamborghini would only appraise at 950K, max, at Sotheby's."

———

I never despaired. Actually, that's a lie. Yet having Marian Wood for my editor at Holt is the best thing that ever happened to me. I think back to the first time we met, downing booze at The Top of the Sixes in New York. She'd just bought *Milagro*. We hit it off immediately. She was only a few years older than me. I was a wise guy. She could be sarcastic, sardonic, caustic, hilarious, no-nonsense, and also fanatically opinionated. I loved Philip Roth; she hated him. We were kin and laughed a lot. She put me at ease in the rough-and-tumble world of New York publishing. Very quickly we became deeper friends. I think of Marian as "my shelter in the storm."

Though I didn't know it at the start, she was going to give me a literary life in New York City publishing. We'd work on my projects for twenty-five, twenty-six years. I was thirty-three when we began and fifty-eight when our string ran out. Between those dates we published eight books. Marian handled all sorts of writers. She kept the alphabet detective, Sue Grafton, on best-seller lists for over two decades. Her other authors included Karen Joy Fowler, Daniel Woodrell, Philip Caputo, Hilary Mantel, John Lanchester, Tim Sandlin, and poet Linda Bierds. Their wide-ranging personalities and styles required from her a great variety of editorial magic acts.

She had enormous patience and insight. Marian was willing to read one draft after another of my submissions. Some she rejected, and with good cause. A couple of others I published elsewhere. Yet the heart of my career and modest reputation was created by works that Marian published with Holt, Rinehart and Winston (later Henry Holt and Company). Those books were *The Milagro Beanfield War* (1974), *The Magic Journey* (1978), *A Ghost in the Music* (1979), *The Nirvana Blues* (1981), *The Last Beautiful Days of Autumn* (1982), *American Blood* (1987), *An Elegy for September* (1992), and *Conjugal Bliss* (1994). We finally parted in 1998 when she moved to G. P. Putnam's Sons and, no matter how often I rewrote it, I couldn't shove my craziest novel, *The Voice of the Butterfly*, down her throat.

24

RINI TEMPLETON AND I became very close. At thirty-eight she was five years older than me and way more experienced. Though married and divorced several times, none of those relationships had lasted long for her. If I queried Rini about her past life, she shut up and glared at me. Once, in a letter, she wrote, "You wanted to know more of me, of my heart? What to say? I guess I have been intimate with multitudes of people, in talk, in bodies, working closely on the really moving things of life and art. But it has never seemed to me that the point was to add it all up or articulate it. It's just all there. In Breugal's *Icarus*, for instance, everything leads to the sun."

Rini labored at least sixteen hours a day on her art and sculptures, chain smoking Mexican Delicados cigarettes while steadily drinking wine. I never saw her even vaguely tipsy. Her drawings consisted of pen-and-ink illustrations, or scratchboard designs that imitated woodblock illustrations. She called them "Xerox art" because they were always political, rarely signed, and free for any radical or progressive group to use on fliers, posters, or in their newspapers. Her sculptures resembled abstract cactus plants, eagle wings, or basalt stones shaped for millennia by strong river currents.

While sculpting she wore acetylene goggles, thick leather gloves, and was usually sweaty, filthy—her face smudged, hair askew, hands calloused and bent, almost deformed from cutting and bending hot metal. Her uniform was dungarees and work boots; never a dress. If I told her she was lovely, Rini would look down, embarrassed, and often reply scornfully, "I am *coja, manca, tuerta.*" Lame, one-armed, half blind.

She was born in Buffalo, New York, in 1935. The family moved to Washington, DC, then to Chicago where she excelled at school and became a brilliant "Whiz Kid" on NBC radio and TV. Her specialties were Shakespeare, opera, and baseball. At age sixteen she left home and hitchhiked through thirty states, washing dishes to support herself. Then she hit Europe for three years, living in Paris and Majorca, Spain, busking for money by playing the guitar on street corners and sidewalks.

Circa 1958 she turned up as the art editor of *El Crepusculo*, a progressive Taos newspaper briefly edited by Edward Abbey. Twelve months later Rini celebrated Fidel Castro's triumphant takeover of Havana, and for several years she worked on Cuban literacy campaigns, cut sugarcane, became fluent in Spanish, and helped found a revolutionary printmaking workshop.

By 1965 she had returned to Taos, married the painter John DePuy, and eventually became art editor of *El Grito del Norte* and the *New Mexico Review*. Her artwork supported the Chicano Movement. She helped Betita Martínez produce the enormous photo-essay book called *450 Years of Chicano History in Pictures*. By 1973 Rini and John DePuy had called it quits, which is when she and I became more than just good friends.

We worked together at her primitive cabin in Pilar, or listened to *Radio Habana* in Spanish on her shortwave radio during the Watergate hearings. Rini played Inti-Illimani, Victor Jara, and Violeta Parra records while we ate quesadillas, drank cheap red wine, and she explained to me dialectical materialism, Cuban socialism, Puccini, and *King Lear*. Her sketchbooks were filled with drawings that depicted striking workers, protestors with upraised fists, or sometimes the bucolic landscapes of northern New Mexico. Occasionally, when together, I read aloud chapters from *The Milagro Beanfield War*. Rini was another important inspiration and critic for that novel.

I remember us standing outside her cabin at midnight in bitter snowy cold gazing at the stars, feeling satiated and happy from talking, working together, and making love. She opened wide my life to more political and passionate levels than I had previously experienced. Her dedication to work, to humanity, to *hope*, was surreal.

Ruby and I had split apart for a year, agreeing to reconsider the marriage after that break, perhaps rejoining our lives for the sake of Luke and Tania. When I explained this plan to Rini she had no problem with it. After the trial separation, Ruby and I chose to reunite at the end of 1973. The difference was I would live in Albuquerque, her town. Before leaving Taos I asked Rini if we could please remain "friends." I won't elaborate, but that did not go over well.

Ruby and I lasted only six months, then the marriage was over, although our close friendship, our politics, and our family connections have remained strong to the present day—fifty-six years since we met in 1964.

By the time I returned to Taos, Rini had moved to Mexico City. She and I remained out of touch until 1977, when we reconnected, but not as before. By then she had lost much energy from overwork, living poor, and lack of self-care. Most of her time in Mexico was dedicated to political art, the *movimento*, and revolution. She founded the Popular Graphic Workshops, helped create the Mexican Cultural Workers Front, joined graphic designers for the left magazine *Punto Critico*, and visited Nicaragua to train Sandinista revolutionaries in how to foster political education. Nobody ever strove harder to create a better world, but that extreme effort sapped her energy, eventually killing her.

Rini died alone in a tiny Mexico City apartment at age fifty-one on June 15, 1986. Stroke? Heart attack? Pulmonary embolism? You tell me. When I last saw her, in March 1986, her front teeth had fallen out because she refused medical help as hypocritical when all the poor she defended possessed no money for health care, no bread at all for amenities. My final glimpse of Rini took place thirty-five years ago, already.

Many comrades refer to her as a saint. I have never met another person that hungry to be of use. She was a beautiful human being.

25 WHEN RUBY, LUKE, and I moved out west in 1969 I bought a secondhand file cabinet and began to keep folders for researching *New Mexico Review* projects and for business and personal letters. I clipped articles from the *Taos News* and the *Albuquerque Journal*, saving them in manila folders. My intent? To build a macroscopic overview of my new town, of New Mexico, of the world. These research files informed *Review* articles and *The Milagro Beanfield War*. However, I pondered a larger book after *Milagro*, a panoramic overview of society that would be like *War and Peace*, a more radical tract than *Milagro*, which I feared was too humorous. Its laughter diminished the power of its political message.

Now I wanted to write an all-encompassing saga about the rapacious economic system that both enslaves human beings and is destroying the biology that sustains us at home and abroad. It's true that survival requires a sense of life-saving humor. Now I needed to make clear that poverty is no fun, and climax capitalist development has a very cold heart.

As she tried to keep my dogma on a short leash, or at least down to a dull roar, Marian Wood regularly dubbed me a "four-foot-tall Stalinoid dwarf." Politicized herself at an early age, Marian's youthful revolutionary sympathies veered toward Leon Trotsky, then tapered off. As I pranced hither and yon swearing to overthrow the capitalist system, Marian occasionally reminded me that if I wished Holt to keep printing my polemics they'd better make a profit. Nobody at any publisher's helm was eager to promote a flop. When her sobering realism reared its unwelcome head, I cavalierly retorted, "Just watch me."

She replied rather guardedly, "I am."

––––

Skip this paragraph if lists bore you.

The manila folders expanding in my file cabinet were labeled "Education Hassles," "County Commission," "Town Council," "Politics/Politicos," "Cops,"

"Community Action Programs," "HELP," "Municipal Bonds," "Water Problems," "Road Paving," "Taos Art Association," "Vietnam Moratorium," "Police Blotter," "Crime," "Ecology," "Hospital," "Teenagers," "Electricity in the Pueblo," "Garbage Problems," "Economic Scams," "Banking," "Sewage Plant," "Local Despots," "Indian Affairs," "Farming," "Poverty," "Lawyers," "Random Subdivisions," "Planning and Zoning," "Electric Co-op," "School Board," "Ecology," "S & L Scams," "Building Inspector Scandal," "Welfare," "Hippies," "Trailer Parks," "Crime," "Legal Suits," "Religion," "Kiwanis and Lions," "Real Estate Developers," "Movies," "Low Wages," "Operation Breakthrough," "Ladies Garden Club," "Absurd Shit," "Personalities," "Child Abuse," "Miscellaneous," "Food Stamps," "Alcoholism," "Drugs," "Jail Pacts," "Car Accidents," "Adultery," and "Divorce."

That's just for starters. I was thorough. Ambitious. Obsessed. Somewhere I had read a Gustave Flaubert quote: "A writer must know everything." As I collected newspaper articles, I also handwrote pages of notes to include with those documents. The notes suggested how specific information of each file would fit into the novel I was planning. Its title was *Home Free*. Think *Jean Christophe*, *Bleak House*, *The Brothers Karamazov*. That is, Romain Rolland, Charles Dickens, Dostoyevsky.

I had plans to be Joe Dimaggio, not his brother Dominic. Or Wayne Gretzky, not his talented line mate Esa Tikkanen. Or Muhammed Ali, not Joe Frazier or George Foreman.

Fair enough?

———

What was my story? An accidental 1930 dynamite explosion in tiny Chamisaville, New Mexico (thirty miles south of Milagro), unearths a hot springs, which an unprincipled developer turns into a religious tourist attraction and spa, leading to much skullduggery during the commercial development of my town for the next forty years until 1970. At that point the local Indian Pueblo attempts to reclaim its sacred land, stolen by the US Government in 1906, while also negotiating an attempt to distribute electricity inside the main Pueblo apartment buildings, an effort promoted by the Mafia. Electricity would "benefit" the Pueblo even as it destroyed a thousand years of Native independence and cultural integrity.

That would cover my first three hundred pages of "the betterment of Cha-misaville"—my "introduction." Which included every corrupt machination that occurs while changing the society from a subsistence-agricultural community in charge of its own destiny into a cash-dependent modern township where the former residents have become impoverished wage slaves for the new ruling class of bankers, realtors, and government scumbags, effectively "destroying the vil-lage in order to save it."

The next four hundred pages of my saga would describe the dismemberment of Chamisaville's society (and ecology) caused by its corruption-driven devel-opment onslaught between 1970 and 1975. Electricity enters the Indian Pueblo (in exchange for returning its "sacred lands," a deal made with the devil). There is no happy ending. A tragedy completes my tale, yet there's hope as the die-hard survivors keep on. Their triumph is that they refuse to despair.

You tell me: What else is life about?

26

FROM 1974 TO 1977 I crammed on the story. Nonstop, daily, ten to fifteen hours a day, seven days a week, fifty-two weeks a year, no breaks, no vacations, no time off. Without question, I wanted to write a masterpiece. Still young and at the top of my game, I nurtured an almost crazed ambition for clarity and luck. This would be "the one that people remembered." A trick was that I could type all night, sleep a few hours, then catch a couple of trout for dinner from the nearby Río Chiquito, fry them up, drink a beer, and return to the magnum opus all night. I managed a "little vacation" every day without interrupting my working hours.

What puzzles me now is that for two of those years I lived with a new girlfriend, Stephanie Sonora, and her son, Tino. Stephanie had a powerful influence on my life and on *The Magic Journey*, but I can't go into that here—it would require too lengthy a digression. After Ruby and I were divorced, Luke and Tania stayed with me for all vacations. So how did I manage that and also fashion the brilliant tour de force? Obviously, I had indefatigable energy and the ability to concentrate. Referring to countless pages of novel notes, outlines, newspaper clippings, and my handwritten commentaries in every manila folder, along with lists of my numerous characters and their chronologies, I plowed ahead full steam. Everything I had learned and experienced since Guatemala crowded into the book. I raged with creative hopefulness. Two granite-patterned cardboard boxes held 5 × 7 alphabetized index cards whose typewritten notes dealt with characters, incidents, and yearly events during the unfolding avalanche of my novel, which would outshine Robert Caro's *The Power Broker* and make *Rise and Fall of the Third Reich* seem as infantile as *Goodnight, Moon*. I'd be the literary Babe Ruth, Rocky Marciano, Tom Brady. *Home Free*'s epilogue would be my Nobel acceptance speech.

"Roll over, Beethoven, and tell Tchaikovsky the news!"

———

Marian Wood did not fall in love with my first clean drafts of *Home Free*. She thought they were too tight, too claustrophobic, too dense, and lacking enough dialogue and lighter moments to make them palatable. Back to the coal mines I trudged, retackling the eight-hundred-page manuscript. Many subsequent drafts I stored on the bottom two shelves of my kitchen bookcase. A few years down the line they were sprayed on by a pet male cat and had to be tossed. Meaning I don't have a complete record of the novel's progress. Maybe Marian Wood put my cat up to it, one of those "secret tragedies" in publishing like the lost love letters of Nora Barnacle to her husband, James Joyce.

After a while I "opened up the story," adding more dialogue that gave it increased vitality and depth. Surreal dream sequences. A few sex scenes. Two of my favorite characters grew exponentially: an elderly progressive lawyer, Virgil Leyba, a refugee from the Mexican revolution. And April Delaney, wayward daughter of the town's chief developer, Rodey McQueen, who works with Virgil to oppose every harrowing scam concocted by her father. Virgil emerged clean from my imagination. April was inspired by my ex-wife, Ruby, and also by Rini Templeton and Stephanie Sonora.

Part headings of the novel were illustrated by pen and ink *calavera* drawings I did expressly for the book (*calaveras* are satirical skeletons).

Without fanfare, Holt released the novel in 1978. At the eleventh hour I changed its title from *Home Free* to *The Magic Journey* because another writer, Dan Wakefield, had weeks earlier published a book called *Home Free*. The "magic journey" was the damage created by the rise of exploitation, poverty, racism, and inequality during the "betterment" of Chamisaville. The Industrial Revolution in miniature. Climax capitalism taking command. Think of Friedrich Engels' 1845 diatribe about Manchester and Liverpool: *The Condition of the Working Class in England*.

Was the book successful? Three guesses, and the first two don't count. I doubt it earned back the meager advance. Only a few hardcovers were sent to market, alongside an overkill of trade paperbacks that plopped onto remainder tables in droves like doves shot during the September hunting season. I purchased fifteen boxes of remainders for about a penny on the dollar, and still have some of those boxes gathering dust in dark corners even though I've given away hundreds of copies like canapes at a cocktail party.

Newspapers reviewed *The Magic Journey*, same as *Milagro*, some with praise, others disgusted by my left politics. *Straight Creek Journal* in Denver called it

The Magic Journey
John Nichols

This part of the cover for my novel *The Magic Journey* features a guitar-playing calavera, one of the illustrations I did for the book's part headings. Courtesy of John Nichols.

"the finest revolutionary novel of the decade, and gets my hands-down vote for book of the year." The *Washington Post* said I had "dodged my duty as a novelist" and "made of *The Magic Journey* not a novel but a shapeless chronicle." The *Chicago Tribune* thought it was more than a novel of social conscience or protest, "It is the story of what can happen to a civilization when it turns against itself—when its exercise in progress consumes and destroys its human and natural resources." My hometown rag, the *Taos News*, let me have it with both barrels. "If you loved 'Milagro' for its humor, alas, don't bother with this one: there's precious little. To get to it you'll have tough slogging through an overly long and wordy book, whose stilted rhetoric masquerading as dialogue sounds embarrassingly like several versions of the same high school essay." The *New York Times* decided, "You can get mighty weary of all that preaching." And concluded, "It is nice, friendly, and fun, and it has about as much depth as 'Tommy' and 'Jesus Christ, Superstar.'"

Ouch! That assessment cut off my head so cleanly that I didn't realize the full extent of the damage until I turned to look sideways.

At least Quality Paperback Book Club advertised it as "a wild, raucous and ultimately chilling indictment of Progress, American style." And, ever since, the few people who write me powerful letters or approach in person to explain how much they love *The Magic Journey* and what it has meant to their lives, touch me to the core.

Is it a masterpiece? Does a bear open your refrigerator door but decide not to eat anything?

27

AS DIFFICULT AS it is for me to believe now, I had another novel going simultaneously with *The Magic Journey*. During each brief lull in that project, I created multiple drafts of *A Big Diaphanous Wild Man*. Only now Bart Darling had morphed from a Maine lobsterman into a wacky New Mexico sheepherder. That sucked, so he remorphed into a corrupt art-gallery owner in a town like Taos. And *that* version stunk so bad he subsequently evolved into a Hollywood stunt man and B-movie director living in a mansion similar to the Taos Mabel Dodge Luhan house (when Dennis Hopper owned it!). And, bizarre as this sounds, I eventually "found" the novel begun thirteen years earlier during my 1965 honeymoon spent running liquor out to Monhegan Island in Maine with Ruby and David Pulsifer. The final title was *A Ghost in the Music*. It reached bookstores in 1979.

The reviews were typical John Nichols reviews.

1. *Best Sellers*: "This book has nothing to offer, no plot, no characters, no style, no elevating ideas."

2. *Los Angeles Times*: "Through Bart Darling's race to suicide, Nichols has written a novel that is a celebration of life."

3. *Library Journal*: "Nichols is excessively long-winded, and not a single characterization rings true."

4. *Chicago Tribune Book World*: "In today's environment, one that seems more like a rerun of a TV sitcom each day, it is refreshing and important to find a book like 'A Ghost in the Music' telling such a complex story of simplicity and love."

5. *Publishers Weekly*: "All this is told in pages of excessive chatter—much of it lewd and lurid. The chatter grows exceedingly dreary and repetitious, unfortunately."

6. *Philadelphia Inquirer*: "This, Nichols' sixth book, and fifth novel, is certainly his tightest, most assured work, shaped in a prose of beautiful

clarity and simplicity, in this composition by an artist who keeps getting better and better."

7. *Santa Fe New Mexican*: "'A Ghost in the Music' is glib, trite, superficial. It is a ghost of a novel and little else."

8. *The Denver Post*: "John Nichols style resembles that of several other contemporary novelists—notably Joseph Heller and J. P. Donleavy. All have a way of combining heart-wrenching sadness and bizarre comedy to come up with memorably bittersweet works. 'A Ghost in the Music' is like that."

And get this: While working on that novel I also helped craft a tome of lovely Taos photographs taken by my friend, Bill Davis, and accompanied by my prose memoir of first arriving in Taos. *If Mountains Die*. Marian Wood disliked photo-essays and refused to publish it, so Bill and I jumped through thirty-seven hoops to broker a deal with Sierra Club and Ballantine Books that Sierra Club subsequently ditched, causing Ballantine to opt out, and we wound up with Alfred A. Knopf. And our book was successful. Who would've guessed? Released in 1979, same as *A Ghost in the Music*, it remained in print until 2018. Forty years. I was seriously on a roll and owe Bill Davis much for his perseverance on *If Mountains Die*. He made it happen. Inspired by his great photographs I believe *every* review was positive.

"Look, Ma! No hands!"

28

THIS LAST BIT of creative history I hesitate to bring up because you'll assume I was crazy. However, in May 1977, a high-end East Coast photographer took an option on *The Wizard of Loneliness* that paid me $2,500 a year. The purchase price would be $25,000 if the option was exercised. He also wanted me to write the screenplay and Curtis Brown negotiated that document for him dated September 1977. Ten grand for the first draft, five grand for the second (the polish). Writers Guild minimum.

The guy wanted my first draft by Thanksgiving that year. We agreed on it, and I went to work fanatically among my other projects. I had a *Wizard* draft in time, but Curtis Brown advised me not to send it on because the producer hadn't yet signed the screenwriting agreement. I pooh-poohed their concern on the grounds that we had shaken hands on the deal. So he received my script the day after Thanksgiving, 1977. I was a man of my word.

However, the gentleman then dillydallied, refusing to sign and pay me for my work while he began shopping the script seeking a deal. I have a file of my protest letters to him that generated little or no response. At least he renewed his option. But then he "hired" another scriptwriter, Nancy Larson, at which point I flared and announced that when his current option expired I wouldn't renew it. Immediately he exercised the option, sending a check for ten thousand dollars to Curtis Brown up front. The other fifteen grand arrived two months later. I had lost control of my book to a man who'd openly stiffed me.

Live and learn. I should've listened to my agent. Now I was helpless to affect *Wizard*'s future travels. For the next eight years the man relentlessly pursued a deal and finally generated interest from Redford's Sundance and TV's *American Playhouse*. Director Jenny Bowen and her cinematographer husband, Richard, signed on to make the film. The Nancy Larson script was awful. Jenny tried to salvage it with my help one weekend before going on location in Vermont the autumn of 1987. That task overwhelmed us, as you shall eventually see.

My main learning experience was "get it down in writing." Sadly, on a few more occasions I would forget that admonition. I had a deliberate, built-in antipathy toward "looking after my own best interests." I think I considered that an honorable political act.

29

AROUND MY FORTIETH birthday (in 1980) I wrote Robert Redford a letter in which I outlined the film option history of *The Milagro Beanfield War* from 1974 to 1980. Although I'd already given a new option to a producer named Moctesuma Esparza, Redford was "interested" in the book (which I'll explain shortly). By 1980 Curtis Brown had created a film division, so Adams, Ray, and Rosenberg were out of the picture. My letter to Redford explained that Bob Christiansen and Rick Rosenberg (Chris/Rose Productions) had held the option for six years, beginning shortly after they made for TV (in 1974) an adaptation of Ernest Gaines' novel *The Autobiography of Miss Jane Pittman* (screenplay by Tracy Keenan Wynn and starring Cicely Tyson). During their first year *Milagro* option, financed by Tomorrow Entertainment, Chris/Rose hired Mark Medoff, of *When You Comin' Back Red Ryder* fame, to do the writing. He didn't work out. The producers then went to Paramount, and Tracy Wynn did a *Milagro* script that was competent, not very funny, and catered to interracial violence that my reaction letters compared to *Shaft*, *Sweet Sweetback's Baadasssss Song*, and Pam Grier's blacksploitation flicks, *Coffy* and *Foxy Brown*. Going for major studio funding, Chris/Rose wanted a famous star to play the lead, like Al Pacino, Robert de Niro, Dustin Hoffman, or—Jesus!—Charles Bronson. The scripts, and those names, gave me the willies. I mean, were they talking about an impoverished northern New Mexico farmer here? Can Dustin Hoffman speak Spanish? And how would the embodiment of *Death Wish 1–5*, a murderous Lithuanian vigilante, look in denim OshKosh B'gosh overalls driving a tractor and planting pinto beans?

After two years at Paramount, Christiansen and Rosenberg moved over to Lorimar in 1977. They hired Michael Wadleigh and Leonard Gardner to collaborate on a screenplay, with Leonard on board to write and Michael slated to direct. Michael's credibility came from his film of *Woodstock*. Leonard had written *Fat City*, a fine novel, and he'd scripted the John Huston movie of it. His *Milagro* efforts were still as flat as west Texas. And there continued the same conflict over wanting a star in order to score funding for a major motion picture.

Lorimar backed the project until November 1979, at which point Chris/Rose threw in the towel. That's when I transferred the option to Moctesuma Esparza, who had about as much chance of pulling off a movie "miracle" as I had of writing a best seller or staying married for longer than seven years.

Redford thanked me for my litany of monotonous failures.

30

FRANKLY, WHO CARED? After *The Magic Journey* I was ready to attack the typewriter for another "big" novel I had up my sleeve that was as different from *The Magic Journey* as a Times Square massage parlor was different from the Taj Majal. I don't think I was motivated by Marian Wood's comments about "profit or perish," but I felt kind of burned out by my radical political tenacity. Though I still had visions of a "masterpiece," I convinced myself it could include a different sort of "kitchen sink." Then, while I was fiddle-fucking around haphazardly typing notes for my next guaranteed failure, the book—on just a single preposterous afternoon—fell into my lap.

Either in 1978 or 1979, Baba Ram Dass (formerly Timothy Leary's LSD cohort Richard Alpert) and some other hookie-mooks brought a Hanuman monkey statue to Taos. I'd never heard of Hanuman, who is a prominent actor in the east Indian epic *Ramayana*, which I've still never read, God forbid. The statue arrived in a wooden crate placed aboard a trailer now parked in a field with picturesque high mountains towering above it in Arroyo Seco, a village near Taos.

Ram Dass and other Hindu, Buddhist, karma, dharma, Neem Karoli Baba spiritual adventurers had brought the Hanuman to Taos. They planned an afternoon party to celebrate its arrival. I had a woman friend who was into the Me Decade, Scientology, Hare Krishna, Eckankar, TM, and New Age yogi America gurus, and she invited me to come with her to the Hanuman unveiling.

You can tell I was leaking scorn and sarcasm out every pore of my body even before we started my car and headed north. Secretly, however, I was aching to set free the other "real me," the one who wasn't a four-foot-tall Stalinoid dwarf but rather a horny, confused atheist eager to meet Erica Jong and worship at *her* temple of the Zipless Fuck while overcoming my fear of flying. Yes, I'm an asshole and not asking forgiveness. All religion in general, and icon-worshiping idolatry in particular, have never been my strong suit. Nirvana, reincarnation, and soul travel aren't my cup of cyanide-laced Kool-Aid. I've never understood how people who skip off to spiritual retreats in India can ignore thousands of Untouchables sleeping on sidewalks, shitting in the gutters, starving to death, or splashing filthy river water on themselves at Varanasi.

Nevertheless, my friend and I attended the Hanuman party, which made a big impression on me. Yet now, at age eighty, I scarcely remember it. So here's my novelist brain reimagining the event. Nice people wandered around in a swoon, eating *raita* with their fingers and putting fruit under the trailer so the *murti* inside could make it sacred *prasad*. Bare-chested men carried incense sticks and sage smudge bundles. Children had tinkling bells on their fingers. Folks flutter-danced in and out of a tipi. Cedar cook fires heated exotic victuals. I'm sure there was music—you know, flutes, zithers, and that instrument Ravi Shankar favors. What's it called? Oh, the sitar. Friends talked about karma, swamis, and euphoric vibes.

Finally, when late afternoon arrived everyone gathered around the trailer as the top and siding of the crate was unbolted and removed. And there was the gleaming white marble Hanuman flying toward Lanka in search of Sita. To me the statue seemed perverse, languorous, prissy, sensual, effeminate, and disturbingly androgynous. One hand held an ornate scepter, the other toted Ram's ring, which I presume was meant for Sita.

The present company ohhed and ahhed, or sat in a semicircle on the ground properly awed after taking LSD. I've never in my life taken LSD or mescaline or eaten a mushroom. A few hippies passed around *leños* that wafted sacred fumes across our nostrils. Then the organizers went back to Taos and built the Monkey Temple right off Valverde Street before it intersects with La Lomita, and the temple is still there. I've never entered it. Hence I have never again seen the Hanuman statue first revealed on that sunny afternoon in Arroyo Seco. Afterward I drove home to my wicked Upper Ranchitos bailiwick, cackling with monstrous glee, and created a scathing eight-hundred-page manuscript spoofing everything from Transcendental Meditation, monkey gods, and primal scream rooms to the Zipless Fuck, a satire called *The Nirvana Blues* that Holt, Rinehart and Winston published without a whimper of hesitation in 1981.

———

I had planned for the novel to cover a year in the life of an immigrant Anglo couple while they struggled to build a house in "Chamisaville" (Taos). At the end of that year, just as the last nail was driven home, they'd divorce because that had happened to most of my newcomer Anglo friends in northern New Mexico. Since I was still effectively broke I pitched the book in a twenty-page

Here are two of the monkey-oriented death threats Joe Miniver receives in *The Nirvana Blues*. I drew the monkeys, of course. They made me laugh! Courtesy of John Nichols.

treatment to my Holt editor, Marian Wood, who replied, "Oh for God's sake, get *real*. I'm not *that* gullible."

Screw her. I wrote the bizarre tract anyway. Yet found myself into the monster—after only six fictional days had elapsed—when I reached page eight hundred! So much for the best-laid plans. No house was ever built. I had about as much discipline as the Three Stooges. The novel was like a 250,000 word rewrite of *The Day of the Locust* meets *Portnoy's Complaint* and *Even Cowgirls Get the Blues*. But when I tendered the completed ten-pound behemoth to Marian Wood she accepted it. Then she bent over, picked up my jaw, and handed it back to me. The advance I received was for a *two-book contract*, my pinnacle in publishing! They didn't offer me the moon, but even a tiny asteroid is bragging fodder to an also-ran like me.

The Nirvana Blues is as off-the-wall ridiculous as *The Magic Journey* isn't. But it's also a futuristic view of what has happened to Taos in the forty-odd years since *Nirvana* arrived at your local booksellers. I laughed and cringed all the way from page 1 to the end. Writing *Nirvana* was fun. My hero, Joe Miniver, kept getting cartoon death threats in the mail for his dislike of the monkey god. Of course, I drew all the cartoons.

Some critics hacked it to pieces, but others praised it, if not to the skies at least to the Puerile Hall of Fame. The *Dallas Morning News* said it "has something to amuse—and offend—almost everyone." *Best Sellers* crucified it: "*The Nirvana Blues* is a funny, entertaining book which should appeal to white middle-class undergraduates. The thinking reader will find it much ado about nothing." Next day my mail brought these words from the *Fort Worth Star-Telegram*: "Here is a novel that begins with a wonder, ends with a bullet between the eyes, and along the way delivers one heart-wrenching laugh after another." The *Denver Post*'s opinion? "The overall bleakness of the human landscape in this, the final volume of his trilogy, on the death throes of the Hispanic and Indian cultures in northern New Mexico, is distressing." According to the *Dallas Times Herald* my story was "contrived and directionless" and "Nichols seems to have forgotten that he's in the business of crafting fiction." The *Mill Valley* (California) *Pacific Sun* disagreed. "*The Nirvana Blues* is a winner. If you have an extravagance of frivolity and a streak of silliness, you will guffaw throughout this shockingly hilarious and gut-tightening 'biography' of Joe Miniver." The *Arizona Daily Star* grumbled that *Nirvana* "cranks up the guilt machine" and "Nichols doesn't see any happy endings ahead for northern New Mexico, for pizzafied America, for the '80s." The *Austin Chronicle* felt *Nirvana* was "entertaining," but "in the real world Nichols sees a kind of chaos enveloping this region as cultural genocide threatens northern New Mexico." The *Los Angeles Herald-Examiner*'s opinion was that "John Treadwell Nichols, self-described 'Stalinoid' and '4-foot dwarf,' is as huge and quirky an American writing talent as has materialized in the past 20 years, and his presence should be trumpeted with banner headlines by the culture journal of your choice." Not to be outdone by a competitor, the *Los Angeles Times* crowed, "If, on an astral plane, Melville and Max Shulman could marry and have a kid, the kid might be John Nichols. This last volume of his 'New Mexico Trilogy' is transcendentally profound; also achingly funny." And Long Island's *Newsday* trumped them both by stating, "I wish to persuade you that this sprawling, undisciplined, stream-of-consciousness novel is a work of genius, the most important novel of the year and, not least, hilarious."

Hey, you can't argue with that. *Nirvana* scored a film option. It was a best seller in Los Angeles, Denver, and New Mexico. Too, Holt sent me on my first book tour ever because Marian Wood said if I didn't hit the road to promote my schlock she would quit publishing those screeds. And hell hath no fury, so I went.

Portion of a large poster in French advertising the Costa-Gavras film *Missing*, showing the three main characters, played by Jack Lemon, Sissy Spacek, and John Shea. Courtesy of John Nichols.

PART V

31

AROUND THAT same time a sommelier opened a bottle of expensive wine at the Throne Table of Ma Maison (in Los Angeles) for our hosts, Jack Lemmon and his wife, Felicia Farr. The Greek film director Costa-Gavras was at the dinner too, with his editor, Françoise Bonnot; yours truly; and Eddie and Mildred Lewis. Costa had directed *Z* and *State of Siege*, two of my favorite movies. The first is a political thriller about a Greek assassination and subsequent state takeover by a right-wing military coup. It won a Best Foreign Language Film Academy Award in 1969. *State of Siege*, set in Uruguay during a conflict between the reactionary government and left-wing Tupamaros guerrillas, is a 1972 picture based on the real life story of an American CIA counterterrorist agent in Montevideo, Dan Mitrione, who was kidnapped and murdered by the Tupamaros.

Eddie Lewis was the producer of *Missing*, which would receive four Academy Award nominations in 1982 and share the Golden Palm Award at Cannes. Long ago Eddie had helped break the Hollywood blacklist by placing Dalton Trumbo's name as screenwriter on the 1960 Kirk Douglas-Stanley Kubrick film *Spartacus*. Eddie's the one who phoned me and asked if I could rewrite *Missing*. I thought it was a crank call from an overwrought fan, but Eddie was serious. *Missing* had Costa-Gavras involved but did not yet have a studio green light. Since I didn't yet fly, Eddie paid for my train ticket to LA, where a hipster driving a limo picked me up, handed over a copy of the script, and told me to read it on our way to the Marina Pacific Hotel in Venice. When I finished reading, I should knock on the door of room 3. An hour and a half later I knocked on the proper door, and a handsome man about six years my senior with a heavy five-o'clock shadow and a foreign accent said, "Vell, John, vot you tink?"

When I explained that I basically had no idea how to write screenplays, he waved his hand dismissively and repeated, "Yoost tell me vot you *tink*."

The movie was based on a nonfiction book by Thomas Hauser, *The Execution of Charles Horman*. It described the September 11, 1973, military coup in Chile backed by United States government embassy personnel and the CIA. During the General Pinochet coup, which overthrew Salvador Allende (and killed him), two young American men, Charles Horman and Frank Teruggi, were disappeared and murdered with US complicity (starting with Henry Kissinger and Richard Nixon). Hauser's research details a search, in Chile, by Charles Horman's wife and his dad to find out what happened. For me, Costa's present screenplay was a thriller in which the main characters didn't really connect.

Five minutes into our conversation I realized that Costa mangled English even worse than I spoke French (he lived in Paris, and French was his "native" second language). So when I began to correct his horrid English by completing the sentences in French, he brightened like the White House Christmas tree and we began zooming intelligibly ahead speaking French. What good fortune *that* was. I've told myself all my life that I must've stepped in shit to be so lucky.

When I asked Costa if I could invent any facts, or at least fiddle with the structure of scenes, he said "No" at first because it was a "true story." Then he allowed I could alter some scenes and add dialogue, providing the changes were consistent with the overall situation in Chile as described by Hauser's book.

That's it. Universal Studios and Polygram ordered me to get cranking immediately. I had three weeks over Christmas 1980 to do the job. Make the main characters in their tense thriller more human, more connected, better at ease with each other. Teetering on the edge of success or failure, they were desperate to bag a green light and big-time actors for the roles. They also suggested that if I wanted to work on movies I'd better learn, fast, how to fly. I was headed that way anyway because of the *Nirvana* book tour.

———

I've entered a few totally foreign and unknown situations in my day, but this one teeters at the top of the list. Those were the most frantic three weeks of my life. My girlfriend and her daughter, and my two kids, were at the Taos house wrapping presents; baking chocolate-chip cookies; decorating the Christmas tree; caroling neighbors; yelling at the dogs and cats; playing punk rock, Black Sabbath, and Motörhead records; and arguing with each other—the usual strident holiday caterwauling. They slept on mattresses spread over the living-room floor while I crammed on the script in my freezing bedroom. Sleep was not a viable option for me. I barely understood how to proceed, yet somehow built a forceful relationship between the two main characters, who'd subsequently be played by Jack Lemon and Sissy Spacek. I delivered the screenplay back on time fully convinced I had botched it royally. My cover letter oozed obsequious apologies. Costa-Gavras, Universal Pictures, and Eddie Lewis were overjoyed. The film bagged a green light and almost immediately went on location in Mexico.

Hey, rewriting successful screenplays was like taking candy from a baby! A really *helpless* baby.

As I mentioned earlier, it garnered four Academy Award nominations . . . and won the 1982 Oscar for Best Adapted Screenplay. But by then the Writers Guild had arbitrated me out of a credit. Costa once allowed me to fondle the Oscar he won with *Missing* for Best Adapted Screenplay, a credit he shared with screenwriter Donald Stewart. The gold statuette sat on a shelf in his Paris home office. I don't remember if it was hollow inside or weighed a lot.

(By the way, that same year, Alan Pakula scored an Oscar nomination for his script of *Sophie's Choice*, but he lost out to Costa-Gavras, Donald Stewart, "and the uncredited John Nichols" according to Pauline Kael's lacerating review of *Missing*).

———

Be advised: The success of *Missing* was not a foregone conclusion. After Costa cut the picture and readied it for release, the studio worried it was too anti-American and would create unfavorable commentary about US foreign policy, and also be sued by the US Government. Or at least by some of its embassy personnel in Chile clandestinely involved with the 1973 Pinochet coup. Hence also not a film to release while the Reagan administration was "illegally" financing the contra war in Nicaragua to defeat the Sandinista revolution.

In December 1981, Eddie Lewis, Universal, and Costa-Gavras took *Missing* for a midnight sneak preview at a Philadelphia theater. The point was to distribute audience opinion cards to obtain a feel for the public reaction. My girlfriend and I were flown from New Mexico to Philly, where we joined Costa-Gavras and the Universal crowd. Also invited were my best friends, Alan Howard and his wife from New York, and my radical pal, Mike Kimmel, a native of Philadelphia. Mike was tight with Juan Ramos, head of the left-wing Puerto Rican chapter of Young Lords in that city.

Mike, Alan, and I met at the theater with Eddie Lewis that afternoon to discuss the late-night logistics. When Mike told Eddie about his chummy relationship with the Young Lords, Eddie reached into his pocket and pulled out a wad of twenty dollar bills held together by a rubber band. He peeled off two dozen of them for Mike, ordering him to contact (and bribe) every Young Lord he knew so they'd enter the theater in time for its *Missing* preview.

And, with his pockets full of cash, Mike took off to stack the midnight audience with viewers who'd automatically cheer the show.

I sat through *Missing* petrified and dismayed, same as long ago for that preview of *The Sterile Cuckoo*. But Mike did a good job with Eddie's bread; the audience reaction was stellar. Viewers were stunned at the end. All their cards came back laudatory. The Universal executives (and Eddie Lewis) beamed happily. Released in February and March of 1982, *Missing* rose to number 3 at the box office for a short time, earning a good profit (and much controversy) throughout the United States. Lawsuits for libel were filed against Costa-Gavras and Universal, in particular by a former ambassador to Chile, Nathaniel Davis. Universal withdrew the film until the lawsuit was dropped, then released it once more. *Missing* had legs.

———

After *Missing*, Costa hired me to write two other screenplays over the next five years. He also asked me to critique, and perhaps polish, a third film, scripted by Franco Solinas, which already had a green light and would star Jill Clayburgh. I disliked the awkward script and its wishy-washy Israeli/Palestinian politics, and didn't become involved. The film, *Hanna K*, is considered one of Costa's disappointments.

But *Missing* is how my "accidental Hollywood career" started for reals. I owe Costa and Eddie Lewis for another of those remarkable "gifts" that have been granted me over my "charmed" lifetime. To generate that sort of charmed lifetime you have to be *very* lucky.

32

ON THE SEPTEMBER 1981 *Nirvana Blues* book tour I visited Houston, Austin, Dallas, Los Angeles, San Francisco, Berkeley, Oakland, and Chicago. En route I received a slew of phone messages from Ann Migden of the Writers Guild during the arbitration of my credit for *Missing*, which the studio had submitted as written by Costa-Gavras, Donald Stewart, and yours truly. I did not fully understand the process. And I was preoccupied by trains, planes, and automobiles, media escorts, radio and TV shows, book signings, constipation, and newspaper interviews.

In total I received twenty thousand dollars for tweaking the *Missing* screenplay. A preposterous fortune to me. I had no idea that sum was worse than slave wages. Nor did I realize the value of a screenplay credit, or how viciously writers competed with each other to restrict the number of credits on a movie in order to earn larger bonus payments if a film began shooting. By rights, I should have been advised by the Guild that Donald Stewart had initiated the arbitration in order to increase his payoff by sharing credit with only one other writer (Costa-Gavras) instead of two. But I wasn't told until a year (or two?) later when the president of the Writers Guild, Frank Pierson (who scripted *Dog Day Afternoon* and *Cool Hand Luke*) revealed that fact as he and I worked together, briefly, on *The Milagro Beanfield War* screenplay.

Bottom line?

Too bad, you lose, tough luck, break out the violins. Life is a constant learning experience. And the making of every motion picture generates a hundred tragedies, so don't cry for me, Argentina. Especially since my philosophy was to "live poor" and "maintain integrity."

I was lucky to have been included.

On Oscar night, April 11, 1983, I did receive these words from Sean Daniel, a top executive at Universal:

DEAR JOHN: I AM SENDING YOU THIS TELEGRAM

BEFORE THE OSCARS TONIGHT, BECAUSE THE VIC-
TORY IS YOURS NO MATTER WHAT HAPPENS OR
HOW THE VOTING GOES. EVERYONE WHO WORKED
ON 'MISSING' HELPED CREATE A MOVIE THAT HAS
EARNED ITS PLACE IN FILM HISTORY AND IN THE
HUMAN CONSCIENCE. YOU SHOULD BE PROUD FOR
I AM PROUD TO HAVE BEEN IN IT WITH YOU. WE
WILL BE THINKING OF YOU TONIGHT. THANK YOU
FOR ALL YOUR WONDERFUL WORK. ALL THE BEST,
SEAN DANIEL.

33

TO REFRESH YOUR memories about the *Milagro* option: In 1979, when Chris/Rose abandoned the project, other parties with deeper pockets wanted to join the game. One was Cheech Marin. Another Robert Redford. A wealthy real-estate consortium in Albuquerque (read "the mob?") planned for Jesús Treviño, a distinguished Chicano filmmaker, to direct. Lastly, an unknown Los Angeles producer named Moctesuma Esparza laid his minor cards on the table.

Instinctively, I chose him. I was not a fan of Cheech and Chong's toilet jokes and pot orgies. The Burque real-estate consortium felt disconcerting. And I didn't want a famous blond, blue-eyed Anglo actor directing the film of a book written by another blond, blue-eyed gringo, a novel in which half the characters spoke Spanish. To boot, I figured involving Redford would blow the whole thing way out of proportion. Admittedly, I was distracted by the fact that Redford's fame and money could guarantee the same kind of "security" offered me by the Putnam's Prize fifteen years earlier. That caused a brief "hiccup" in my decision to choose Esparza. My kids were older, they needed clothes, child support, health insurance, bicycles. I cursed my desire to select "integrity" over a more guaranteed livelihood.

During the late sixties and early seventies, Moctesuma had participated in the Chicano Movement. He spoke Spanish. During a demonstration he'd been arrested. Recently he had acquired the rights to form a cable TV station in a largely Chicano community outside of Los Angeles. A regular homeboy.

Mocte had a deal with the National Endowment for the Humanities to make three movies—*The Ballad of Gregorio Cortez*, *Revolt of the Cockroach People*, and *Pocho*. All were geared toward small films or public television. His six-month option with me for *Milagro* allowed him to petition the NEH for more bread, including bargain-basement dollars to hire me as the *Milagro* script-writer.

He obtained the grant and an additional helping hand from the National Council of La Raza. My deal was to write a step-outline, a couple of scripts, a revision, and a polish for $27,500, approximately Writers Guild minimum for work that could last two years. If Mocte exercised the option I'd be paid $35,000. Sounds like a great deal, *qué no*? Truth is, it was a steal tailored to a small production financed by government grants. Still, it beat anything I'd ever earned in publishing. You wonder why literary giants like Fitzgerald and Faulkner wound up in Hollywood? *That's* why.

Not to worry. Robert Redford promptly met with Esparza, and they signed a joint-venture agreement to produce a major motion picture. Whereupon Bob began working with me on the screenplay. A collaboration of two blond, blue-eyed *gabachos* that I'd hoped to avoid when I also avoided the millions I might have grasped by signing with Redford in the first place. Bob and Moctesuma exercised the option in 1983 because the purchase price was so cheap and they wouldn't have to pay any more option fees. It's rare for producers to do that unless the movie is a sure thing. But at that time *Milagro* was like a 100–1 glue-factory hay burner on a very wet track.

Some friends called me a schmuck for cutting off my financial nose to spite my bank account. My reply? I pointed to the halo sparkling above my head.

———

In LA during those 1980s heydays working on other pictures for Costa-Gavras (and Karel Reisz, Redford, Louis Malle, plus a miniseries for CBS), I rented roller blades during breaks and skated on the bike path from Marina del Rey up to the Santa Monica pier and back. I was loose as a goose, in shape and happy. I enjoyed staying at the Marina Pacific Hotel and got high from the girls on the Venice boardwalk wearing pink satin short-shorts, skimpy bandeau tops, and white roller skates. The muscle dudes were also fun. As was the guy who juggled throbbing chainsaws *and* apples simultaneously, taking a bite of each apple now and then.

When Costa-Gavras and I were driving to a meeting with the suits at Universal, he told me about wanting to make a film of an André Malraux novel set in China: *Man's Fate*. It was based on the Shanghai insurrection of 1927 (look it up!). Costa went to China and parlayed with the authorities for a spell, but their restrictions and demands were impossible, so he forsook the project.

"In this business," he remarked, "we don't have the money, or the studios, so that's the only real power we have—to take a walk."

Words to the wise. But right then I was having too much fun. And anyway, we were headed to Universal because Costa wanted to pitch a movie developed by him and me about science and human values in the twentieth century. The first I'd heard about this was on that ride to the studio. When I asked Costa what he had in mind he waved a hand carelessly, saying, "I don't know, but the idea interests me." I thought, *Okay, I'm about to get a lesson on how the real pros convince the real gangsters to cough up development bread.*

So we park, take an elevator to the top floor, and sit down with Eddie Lewis and eight tanned moguls wearing Armani suits in a room whose windows offered a 360-degree view of the greater Los Angeles area and the foothills surrounding it.

Everybody gets comfortable, politely eats a delicate little cucumber and sprouts sandwich, takes a sip of Pellegrino sparkling water, and then the head honcho addresses Costa: "Well, Costa, tell us what you have in mind."

Costa says, "I vant to make picture about science and human values in twentieth century. And now John vill explain."

All eyes turned toward me. If this had been an episode of *The Honeymooners* starring Jackie Gleason I would have exclaimed in panic, "*Hamma, hamma, hamma, hamma!*" But it wasn't. So I forthrightly admitted I had no idea what Costa and I would do since we hadn't discussed it at all. But I'd schmooze with nuclear physicists in Los Alamos near my Taos home, do much research and many interviews, and Costa and I would come up with something brilliant.

Everyone nodded, smiled, and stood, then we all shook hands congratulating each other, and they guaranteed Costa and me the development funds.

More candy from another baby!

In the elevator on the way down with Costa and Eddie Lewis, I asked, "What just *happened* up there?"

Eddie said, "Don't ask. Before the meeting even started it was a foregone conclusion. You should've had another of those little sandwiches."

34

ADMITTEDLY, I HAD trouble with money. Still do. You already know that. I don't trust big lumps of it. One day my agent, Perry Knowlton, called saying that Liza Minelli wanted me to write another novel (like *The Sterile Cuckoo*) featuring a heroine she could play in its film version. G. P. Putnam's Sons would publish the book, and Phyllis Grann, my editor of *Cuckoo* at David McKay, who was now a big shot at Putnam's, had okayed the deal. There would be a large advance, maybe fifty or a hundred grand, I forget. Typically I was broke, and it was a lot of money (to me "a lot of money" was ten thousand dollars). Perry asked me not to say "No" right then on the phone but to think it over for at least a few hours, then call him in the morning. I already knew I wouldn't take the job. Who did they think I was, some kind of opportunistic scumball with a big-time addiction to greed? Excuse me, but I'm an *artiste* not a *prostitute*! And what about all the poor people on earth? What would *they* think?

I dialed Perry next day and politely declined the offer. He must have rubbed his eyes, spun around in his leather office chair, and contemplated the pigeons cooing on his outside window ledge. Why was he representing a client who kept escaping every possible lucrative deal Perry might set up for him with his so-called integrity in tact?

I mean, we all know (don't we?) that in America "integrity" is just another word defining "shit for brains."

———

Speaking of Perry, he had issues with the fact that whenever I finished a novel I gave it directly to Marian Wood and accepted whatever advance Holt offered without asking Perry to negotiate the deal. He suggested a few times that this was unproductive because he'd like to pass the novel around to other publishers for auction in order to gain negotiating leverage with Holt. I said, "But if another publisher offers an advance that Holt won't meet, then I'm obligated to go to them?" Perry indicated that would be the logical course. My reply? "But then I would lose Marian Wood." Perry said, "Or, she'd raise her offer to counter the other publisher, and you'd pocket a better advance from Holt." I said, "Or not, and then I'd lose Marian." He said, "But right now she *knows* you won't go to another publisher, so she can offer you bargain-basement advances." I said, "I don't give a hoot about the advances. I want loyalty to Marian." Perry said, "You're a dope. That's not the way this business works." I said, "Well, I'll be damned if I'll play New York's game of musical chairs in publishing."

Perry had the courtesy not to remind me that I was refusing to let him do *his* job and thereby earn the living *he* was entitled to.

So after a while he gave up, saying if I wanted he'd read my contracts to make sure there weren't too many screwups. But mostly we just became friends. Curtis Brown did earn some minor commissions when I wrote screenplays. But killing themselves to swing deals making me richer was obviously a fool's gambit.

———

While I worked on *Missing* in 1981, Costa-Gavras flew me to LA for a week's final polish on the script. When I arrived in town Universal Studios handed me a manila envelope containing a thousand bucks cash as per-diem spending money during my stay. Please return any bread leftover along with my receipts. They'd already paid for my flight and lodging.

That week I bunked at the Marina Pacific Hotel in Venice and found a nearby grocery store that sold me a loaf of bread, two packages each of Swiss cheese and baloney, small jars of mustard and mayonnaise, a bag of lettuce, and a six-pack of Miller Lite. When the work day ended I made sandwiches in my room, drank a beer, and watched TV.

After the seven days were up I returned the manila envelope to the studio with my receipts and $983.12 in change. They didn't understand. Apparently, nobody had ever returned zilch from the thousand in per-diem money, which was considered very small potatoes anyway. Back in New Mexico I received several puzzled letters from Universal's accounting department, until, unbidden, they sent me a check for $983.12.

I felt super guilty. Yet eventually, despite all the starving Armenians on earth, I mustered enough courage to secretly deposit that sum in my bank when nobody was looking.

More recently, Northern Arizona University in Flagstaff invited me to speak for an honorarium of $5,000. I was horrified. I thought NAU was a small college with mostly Navajo and other Native American students. Hence, in a couple of back-and-forth letters, I successfully negotiated my pay down to $2,500, which still seemed exorbitant. Yet they were adamant. When I arrived at NAU for my presentation I realized it was a big university and they probably had money to burn coming out their ears. However, I *think* I felt proud about the compassionate downsizing of my fee.

Exasperated, my friend Demetria Martínez offered to become my manager. Basically, she thought I was an idiot. She explained how you're supposed to handle the payment of speaking fees. She said, "When people call me up to ask what is my honorarium, I immediately tell them, 'You can't afford me.' And *then* we start to negotiate."

This is me skating on a rare frozen stock pond on the Taos west mesa, with the Tres
Orejas Mountain in the background. Early 1980s. One of the happiest days of my life.
Selfie by John Nichols.

PART VI

35

SO ROBERT REDFORD signed a joint-venture agreement with Moctesuma Esparza and began working with me on a screenplay draft I'd started for Mocte. We conspired together on another draft, although "together" may not be the appropriate word. Pinning Redford down was like trying to find a needle in an airborne haystack flying past you at the speed of light. Aside from the president of the United States, Robert Redford is probably the busiest man in America. If we're talking and the phone rings, Bob has to answer it. And the phone is *always* ringing.

Late June of 1981 he invited me to his first Sundance Institute in Provo, Utah, intending for us to confer during the weeklong event. The Writers Guild promptly went on strike, forbidding us to discuss the project. Bob proposed I attend anyway, suggesting we'd chat "off the record," so to speak. I demurred, insisting I couldn't even eat an enchilada with him for fear of scabbing. He frowned, then welcomed me to Provo as a simple friendly gesture, no strings attached.

I had fun being a spectator at the Institute, rooming with Waldo Salt and Tony Bill. Tony was an actor, director, producer, distant friend, and the first person to give *The Sterile Cuckoo* to Liza Minelli and to hand a prepublication manuscript of *Milagro* to Bob Christiansen and Rick Rosenberg. As an actor he'd been in *Come Blow Your Horn*, *Flap*, and *Shampoo*. Among other films he directed *My Bodyguard* and *Untamed Heart*. His biggest triumph producing movies came with an Oscar for *The Sting*. His office was in Venice, where he often flew his aerobatic plane offshore alongside a remote friend of mine, Forest Murray, who once lived in Taos.

Waldo was an old-guard screenwriter blacklisted for refusing to testify before HUAC who'd killed it during his last-hurrah years, winning Oscars for *Midnight Cowboy* and *Coming Home* and a nomination for *Serpico*. He lolled on a couch in our pad smoking joints the size of .38 pistol barrels while I played boogie-woogie piano to amuse him and Tony. Waldo amused us in return by stating repeatedly that his 1979 original script for, and the film of, *Coming Home*, starring Jon Voigt and Jane Fonda, was just a bunch of malarkey.

Characters from Hollywood I met at Sundance who were Redford's friends called him "Ordinary Bob" because he tried so hard to be just one of the guys. When he drove a carload of us to a rodeo in Park City, all aboard wanted a couple of six packs of beer to see us through the calf-roping and bull-riding events. When Bob swerved into a 7-Eleven and hopped out to grab the booze, everybody screamed, "No, no! Let *us* go in or we'll never reach the rodeo!" But Redford insisted, and he didn't escape from the store with our Budweisers for thirty minutes.

After that I never again corralled him long enough to talk turkey for more than forty seconds. We shared a few long phone calls during which I scribbled pages of notes. Redford had a famous problem arriving at meetings on time. In 1981 I hitched a ride after the Sundance Institute from Provo to the Salt Lake City airport in a rental car driven by the director Sydney Pollack. It's about a one-hour drive, but took longer because a state cop car tailgated us from Provo to the airport entrance gate. Almost the entire distance Pollack ranted about Redford's habitual lateness. They're close friends. Sidney had directed him in *This Property Is Condemned, Jeremiah Johnson, The Way We Were, Three Days of the Condor*, and *The Electric Horseman*. Yet during our entire ride Pollack decried how frustrating it was to work with an actor who never showed up on time at meetings, or on the set, or anywhere for that matter. Bob's erratic habits drove Pollack over budget, almost destroyed his movies, and triggered repeated heart attacks. You'd have thought he hated Redford. Not so. By the end of our brief journey it was obvious Pollack loved Robert Redford. Or, if nothing else with Bob, I imagine he's *always* money in the bank.

––––––

My own few experiences were similar. One day, spring of 1982 or 1983, I'm supposed to meet Redford at his rental house in Santa Fe. Our meeting is planned for 1:00 p.m. I drive down from Taos, conscientiously arriving at Bob's house on time. He's not there, but the door is open. I walk inside and commandeer a comfortable chair waiting for the director to arrive. Fifteen, twenty, twenty-five minutes go by. Nobody shows. Since there's a remote lying on the coffee table, I click on the TV and watch something. *Oprah? Jerry Springer?* A rerun episode of *Bonanza?* Then I'm hungry, peruse the kitchen refrigerator, and fashion myself a baloney, cheese, lettuce, and tomato sandwich with mustard and mayonnaise, and also pop open a beer. Proceeding to the outdoor portal, I make myself comfortable on a chaise lounge gazing at the placid swimming pool while I eat. I'm in heaven because that sandwich and cerveza contain all my favorite food groups.

After finishing the snack I was bored. Searching the house I found a bathing suit hanging over the bar of a shower curtain. Grabbing a towel I went for a swim. Half an hour and twenty laps later I dry off, redon my clothes, and *then* Bob arrives for our meeting between 3:30 and 4:00 p.m.

We smile, shake hands, and settle down to business. I don't believe anybody like me ever complains openly about his lack of punctuality, because, after all, he *is* Robert Redford.

36

WHEN THE WRITERS Guild went on strike in 1981 I wrote a memoir in six or seven weeks. *The Last Beautiful Days of Autumn* is part of a trilogy that begins with *If Mountains Die* and ends with *On the Mesa*. *Autumn* is a joyful recollection of my adventures with the landscape and friends and lovers in Taos, illustrated by my own photographs. Book two from Holt's *Nirvana Blues* deal. Marian Wood accepted *Autumn* only because *If Mountains Die* had been successful. I already told you she didn't like photo-essays. My manuscript was longer than the contract called for, she complained. The Holt designer and art director thought my photographs sucked. The book was remaindered almost on the day it was published.

But, hey, one internet reviewer named Peter says,

> This is my favorite book of all time. I'd describe it as the 'Walden' for those who grew up (or even spent some time) in Northern New Mexico. His recounting of anecdotes about living in Taos, N.M., interactions with his friends, family, acquaintances, fishing the Rio Grande, wandering the high desert and the mountains, and making love inspired me to take more pleasure in the life I live. What's more, his descriptions of Northern New Mexico just plain made my heart hurt with homesickness. I love Northern New Mexico and it is so great to read work from such a talented author who loves New Mexico just the same."

Brandi Hughes chimes in with equal enthusiasm. "John Nichols is by far one of my favorite authors and this is one of my non-fiction favorites. An environmental love story between the man and the area in and around Taos, New Mexico. Check out 'On The Mesa' as well. I can't say enough about this man and his writing."

But we know that every scintillating accolade has a flip side. According to David Roberts: "Note that there is quite a bit of explicit erotic writing in parts of the book. I think Nichols was horny when he wrote the book."

Life is chaotic. Always, in Taos, I go fishing on the Río Grande. I initiate photographic expeditions. Doves and grouse can be hunted in September. And every night is a work night. If my kids are in Taos for the summer, I play with them, and when they sleep I type, logging very little shut-eye myself. I juggle and juggle, always exhausted. My friend Mike Kimmel flies out—from New York now—to hunt and fish with me, and when he sleeps I type. I develop Menière's disease that causes vertigo attacks and much vomiting. That calls for a no-salt diet, diuretics, and an absence of caffeine. Absence of caffeine cuts my productivity in half.

1981, 1982, 1983, 1984. I'm off to visit Costa-Gavras in Paris. I start rewriting a script for Karel Reisz (more on that soon). I go back to work on *The Milagro Beanfield War* screenplay. I'm trying to write short novel versions of *American Blood* and that nonfiction book, *On The Mesa*. Published in 1987, *American Blood* is steeped in the violence underlying our culture. Murder, racism, guns, and a tragic love story.

On The Mesa speaks of solitude, serenity, wide skies, and the complicated life cycles of a tiny stock pond.

"Which one will the fountain bless?"

———

Predictably, Redford soon dropped me from the *Milagro* screenplay like a bad investment at the start of a Bear Market. He switched to his pal David Ward, who'd written *The Sting*, a successful movie for Bob and his friend Paul Newman (and my distant acquaintance Tony Bill). Over the grapevine I heard that Ward received four hundred thousand dollars for his *Milagro* first draft. I don't know if that's true or simply *chisme* (gossip). When Ward's initial script arrived in my mailbox I went postal. The thing was flat as a restaurant griddle, but that could be improved. It was his climax scene that almost drove me to buy a gun at Walmart. My hero, Joe Mondragón, who's farmed all his life in northern New Mexico, makes a mistake while planting his illegal beanfield. And when triumphant locals arrive to harvest his pinto crop, they discover Joe has irrigated *peas* instead of beans all summer, *and he never once noticed his faux-pas!*

You can't be freakin' *serious*. Redford apologized, and Ward rewrote his ending. But I never managed to erase the taint of that first ending. The implied ignorance was insanely scary. What next? The Hispanic small farmers of Milagro sponsor an "After Harvest Czech Festival" where they dance polkas in the main square and sell Pysanky Easter eggs to Bavarian tourists?

Nevertheless, Redford seemed eager to self-destruct after the success of his first directorial effort, *Ordinary People*, which starred a modest, grief-stricken, mid-America family of middle-class Anglos mourning the accidental death of their oldest son. It won almost every award that the Oscars and Golden Globes could throw at Bob in 1980, including Best Director, Best Picture, Best Adapted Screenplay (by Alvin Sargent of *Sterile Cuckoo* fame!), best Supporting Actor for Timothy Hutton, a Best Actress nomination for Mary Tyler Moore, and Best Supporting Actor nomination for Judd Hirsch.

So why *not* choose for your second directing effort a turbulent, irreverent ensemble piece featuring two hundred characters, half of them raucous (sarcastic) Latinos (Chicanos, Hispanics), set (on location) in America's poorest state, New Mexico, which three-quarters of United States residents (and moviegoers) don't even realize *belongs* to the United States?

Made sense to me, particularly given the project choices I was making for my own creative life, where you could say I kept cheerfully lurching ahead way outside my own comfort zone.

37

FOR EXAMPLE: DOLLY IN CLOSER to the many convolutions of working with Costa-Gavras on our original film called *The Magic City*. The one about "science and human values during the twentieth century." Our intention was to inspect contradictions inherent in great scientific discoveries like atom splitting, radar, airplanes, and automobiles that were transformed into nuclear warheads, tanks, dive bombers, and Hiroshima. In his autobiography, *My Life and Views*, the noted physicist Max Born bequeathed me this philosophical road map:

> I am haunted by the idea that this break in human civilizations, caused by the discovery of the scientific method, may be irreparable. Though I love science I have the feeling that it is so greatly opposed to history and tradition that it cannot be absorbed by our civilization. The political and military horrors and complete breakdown of ethics which I have witnessed in my lifetime may be not a symptom of social weakness, but a necessary consequence of the rise of science—which in itself is among the highest intellectual achievements of man.

Jacques Monod, a French biochemist and Nobel winner, believed that "any mingling of knowledge with values is unlawful, forbidden." That was thanks to the creation of the "scientific method."

———

For almost a year I researched the project, reading books, talking with atomic physicists, learning the history of automobiles, airplanes, the Green Revolution, and Coca-Cola. I kept returning to the creation of nuclear weapons, which demanded both genius and total "innocence" (translated as catastrophic stupidity). I contrasted the lives of two brilliant scientists: the hawk, John von Neumann (who'd advocated nuking Russia immediately after they tested their first

My portrait of a physicist at New Mexico's Los Alamos lab walking his bomb. A comment on "science and human values." Courtesy of John Nichols.

atom bomb in 1949), and the dove, Norbert Wiener, who invented cybernetics and swore "never to publish further work of mine which may do damage in the hands of irresponsible militarists."

Of course Henry Ford and Andrew Carnegie created miracles that evolved into disasters. Many folks developing nuclear weapons had little or no emotional connection to the potential consequences of acquiring the knowledge to destroy our planet. Most had never seen newsreels of Hiroshima and Nagasaki. No one building automobiles thought about cancer caused by carbon monoxide, let alone the threats of climate change or how many drivers and passengers would be murdered or maimed in auto accidents. Very few Delaware workers at Dow Chemical making napalm to incinerate peasants of Vietnam's Mekong Delta considered what their product *did* to those people.

My studious explorations comprised a "bible" of information that Costa could study. After he was up to speed, we considered the material, inventing plots, stories, and personalities. I wrote a handful of treatments outlining ways to structure a movie.

My initial suggestions leaned heavily on astrophysicist Freeman Dyson's 1979 memoir, *Disturbing the Universe*, and a 1974 book, John McPhee's *The Curve of Binding Energy*, which features a Los Alamos nuclear physicist, Ted Taylor, who developed the smallest fission bomb ever invented. Called Davy

Costa-Gavras at our New York hotel while we were working on *Warday*. The float bowls of roses came with our room service for coffee and snacks. Hollywood, love it or leave it! Photo by John Nichols.

Crockett, it was twelve inches across and weighed fifty pounds. I also held a grim fascination for Herman Kahn's reflections in *On Thermonuclear War*, where he saw little difference between "the horrors of war" and "the horrors of peace" generated by cancer-causing toxins from chemical fertilizers and the like.

Another path I followed was the life story of Samuel Cohen, father of the neutron bomb, a weapon that exploded above a town and killed every person below with its radiation yet caused no damage to buildings or manufacturing plants, which could be reoccupied swiftly.

Ted Taylor and Freeman Dyson had worked together on Project Orion from 1957 until 1963, when a nuclear-test-ban treaty killed it. Their idea was to develop a rocket ship for interstellar space travel propelled by small nuclear bombs. Orion was referred to as an "Intersteller Ark." It mandated peaceful use of current nuclear stockpiles. Major problems included the development of small fission (or fusion) blasts below the rocket that wouldn't damage a "pusher plate" aiming their spaceship through our solar system and beyond.

I developed a treatment featuring six nuclear physicists and their families in a lovely all-American village (like Los Alamos) during their attempts to develop a viable rocket, Ganymede, propelled by controlled nuclear explosions from tiny "grapefruit bombs."

They were super excited by the possibility of peaceful space travel, then dismayed when government financiers of their project decided the grapefruit bomb was a perfect weapon to use against the Soviet Union. The director of Ganymede was awarded an Enrico Fermi Prize for inventing the grapefruit bomb. But in his acceptance speech, when the director starts rejecting military use of his invention, government handlers abruptly clear the hall because of a bomb scare. Next day the disillusioned eldest member of Ganymede explodes a tiny homemade nuclear bomb, leveling the village.

Complex material. Most of the movie focused on the excitement generated for my physicists by their rocket-testing experiments, along with their idyllic, often humorous daily lives in a dreamy 1950s American "baseball, Chevrolet, and apple pie" small town. Their innocent enthusiasm is meant to be heartbreaking.

Of course the tragic surprise ending would leave audiences gasping, and with much to think about.

———

A cartoon portrait of myself while I was working on the Warday script with Costa-Gavras. Courtesy of John Nichols.

Following a slew of discussions, Costa asked me to cobble my treatments together as a novel. A *novel*? Of the movie before I'd even written the *movie*? Costa said, "*Bien sûr.*" That was a first. So I wrote a novel that ran 279 pages. Then Costa gave me the okay to invent a first-draft screenplay. Our process had entailed a barrage of nitpicking trials and errors. Collaborating with Costa was like trying to develop a viable nuclear-fusion reactor.

However, easy come, easy go. Costa didn't like my script and switched me over to our next project, a film based on the novel *Warday*, written by Whitley Strieber and James Kunetka.

Out of the frying pan I jumped, and right into the inferno.

38

BACK FROM A Paris meeting with Costa-Gavras and on the way to Las Cruces, New Mexico, for an anti-Reagan rally on April 24, 1982, I picked up a road-killed turkey vulture, stashed it in the trunk of my 1973 Impala, and stopped for ice at a 7-Eleven. I piled more ice onto the bird that night, and again next day, planning to skin the vulture, stuff it, and hang it from my living-room ceiling with the other roadkill birds I'd prepared years earlier for my kids.

At the Las Cruces house where I stayed, a visitor had left a copy of the *Washington Post*. In it was an article about the recent murder of a twenty-two-year-old young woman after her car broke down late at night on a deserted road in rural Maryland near her home. Two guys stopped to help, kidnapped her at gunpoint, drove her to an empty shack, tortured and repeatedly raped her, cracked her skull with a logging chain, then shot her, cut off her hands, and burned the body. They were caught and remanded to life in prison. That awful story helped spur me to write my novel, *American Blood*. A comparable atrocity is at the heart of the book.

On Sunday I drove back to Taos from Las Cruces. Come Wednesday I smelled a stench and abruptly realized I'd forgotten all about the buzzard in my trunk.

Another experience that elucidates my life.

———

The *American Blood* I published in 1987 was not the one I had originally planned. I never realized the long book I'd researched and plotted through the late 1970s and early 1980s. It would have covered the rise of industrial capitalism in America from 1870 until Vietnam's My Lai Massacre on March 16, 1968. I would begin with a travesty like the 1864 Sand Creek slaughter of Arapaho and Cheyenne Natives in eastern Colorado, then segue to the killing of the buffalo, a perfect metaphor explaining the brutality of our economic system. In my novel

I'd build a city of a million people on the massacre site. My two main protagonists would be a man born from the rape of a Native woman by a white cavalry officer during the attack, and another man who was the Anglo son of a captain leading that charge. Each protagonist would live to be a hundred.

For years I read and underlined books on US history, the aftermath of Reconstruction, lynching and Jim Crow laws, Plessy v. Ferguson, the cruelty to Chinese immigrants building our railroads and to the immigrants from Eastern Europe, Russia, and Scandinavia recruited by railroad barons to settle Minnesota and Nebraska lands, thus giving those tycoons free government rights of way. I studied the Gilded Age of scurrilous exploitation, poverty, and crippling inequality as seen in the lower east side slums of New York photographed by Jacob Riis, or in the Chicago stockyards described by Upton Sinclair's novel *The Jungle*.

Included would be genocides connected to Manifest Destiny, the Mexican-American War, and the mass extinction of Native Americans. I read union chronicles by the controversial radical Philip Foner, Ida Tarbell's *History of Standard Oil*, Matthew Josephson on *The Politicos* and *The Robber Barons*. Harriet Tubman and Sojourner Truth inspired me. As did Ray Ginger's biography of Eugene Debs. And histories of mining towns like Butte, Montana. Brown v. Board of Education would be important. And Malcolm X, Crazy Horse, Joaquin Murrieta. Prohibition called with its Dillingers, Capones, Pretty Boy Floyds, and Bonnie and Clydes. Howard Fast's novel *The American* celebrated the life of John Altgeld (who, as governor of Illinois, pardoned three of the Haymarket Square bombing anarchists) and the corrupt election of 1896, when McKinley defeated William Jennings Bryan as bankers across America threatened to foreclose on farmers if Bryan won. Mark Hanna was a Republican millionaire pulling their puppet strings.

I couldn't stop doing research, underlining pages, filling manila folders as I had for *The Magic Journey*, recreating the great panorama of robbery, larceny, and inequality initiated by the Goulds, Fisks, Harrimans, Vanderbilts, Morgans, Carnegies, Rockefellers, and presidents who stole, murdered, and enslaved our way to becoming the "Richest Nation on Earth."

Our impeccable "Democracy."

I felt no shame blustering loudly from a soapbox. However, midway through 1984 I realized my chaotic life could never pull off that macroscopic overview of our nation's history. And, throwing up my hands in surrender, I opted for a way less ambitious *American Blood*.

39

THERE'S THUNDER AND lightning over the Gulf Stream. The English film director Karel Reisz and I have been scouting locations for a movie called *Cabo Rio* during the summer of 1983. I am forty-three years old (and also working on a *Milagro* script, a *Warday* script, the short-version *American Blood* novel, and the memoir, *On The Mesa*). Karel and I needed a tiny island to support a group of shipwrecked Haitian refugees. Ronald Reagan was our president, and he didn't want any of those black misfits to reach Florida shores. In Port-au-Prince the Haitian dictator, Baby Doc Duvalier, was okay with Reagan.

Karel Reisz is actually Czech. His parents put him on the last train out of the country in 1938 before the Nazis took over, then they died at Auschwitz. Karel was twelve years old. He became a British citizen and, subsequently, part of the New Wave Cinema that included Tony Richardson (*Tom Jones*) and Lindsay Anderson (*O Lucky Man!*). Karel directed *Saturday Night and Sunday Morning*. America gave Meryl Streep an Oscar nomination for acting in Karel's film of *The French Lieutenant's Woman*. Our movie was about some Haitian boat people shipwrecked on a tiny cay among the Bahamian chain of islands. Nobody would rescue them. True story. The Bahamas refused, and neither the Haitians, Cubans, nor Americans would violate international law to cross the Bahamian sovereign boundary. *Cabo Rio* featured an American Coast Guard captain who finally broke legal tradition in order to rescue the Haitians, and that act destroyed his career.

Our moral was: individual conscience supersedes international laws.

———

In Miami we toured the Krome Detention Center for Haitian boat people— think of Donald Trump's holding pens for Central American asylum seekers. We interviewed Haitian immigrants living twenty to a small cottage or apartment in Little Haiti or Liberty City, then chugged around Biscayne Bay and its estuaries with the Coast Guard, who explained their own Gestapo tactics. The Reagan administration had signed a rare treaty with Haiti's Baby Doc giving American ships the right to board Haitian vessels on the high seas, arrest the occupants, and forcibly return them to Haiti. A travesty of international law.

Driving from Miami to Key West with Karel, he asked me to sing rock and roll songs. So we headed along those causeways above the water with me bawling "Blue Suede Shoes," "Rock Around the Clock," "Be Bop a Lula," and "Johnny B. Goode." When movie financiers promoted stuff that Karel didn't like, he'd remark in his upper-crust British accent: "I wish I could give them *a little bit of the whip*." Other films he made in America were *Who'll Stop the Rain* with Nick Nolte and *Sweet Dreams*, the life of country singer Patsy Cline that starred Jessica Lange. According to Karel he had trouble raising money because producers always balked, saying, "Here comes Karel Reisz begging us to fund another one of his bummers."

During our work sessions Karel outlined perfectly, word for word, every scene for the movie while I scribbled furiously in my notebook. At one point I asked him, "Why don't *you* write the script yourself?" Karel replied, "Because, John, the minute I put pen to paper it all turns into shit."

———

From Key West a bubble copter whisked us to the Dry Tortugas. I peered down at sea turtles swimming slowly as well as a couple of tarpon. Our pilot had earned his sea legs in Vietnam. When I cried, "Look, sharks!" he dove to just above the rotor wash so we could see more clearly. Later he zoomed six feet atop the waves toward Fort Jefferson like Robert Duvall in *Apocalypse Now*, and at the last moment flipped us up and safely over that Civil War prison relic. I almost blew my lunch.

Karel wasn't afraid of airplanes. For him, "They're just like getting onto a bus." Toward the end of World War II he joined the Royal Air Force in Britain, learning to fly, but crashed a couple of planes nose first trying to land them, digging a furrow on the dirt runways. So authorities canceled his license. He commented, "I just never could get the hang of it."

———

"Aren't we lucky," Karel once said, "to be paid millions of dollars for playing with toys like little boys in our profession?" I never banked millions of dollars from Hollywood, but for stretches I might average forty grand a year with family health insurance thrown in. And after twenty years of haphazardly working on films I qualified for a Writer's Guild pension that nowadays pays me $1,700 a month. The American dream! If you can't stand the money, they throw it at you, even at a renegade like me. My friend Mike Kimmel used to say, "I'm no push-over . . . but I can be had." The assumption is: *everyone* has a price.

———

Warner Brothers was funding *Cabo Rio*. Karel had it budgeted, nailed down, viable. His current storyboards were completed and astonishing. But there was one problem: Karel wanted the Haitians shipwrecked on our plot of sand to be saved by a Coast Guard cutter during a fierce tropical storm. The cutter couldn't just be anchored offshore and the Haitians ferried to safety in rubber rafts, dinghies, or government launches. Our rescuers had to fire lines from their boat's harpoon cannon to shore, and then the Haitians would be transported to the cutter in precarious bosun's chairs swinging wildly above turbulent waves leaping to catch and drown them. The lead producer of the film told me, "He's crazy! It'll cost a million dollars just to shoot that scene! There's only one tank on Malta we could use! The studio will be crapping gold bullion to pay for it!"

Fair enough. In the screenplay I repeatedly modified the rescue scene. But Karel would have none of that. "Oh, John," he intoned morosely, "I *do* wish you'd quit trying to de-James-Bondify my film."

Cabo Rio never got made.

———

Here's a brief moment I treasure, though. I'm waiting in line at the Miami airport to purchase a return ticket for New Mexico or maybe obtain a boarding pass. Behind me waits a middle-aged man from Bolivia anxious to get his ducket for La Paz. We begin chatting in Spanish. He wonders where I'm from and what I'm up to in Miami. I explain that I'm working on a picture to be set in Miami and on a miniscule Bahamian cay where shipwrecked Haitians are dying.

The man is interested in American films. I return the favor by relating how impressed I was with two movies made by the Bolivian director Jorge Sanjinés: *El Sangre del Cóndor* and *El Enemigo Principal* (*Blood of the Condor* and *The Principal Enemy*), both virulent anti-American tirades starring mostly amateur Quechua actors.

My conversation buddy was astonished I'd heard of the obscure director, let alone thought favorably of his films. I explained that in my New Mexico hometown, about five years earlier, some friends and I had put together a program of progressive Spanish-language features in the Catholic Church gymnasium. The effort had drawn large crowds of Hispanic locals. Other movies shown were Luis Buñel's *Los Olvidados*, a Peruvian effort called *La Muralla Verde*, and the Spanish flick *El Jardín de las Delicias*, directed by Carlos Saura. Each of those works contained strong political opinions.

When we parted the Bolivian gentleman did not shake my hand; he gave me instead a spontaneous *abrazo*.

40

IN MANAGUA, NICARAGUA, a few months later, during the Purísima celebrations before Christmas 1983, I chatted with citizens digging air-raid shelters at midnight. I was a guest of Blase and Theresa Bonpane's group, the Office of the Americas, in Los Angeles. Our delegation stayed in apartments formerly belonging to the deposed dictator Anastasio Somoza's National Guard. Somoza had fled to Paraguay in 1979 when the Sandinista revolution triumphed; he was assassinated a year later. Incongruous life-sized cardboard Santas decorated Managua's doorways, also pictures of the pope (who was visiting soon). We fifteen Americans were the only people with cameras throughout the entire country. Our purpose was to listen close, observe carefully, then return home determined to call off Ronald Reagan's dogs of war.

I wrote a long article, "After the Triumph," that was courageously published by Pat Reed in the *Albuquerque Journal*'s Sunday *Impact* magazine. Any American journalist or politician who would listen got an earful from me about the hopeful promise of the Sandinista revolution. After I spent an hour explaining to reporters what I'd seen in Nicaragua, the first question they invariably asked was, "What is it like to work with Robert Redford on *The Milagro Beanfield* movie?"

You can't keep a good press down.

———

That December, from a trench in northern Nicaragua, my group can look past a burned-out village to Honduras, where American-financed contra troops patrol the border. We are all nervous. Our leader, Carol Fonte, was friends with Ita Ford, one of three US nuns and a missionary murdered in El Salvador December of 1980. Noel Corea is our guide and spokesperson for the Sandinista revolution. He claims to have smuggled the first AK-47 from San Francisco into Nicaragua at the start of the war against Somoza. In Managua everybody is digging those bomb shelters, expecting US planes to fly over any minute. Even twelve-year-old kids are toting AK-47s, protecting stores, schools, and open-air markets. The Nicaraguans have decided that Ronald Reagan and George Schultz will have to kill every last one of them if we invade their country.

What impressed me most on my short visit is that humans could throw off centuries of oppression, hoping to install an egalitarian system from scratch. In America I rarely converse with persons who share my call for radical social, economic, and environmental change. In Nicaragua nearly everyone I spoke with was eager to implement my agenda. It was the most hopeful situation I've ever experienced.

The United States' contra war helped make sure it didn't last. I don't blame that all on us, because the Sandinistas also shot themselves in the foot. Nevertheless, we worked hard to create in Nicaragua a situation like the nightmares we've helped foster today in Afghanistan, Iraq, Syria, and Iran.

It's our democracy's "magic touch."

41

SINCE I CAN scarcely describe the book *Warday* from memory, please look it up on Wikipedia. Costa-Gavras and I began imagining the movie version in 1983, and we continued through 1984. Briefly, it concerns the United States five years after a "limited" nuclear exchange between America and the Soviet Union. Though New York City is bombed at the start, much damage around the country results from Soviet weapons exploding in our atmosphere. Their electromagnetic pulses shut down electronics across the nation. Computers don't work, the banking system collapses, and anarchy reigns. "Only" seven million US citizens are exterminated, yet five years after the war our society, and environment, are completely derailed. Texas and California are independent countries. *Atzlan* controls the Southwest, Chicanos having expelled all Anglos while creating a libertarian socialist state. Citizens are dying in droves from the Cincinnati Flu. The Soviets and the rest of the planet have suffered equally. The UK and Japan are superpowers. It's an exhausting vision of Armageddon, a panoramic disaster scenario on steroids.

———

That said, I'm kneeling beside Costa at the window of his Helmsley Palace Hotel suite in New York, and we are arranging single file, along the sill, a group of float bowls with a pink rose decorating each one. The bowls arrive on our room-service trays. The flowers are beautiful. I snap twenty photographs of Costa posing beside the float bowls while staring out the window. Below us is the back of St. Patrick's Cathedral. It's spring, 1984, soon I'll be forty-four, and we are writing a script of *Warday*. Preparing for the project, Costa and I rode our ever-present curbside limo to a Manhattan screening room where, for several hours, we studied newsreels of Hiroshima's aftermath. Japanese doctors peeling chunks of roasted meat off victims' necks and shoulders was gruesome to behold. As were babies burnt to a crisp, survivors crawling through the ashes, and people without fingers rubbing clumps of hair off their blistered heads.

I recalled that years earlier, on a seventh-grade class trip from Forestville, Virginia, to the Smithsonian in Washington, DC, I had puzzled over a jar of formaldehyde that held a Japanese fetus deformed by the atomic radiation of Nagasaki.

———

Warday was not so much a novel as a travelogue across the United States recounting Strieber and Kunetka's fictional reporting of Armageddon. I wound up inventing characters who occupied the tale of a New York father crossing devastated America hoping to reach his family in California. Today, my elderly brain doesn't summon a coherent memory of that scriptwriting process, but it required super stamina. Costa was a demanding taskmaster who worked ferociously hard on every scene and line of dialogue. I wasn't skilled enough to write at the level he required for such a complicated disaster film.

Listen to this, however. After finishing a first draft of the script, I fired it off to the producer—Eddie Lewis once again. Costa was out of touch in Europe. When Eddie gobbled my portrait of Armageddon he swore it was "the greatest script he'd ever read." (All producers are obligated to say that. "Extreme enthusiasm" is the name of the game, no matter if they're dealing with a piece of crap that even John Waters wouldn't touch with his magic wand of sordid lechery.) Eddie ordered me to overnight the screenplay to Robert Redford immediately. I protested. That was *his* job—he's the *producer*. His answer was that I'd worked with Redford, I *knew* him, and Eddie had never even met the guy. Hesitantly, smelling a sour apple in the mash, I said, "Well, I can mail it to Bob's assistant, Robbi Miller. She's my friend, but shouldn't Costa first—"

"Send it," Eddie interrupted. "By Purolator. Right now. Time's a wasting."

Puzzled, I expressed *Warday* to Robbi Miller, who gave it to Redford. Bob refused even to read it because Costa had promised first glimpse of the draft to Paul Newman, Redford's buddy. By this time Costa had discovered that I'd zipped the script to Redford, and he (Costa) was furious at me. I blubbered that when Eddie Lewis insisted I forward the manuscript to Redford he didn't say anything about Paul Newman. I don't know what then transpired between Eddie and Costa-Gavras, but next thing that happened is Eddie called to say Costa needed me in Paris working with him daily for three months rewriting the *Warday* screenplay.

By then I was pissed at all the machinations. And I'd made it clear in my contracts that I would take brief meetings in LA, New York, Paris, or Timbuktu, but I didn't work for extended periods anyplace except Taos, New Mexico.

And *that* killed the project.

———

Costa and I got along, though. Apparently my peccadillos were instantly forgiven. I never understood what was happening behind the scenes anyway. Hence I often reflect on my good fortune to have accidentally fallen into the world of Hollywood and to have enjoyed all that I learned through researching various projects, each one offering a college education about the subject matter. Despite the aspersions cast on the LA movie scene, for me it was (with one notable exception I'll explain shortly) a domain of little bullshit and a few directors who worked very hard on their craft and sullen art. As I said, I rarely spent more than several days in Los Angeles (or New York or Paris), and accomplished all scriptwriting at my Taos home. Having no desire to integrate with the West Coast world, I pursued zero "networking" there. I was in and out like a thief in the night. And never did a script on spec or tried to sell it—are you crazy?

Gigs haphazardly fell into my lap. People called out of the blue asking if I was available. Sometimes I signed on, or else I wasn't interested. I turned down a lucrative polish of *The River*, a film starring Mel Gibson and Sissy Spacek, because I thought it was a lousy screenplay. The movie crashed and burned. Likewise, I passed on writing a script of *Prisoner Without a Name, Cell Without a Number* because I disliked its author, Jacobo Timerman, an Argentine journalist kidnapped and jailed by the country's military junta in the late 1970s. He was repeatedly tortured, then exiled to Israel in 1979. The book was an international best seller. Politically, I should have been drawn to the project, to Timerman's beliefs and his courage. But something about his attitude, his ego, stopped me.

And Karel Reisz once asked me to rewrite a Harold Pinter script of *The Handmaid's Tale*, making it "more North American." I read the book, disliked it, and declined to become involved. The film eventually got made, directed by Volker Schlöndorff, not Karel. It starred Natasha Richardson, Faye Dunaway, and Robert Duvall, and was a victim of bad reviews, a financial disaster. Pinter disowned his screenplay, trying to remove his name from the credits since many others had meddled with his original vision. He also pilloried bastardized versions of his work on *Remains of the Day*, this time successfully avoiding the credits. Frankly, I loved that movie.

So I suppose the "real" Hollywood has remained a mostly unknown foreign country to me. I existed on its very fringe, picking up crumbs that fell off the table. Never drove a car in LA, tooted cocaine, or romanced a starlet. I once explained it like this: "I never jumped over the moon, but, when nobody was looking, I did run away with the spoon."

42

YILMAZ GÜNEY WAS a Turkish Kurd communist director friend of Costa-Gavras in Paris. Turkey had often jailed Yilmaz. He achieved exile in France. Güney's 1981 film, *Yol*, shared the Golden Palm Award at Cannes with *Missing*. But a day came, in 1984 Paris again, early September, when Costa told me we were taking a day off from *Warday* by going to Père Lachaise Cemetery for his friend Güney's funeral. Cancer had killed him. While we were entering the cemetery Costa revealed that my all-time favorite movie director, Francois Truffaut, was dying of a brain tumor. Truffaut succumbed six weeks later.

I'm guessing that several thousand Kurds and communists, from Turkey and elsewhere in Europe, carried Güney's coffin on their shoulders from the Place de la République to Père Lachaise. Nobody talked. The women wore dark head scarves, the men smoked black-tobacco cigarettes. Because Costa was head of the French Cinémathèque we were led to the grave site. Photographers and TV cameramen perched above us on granite angels and mausoleum roofs. Bystanders were packed very close together. Some women near the open grave fainted and were passed back by many hands over the heads of mourners. A claustrophobic man crawled between peoples' legs to escape the crush. A short speech in French, a short talk in Kurdish while the coffin was held on ropes by pallbearers. When they began to lower Güney into the grave, thousands of fists raised into the air as the crowd sang "The Internationale."

That's among the most powerful and unique moments of my life.

Another cartoon portrait of myself after investing all my Hollywood money in a tax shelter to spite the IRS. Courtesy of John
Nichols.

PART VII

43

MY MEMORY OF the 1980s is often a blur. I'm working on two novels and two screenplays, and I'm doing a nonfiction book also. I fly to Los Angeles and meet with the French director Louis Malle. Then I fly to Oakland and do a signing at Cody's in Berkeley. I fly back to LA for another signing and a meeting with the producer Eddie Lewis. Possibly I have more energy than a hummingbird. I fly to Albuquerque to do a benefit for the Writers Union conference in New York. I give my talk in Las Cruces against the Reagan Administration. I travel to some meetings with Robert Redford in Provo, Utah. Louis Malle comes to Taos and I give him the tour for two days. He's directed films like *Murmur of the Heart*, *Pretty Baby*, *Atlantic City*, and *My Dinner with André*, and now he's interested in my novel *The Magic Journey*. I'm working with Redford on a *Milagro* screenplay. In New York there's another meeting with Costa-Gavras on our new script, *The Magic City*, and then on our newer creation, *Warday*. On my *Nirvana Blues* book tour I conquer Seattle, Portland, the Bay Area (again), Los Angeles, Phoenix, Tucson, Flagstaff, Denver, Boulder, Colorado Springs, Austin, Dallas, Chicago. Up high I'm terrified of even modest turbulence. Once I grabbed the hand of a passenger seated next to me, and, although startled, he let me hold his hand until the plane landed safely. I apologized profusely. He replied, "No problem."

———

My kids are with me for vacations and for all their summer and winter breaks also. My house in Upper Ranchitos is a disaster case, but comfortable. When it's cold, Luke and Tania sleep on mattresses in the living room, which has a heater. Tootie and I watch MTV together. I'm supposed to dig Ted Nugent's *Scream Dream* and Madonna's *Like a Virgin* and "Material Girl," songs like that? Or all the punk rock, thrash, grunge, alternative groups like the Dead Kennedys? The Butthole Surfers? The Ramones? Nine Inch Nails? Depeche Mode? Skid Row? And the *Sid and Nancy* movie? Hello? Earth to the Nichols Galaxy? Gag me with a spoon!

During winter vacations Tania and Luke and I had snowball fights *inside* the house. We played hockey with hockey sticks and tennis balls in the kitchen, smashing everything and bruising ourselves. A little hoop hooked at the top of the kitchen door inspired raucous Nerf basketball games. While I slept they had "totonie" wars outside, throwing egg-shaped cottonwood seed pods at each other. I don't know where they found the word "totonie." Kids make up stuff.

Fortunately, Tania and Luke never drowned in the Pacheco irrigation ditch that ran by our dilapidated adobe. Nor did they fall out of their tree house, either, breaking arms and legs while their daddy was snoring.

———

I'm writing a nonfiction book and another screenplay. Conscientiously, I always deliver the scripts on time. Because Louis Malle is courting Candace Bergen back in New York, we have to stop at every pay phone during our tour of Taos so he can call her. My fingers tap on the steering wheel while they palaver. I have a prolapsed mitral valve and asthma, tachycardia attacks and atrial fib. So what? I always carry an inhaler. I drink a lot, eat too much, and never gain weight. Jack Daniels before my meals and wine with the meals—and beer. Apparently I have great capacity. I swallow my heart pills and take the diuretics and avoid salt to keep Menière's at bay. Always go jogging every day. My exercise is out on the mesa, off in the woods, down at the river, or up in the mountains as often as possible.

The problematic ticker is no big deal. I've been on and off cardio pills like digitalis, digitoxin, Tenormin, Quinaglute, Verapamil, Carvedilol, Lanoxin, Triamterene, warfarin, and Lasix since I was thirty-five. When I have tachycardia or A-fib problems I perform the Valsalva maneuver. You squeeze yourself downward as if constipated trying to move your bowels. That stops your heart, then it restarts in sinus rhythm. I sense that dying is banal; it's easy. Often I joked, "Live fast, die young, have a good-looking corpse."

Then I reassess chapter 12 of a novel or scene 126 in my *Magic Journey* screenplay for Louis Malle. I've boiled down the massive novel's first three hundred pages to a single scene. Brilliant! I was a genius . . . until Louis skipped town at midnight for Galveston to shoot a movie called *Alamo Bay* about a fishing war between macho Texas shrimpers and Vietnamese refugees, and I never heard from him again.

44

GETTING PAID TO work on movies had a serious drawback. Here's a chronicle of my crass inability to manipulate the capitalist system. Grab a beer and stretch out on the Barcalounger; this tangent will take a moment. My account just goes to show that no matter how leftist we might consider ourselves, there's always room to mangle whatever because of our contradictions. And wallow in shame afterward.

Get out your hankies.

During the 1970s money had been hard to come by. Five grand a year, perhaps six. Maybe I'm low balling, though not by much. The *Sterile Cuckoo* salad days were long over. However, when I began working on films in the 1980s my income jumped. As did my taxes. One year I earned eighty thousand dollars, but in those days the US tax code was almost fair (before Reagan dismantled it), and I delivered a hefty amount to Uncle Sam. "You're nuts," my radical friends said. "You're just financing American imperialism abroad and Wall Street fat cats at home. Wise up, get a tax shelter, don't be stupid all your life."

I asked an accountant friend, "Larry, is there anything I can invest in that wouldn't wind up financing a Rockefeller resort in the Caribbean or a diamond mine in South Africa?"

He said, "No. But you could buy a house, fix it up, and rent at a fair price that helps cover your mortgage. It's guaranteed to appreciate."

Bueno. I bought a house. My realtor, Chuck Holden, called himself "Marxist Real-Estate Man." And did he have a deal for me. An old adobe home, four rooms, on two-and-a-half acres of irrigated land with the Pueblo River running through it. Owner financed. Seventy-two thousand dollars. "You can't miss."

Hook and sinker I swallowed the bait. And, because I'm not a "conniving capitalist pig crushing tiny third-world people like bedbugs under my thumb," I didn't ask for an appraisal, an inspection, or a lawyer to check the contract. And Chuck didn't request that stuff on my behalf. Scanning the written deal, I skipped over clauses that said I was purchasing the house "as is." Everything looked kosher to me. Because I'm "honest and trusting," I merely shook the owner's hand, gave him a down payment, then put my girlfriend and her kid in the dwelling and waited for the property to appreciate.

Surprise!—soon enough the toilet didn't flush. Why not? Well, the septic tank was filled to the brim with dirt, the ancient pipes under the floorboards were totally corroded . . . and the roof leaked. Also the joint was infested with earwigs. The contract's "as is" clause meant that was all my responsibility.

Okay. Plumbers resurrected the septic. They crowbarred up some floorboards and laid new pipes. Then pest control arranged a plastic bag over the entire house, kicked out my girlfriend, and pumped skeleton-brand insecticide into the quaint old adobe for a day. A week later they removed the baggie and entered my new investment wearing hazmat suits. Upshot? "Everything is fine."

My girl and her child moved back in.

When next it rained the roof leaked. So Luke and I climbed up there and tacked down new rolls of ninety-pound granulated tar paper. Then hurricane-force winds knocked over a dead cottonwood tree behind the house. It crashed into the neighbor's yard and smashed his commercial rabbit hutch, setting free thirty bunnies, and wasting another couple dozen. I apologized and hired a lumberjack to buck up and cart away the felled cottonwood. Next, a group of finish carpenters reconstructed the rabbit hutch. And of course I paid for the dead *conejos*.

———

There's more. Though my rental investment is located only thirty yards from the Pueblo River, unexpectedly the hand-dug well dried up. Come to find out it was only sixteen feet deep. No water in the kitchen, the bathroom, no water anywhere. My girl and her daughter can't pee, poop, or take a shower. In back of the house Luke and I hastily built a two-seat outhouse, which the child refused to use "because of the black widows."

Costs on my tax shelter were skyrocketing. My girlfriend was tired of switching back and forth from motels to that shelter. Naturally, I coughed for the motels. Then I hired an experienced but modestly priced well driller to dig a new well.

Great move. "Modestly priced" is a dead giveaway. He probed down to the second aquifer, hit an artesian pocket, and panicked. Water spouted from the ground like Old Faithful in Yellowstone.

"Fix it!" I begged the driller.

"I don't know how," he replied. "I never hit an artesian pocket before."

"But it's creating a sinkhole my house is gonna fall into!"

"We have to call the state engineer," he said.

Two of those bespectacled water lawyers drove up from Santa Fe and stared at my gusher. "You gotta cap it," they told the well driller.

"I don't know how to do that," he explained.

"Then call Halliburton over in Farmington," the suits told me. "They put out oil-well fires and stuff like that. If you don't have this thing capped, we'll start fining you a hundred dollars a day."

Halliburton drove two mammoth cement trucks from Farmington to Taos and began pumping their pressurized product down toward the artesian pocket. Meanwhile, my "modestly priced" guy said, "I'll bore you another well over here, just at the cost of the casing." Because my unhinged brain had gone on vacation to Cancun, I replied, "Okay, fine, whatever."

Oops. You guessed it. My water expert hit another mistake and freaked completely while Halliburton was still there. Hence when the Farmington hotshots finished with their first rescue mission, they moved over and commenced their second job at double the cost.

End result? The well driller actually *sent me a bill* for his services to go along with Halliburton's request for immediate payment of the multiple thousands I owed them. And the tax shelter still had no water.

———

Back to my senses, I fired Marxist Real-Estate Man and found another realtor to put my investment on the market. By then I was broke, facing a Chapter 7, possibly Chapter 11, so I told the new agent, "I bought it for seventy-two, but put it on the market for sixty, and there should be some takers. I've fixed everything except the well, and I've since learned that a competent driller would first seal the *malpaís* before they went any deeper, so that stitch in time should make a new well easy."

I was right. Smart hustlers immediately pounced on the deal. It's not every day in Taos you can find a house on two and a half fertile acres with a river running through it. Not so fast, though, there was a catch. Turns out another clause in my real-estate contract allowed the owner to quash any deal I made with a buyer if he (the owner) felt the buyer wasn't as good for the money as yours truly. Ergo, the first two candidates eager to buy were rejected by the owner. I asked my new realtor, "Can he really *do* that? I'm paying an exorbitant mortgage. I'm broke. I'm going crazy."

The realtor pursed his lips. "I dunno. I guess he can. I've never run into this problem before."

My girlfriend seriously tried, though failed, to commit suicide. Finally, the third potential buyer, who really wanted the property at such a cheap price, hired an educated lawyer slicker than the house owner's shyster and swung a deal to take that turkey off my hands. I was rid of my investment, all my Hollywood money, and minus other savings I'd managed to accumulate. That left me stressed to the max after the worst deal I ever made in my life, bar none. And off to live in a distant city went my girlfriend and her child.

Fool me once with the Putnam's Prize in 1966, shame on you. Fool me twice by convincing me twenty years later to invest in a "tax shelter," shame on *me*. Take me out back to the woodshed for a good whupping. I certainly deserved it, and still have the scars.

———

Final words: Marxist Real-Estate Man owned a plane. And one day, flying it west toward Tierra Amarilla the next county over, the plane apparently crashed and was never found. Chuck Holden disappeared.

Robert Redford and John Nichols on *The Milagro Beanfield War* set in Truchas, New Mexico, autumn 1986. Photographer unknown. Courtesy of John Nichols.

PART VIII

45

FOR WHAT IT'S worth, I shouldn't have snidely reproached Robert Redford for his obsessive tardiness, career distractions, or absurd ambition to take on *The Milagro Beanfield War* after the successful simplicity of *Ordinary People*. Listen to how I was ruining my own life.

When, in 1985, I took on a six-hour miniseries for CBS about Pancho Villa and the Mexican revolution, I commenced slogging on the "bible"—another gig that just "fell into my lap." After reading *The Magic Journey* novel, Kim LeMasters at CBS proposed me for the job. The bible is a treatment of all three two-hour teleplays in the series. First you have to read ten different books about the Mexican revolution *and* the life of Pancho Villa, and you should memorize a few newsreel documentaries while discussing the project with the independent producers, Philip and Mary-Ann Hobel, and their handlers at CBS (one of the Hobels' successes had been *Tender Mercies*.) Then you gotta rewrite the bible three or four times after discussing it with the Hobels, and CBS, and "other people." This requires a year and a half of hard labor, at which point you must write the first draft "teleplay" of the initial film, followed by the second draft "teleplay" of the initial film, and next the third draft "teleplay" of the initial . . . and so on.

You might ask, "John, we don't mean to be impertinent, but *why* did you accept this project in the first place?"

My simpleton's answer is, "I thought I could educate a prime-time American TV audience about US imperialism in the third world."

Right. I'll believe that when it rolls over and kisses my butt. If you really want to know the truth, my life was too complicated so I had gotten remarried. Which, it turns out, was hardly the right move. Yet I thought I wanted *stability*. If I'd *really* wanted that I would've shot myself or fled to Antarctica. Instead, I took on Pancho Villa partially because I had a bigger family with a new wife, my two kids, and her two kids, and it seemed obvious, politics aside, that I could use that old bugaboo, the money.

Of course my new bride and I exalt in our dangerous excitement. Working, playing, hiking, jogging together past the autumn cottonwoods, going to the movies, arguing about poetry, novels, art, children, politics, drugs, emotional codependencies, Freud, Jung, Ezra Pound, sex, money, and Ronald Reagan. You know the drill. Either we make up or break up, but we discuss everything. I can't stand her jealousy or my jealousy in revenge. There's too much euphoria, too many emotional minefields. It's up, it's down, it's up, it's down, there's no in-between, no allee-allee in-come-free—it's either ecstasy or agony, all bound up in sexy arousal all the time. The angry times are just as passionate as the joyous times. It's *interesting*. It's *exciting*. It's like David Carradine autoerotically asphyxiating himself in a Bangkok hotel closet while attempting to stimulate an out-of-this-world orgasm.

———

Perhaps I might mention here that while I and my newly betrothed were jogging, drinking champagne, climbing mountains, and arguing about who's a greater artist—Picasso or Walter Keane's wife?—I had begun writing the "short version" of *American Blood* along with a thirty-fifth draft of *On the Mesa*, my nonfiction homage to the treeless sagebrush mesa west of Taos with a minute stock pond in the middle. I envisioned *Mesa* as a political-environmental diatribe, yet also a beautiful portrait of the high desert as home to amazing species. When the book was an environmental diatribe, it stunk, period. Yet as a peaceful hosanna to fairy shrimp, prickly poppies, and spadefoot toads it bored Marian Wood, who yawned while explaining to me that my pastoral rambling had no interesting *definition*.

Eventually, I solved that problem by introducing three fictional characters: a mysterious attractive woman, Cassandra; a good-old-boy petroleum landman, I. J. Haynes, from Shreveport, Louisiana; and a petty gangster, Bill Bones, who planned to build a hippie café near the isolated stock pond. And once it's up and running, he'll wrangle a beer and wine license, too.

That's called "creative nonfiction." Much like the memoir you are reading right now.

By then, sadly, Marian had dropped out, and a freelance editor named James Thomas, getting paid by Peregrine Smith Books in Layton, Utah, was masterfully guiding my finishing touches, leading to the book's 1986 publication.

On the Mesa reviews were universally sweet. *Publishers Weekly* called it "a beautifully written appreciation of the wilderness." *New Mexico Magazine* said, "The book has all the elements of a classic." According to the *Fort Worth Star-Telegram*, "*On the Mesa* is a *Sand County Almanac* of the '80s." The *Dallas Times-Herald* felt, "This is a rhapsody on the healing power of the earth." The *Denver Post*'s comment? "In *On the Mesa* he captures the wild, austere splendor of the Taos mesa" where "a fragile little stock pond becomes a metaphor for the tenacity—and dignity—of life on earth." Kind words from the *Salt Lake City Tribune* were, "*On The Mesa* is John Nichols at his best." And a local blat, the *Albuquerque Tribune*, quipped, "This book is a medicine bundle, especially gathered for us. And what good and strong medicine it is."

46

IN THE SPRING of 1986 Robert Redford asked me to rewrite David Ward's latest script of *Milagro*. It was "flat," nobody liked it, David had no "sense of the people." He was pooped and unhappy—"He just doesn't have it." Robbie Greenberg, the cameraman, didn't like it either. In fact, Robbie phoned me and said, "You gotta rewrite the screenplay and save it." One of Bob's assistants, Sarah Black, came to New Mexico to confer with me. She read every version of my scripts. She knows the book by heart and is "pasting it all together." She tells me that David Ward is "tapped out" and it's "a shame all the money that has been wasted." She admits, "Everyone is panicked."

Sarah asked if I'd work on the script again. I said, "Sure." They pushed to sign me for the five grand I owed Moctesuma Esparza on the former contract I was fired from, but my agent shit a brick. The new rewrite earned me twenty thousand dollars (EXTRA! EXTRA! READ ALL ABOUT IT! JOHN

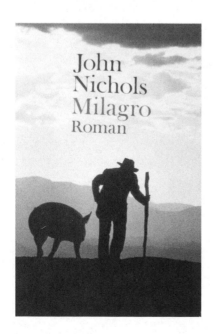

Cover on the 1988 Dutch translation of my novel *The Milagro Beanfield War*. Courtesy of John Nichols.

NICHOLS DRIVES A HARD BARGAIN!). Sarah wished to know why my involvement with Bob had gone awry. I explained how difficult it was to arrange meetings; the Writers Guild strike; and possibly the fact I was at work for Writers Guild minimum gave me a "lack of credibility." Maybe Bob thought paying David Ward a fortune would assure a great product. Moctesuma told me that a million dollars had gone for screenplays (not including whatever was paid to Tracy Keenan Wynn and Leonard Gardner when Chris/Rose held the option). Forty grand of that million spent under Esparza was earned by me. That's called being a very low man on the totem pole. Another euphemism for "integrity."

"Bob listens to anybody," Mocte said. "He'll take input from everybody. He reads everything. Just never knows in what direction he's going."

———

May of 1986 was an interesting month. Redford had determined to shoot the movie on location in New Mexico. When first we'd met I suggested that was a crazy plan. When he asked, "Why?" I explained that when I worked on *The Sterile Cuckoo* with Alan Pakula, I'd asked him if *To Kill a Mockingbird* had been filmed on location in Monroeville, Alabama, Harper Lee's hometown and the model for "Maycomb, Alabama" in her novel and the film. Pakula had thrown up his hands, exclaiming, "Are you fucking *kidding* me?" Something that racially loaded in small-town Alabama would've gotten the entire film crew and all the actors killed. So Maycomb was recreated on the Universal Studios Hollywood backlot. My advice to Redford was, "It'd be a good idea to treat *Milagro* the same way."

Bob looked askance at me and said, "Times have changed."

Pretty soon Hollywood characters were invading northern New Mexico—location managers, cameramen, art directors, and slick Mr. Fixits toting carpetbags full of unmarked bills to pay homeowners for location spots. Redford's team picked the picturesque small-town Chimayó plaza (a half hour north of Santa Fe) as their principal location until Chimayó told them to go take a flying douche at a rolling sopaipilla. That created local and national headlines for two weeks, driving my testicles up into my abdomen for the duration. "FUCK REDFORD!" is what most headlines gleefully implied. The press loves to topple an icon. But "FUCK NICHOLS!" was also implied. And Chimayó's rejection was a disturbing omen of bottlenecks to come.

Friends of mine began asking me to finagle them jobs on the movie, from building sets to acting or having their girlfriend's *corrido* on the film's soundtrack. Santa Fe's mayor, Sam Pick, and two former governors, Jerry Apodaca and David Cargo, were angling for parts in the picture. A casting agent wanted me to find her a bunch of "colorful old timers" to use as extras for the film. I am not a hustler, and I *hate* asking people for money or favors. It didn't take long to realize I was up shit creek without a paddle.

––––––

As for the novel *American Blood* that I was also creating? I had a library of 120 books about the Vietnam War (which I'd protested from 1964 until 1975), and I chose to begin my story with forty pages of our graphic war atrocities, one of the worst decisions I ever made. I've regretted the introduction since because it loudly declares, "THIS IS A VIETNAM WAR NOVEL!!!" But it wasn't. The book intended to explain the violence underlying American history and culture since our beginnings, interwoven with a powerful and tragic love story that confronts the heart of American despair, ultimately rejecting it.

Oddly, Marian Wood was behind this angry Jeremiad all the way. She felt the initial drafts were too long and relentless, so cut them. But after I chopped them down to size she suggested, "You cut too much, add more of what you had before." So I puttered with the manuscript, hoping to strike an unhappy medium as the *Milagro* film melodramas swirled around me.

47

NOT TO BE evasive, but while I'm on the subject 1987 would be the year Peregrine Smith published a large coffee-table book of my photographs accompanied by excerpts from my other writings alongside an introduction of how I came to New Mexico, wrote *The Milagro Beanfield War*, and it evolved into a movie. *A Fragile Beauty* would hit the stands simultaneously with *Milagro*'s release set for March 1987. Yes, I had compromised my "integrity" in order to publish the photographs. Without the film, nobody would've released the pictures.

All the same, I argued ferociously with Peregrine Smith about the design of *A Fragile Beauty*, over which I had contractual control. They just couldn't get it from my point of view, which was to minimize the movie connection. Their designer, and the publisher, Gibbs Smith, wound up in Taos working at my kitchen table while I presented them with a page-by-page dummy I'd drawn by hand for every page of the entire book.

I know that sounds obnoxiously arrogant on my part, but I wanted the finished product to be clean, simple, and dignified, without all the bells and whistles designers feel they *have* to add because they are *designers*. No full-page photos bleeding off the page here followed by much smaller images surrounded by wide white margins and then another picture cut in half by the gutter. Way back during the *New Mexico Review* days, Rini Templeton had taught me how to make a design clean, elegant, simple, very readable, and beautiful.

Less was more.

Of course, bells and whistles, no matter how inappropriate, sell better.

Given the choice, what do *you* think publishers want? Especially from a book whose raison d'être is its tie-in to what should be a popular movie?

Gibbs Smith, the head honcho of Peregrine Smith Books, wanted the photo-essay to be called *John Nichols' Milagro Country*. I balked. "Hell no, that's embarrassing. I don't *own* that country. It's a white, imperialist title. Just call it *A Fragile Beauty*." We argued. I got my way, sort of, except that Gibbs insisted on *John Nichols' Milagro Country* as a subtitle, albeit in smaller print, but still connecting *A Fragile Beauty* to the movie. I felt obliged to give in on that point because I wanted my photos published in a decent venue, color-corrected, and viable. And I understood Peregrine Smith was publishing the book solely to cash in on the film. They weren't just in it to honor my photographs or my writing skills.

However, listen to this: Gibbs Smith tells me to ask Robert Redford to produce a foreword to the book so *his* name will also be on the cover. I said, "Not in a million years. Forget it. The humiliation of riding on his coattails with the film is already unacceptable. Plus Redford gets asked by five hundred people a day for this favor, that favor, this endorsement, that ancillary commitment, you name it. He's trying to finish one movie, direct another film (*Milagro*), take care of his family, support liberal environmental political candidates, fight off the press and gossipmongers and the scandal chasers every minute of every day. He doesn't need one more distraction, and I would rather rot in hell than ask him for such a blatantly cynical task simply so you can put his name on the cover of *A Fragile Beauty* in order to sell it." I emphasized, "It's *my* book. And I've worked hard putting it together." I added, "And Redford has no time for that kind of bullshit."

Gibbs Smith raised his open hands and backed off, saying, "Okay, okay, I see your point, you win."

Then he went to one of Redford's assistants, telling her that John Nichols wanted Bob to write a foreword to *A Fragile Beauty*. The assistant approached Redford, and Bob generously replied, "Okay, I'd be delighted to help out John in any way I can."

On hearing that news I went through the roof. But I didn't have the guts to tell Bob that Gibbs Smith was a liar, so instead I thanked Redford profusely for his willingness and waited for the foreword.

Weeks, a month, two months go by. Gibbs Smith asks me, "Where is Redford's foreword?" My reply is, "I told you, he's a very busy man." But Gibbs won't take that for an answer. "We're designing the book. We have to have that foreword." My reply is, "So go ask him yourself if you want it so much." Obviously I should have been obsequious and grateful that Gibbs was willing to publish my book in the first place.

Whatever Gibbs did, or didn't do, never produced a foreword. So I wrote Bob a letter giving him the straight skinny on how he got asked for a foreword in the first place. He replied by sending me a very short foreword. I complained about some of the grammar and the use of patronizing words. He answered back through an assistant, Lois Smith. I fussed about a split infinitive and a remark about "sex." He took out "sex" and the split infinitive but left in my other complaints. I couldn't believe that with all the work he had to do, and I had to do, Redford and I were in a nit-picking back-and-forth quarrel about the finer points in a three-hundred-word puff piece!

The entire time I was deeply humiliated at so pathetically "asking" for the foreword to assure that Redford's name, and "*Milagro*," would wind up on the cover, guaranteeing that Peregrine Smith could make a quick killing with the book then stiff me for half my royalties due.

The upshot? Movies and books are not a great métier to choose if you have a problem with feeling ashamed.

48

IN JUNE 1986 I had a paying gig at the Park City, Utah, Writers Conference. Wednesday through Saturday. I was scheduled to deliver the closing speech Saturday night. By then I had formerly committed to rewrite the *Milagro* screenplay (while still struggling with *Pancho Villa* and *American Blood*). Redford called me from Provo demanding I come down to Sundance in Provo on Saturday for meetings that day and Sunday. He'd send a car. I explained about my important closing speech at the Park City conference on Saturday. Bob said, "Change your speech to Friday, we need to meet." Conference organizers had a fit because my talk was intended as their climactic grand finale. Yet they reluctantly agreed to shift my spritz to Friday so I could leave early, which I did on Saturday morning.

Upon arriving at Sundance, Bob immediately had me attend a read-through of the last David Ward *Milagro* script with actors Lee Grant, Alan Alda, Laura Dern, John Shea (who'd starred in *Missing*), and the director of *Butch Cassidy* and *The Sting*, George Roy Hill.

Before they started reading, Bob snowed them with a pitch that elevated the screenplay of *Milagro* to the level of *Citizen Kane* or *Chinatown*. Then the actors knuckled down to business. Before five minutes had passed I began shrinking in my chair; it sounded so awful—slow as molasses and running over two hours. I was mortified. All the readers seemed to be on Thorazine. At the finish they clapped politely. After the run-through I asked Bob if he was panicked. He said no, he thought David Ward's script was three-quarters toward a shooting script. Gulping, I queried, "Really?" He replied, "Sure." I wondered how, because to me everything seemed freakishly discombobulated.

Supposedly we would meet Saturday night and Sunday morning at Redford's house. Good luck with that. Bob began racing around and was never available. Our meeting was rescheduled for Monday at 9:00 a.m. He showed up at 11:00. We schmoozed for four hours as I scribbled ten pages of random notes. Bob is antsy because he can't lock in locations without having a script. He mentioned actors he wanted: Sonia Braga (Brazilian), Rubén Blades (Panamanian). All the Chicana actresses he'd talked with "came on too strong," he didn't like them. I thought, *Great, there's gonna be no Chicanos in this movie?* He was testing Ricardo Montalban's elder brother to be Amarante Córdova. That fell through because insurance wouldn't cover the old fart. The fact is, I realized, my director had no signed-up cast at all!

I explained to Sarah Black I could commit three weeks to the script before the deluge of my other obligations drowned me. And that's what I did, working eighteen hours a day, killing myself with booze and cigarettes. Kool Filter Kings. I'd quit smoking when I was twenty-two, yet began again after remarrying at forty-five only nine months earlier. A pack a day. And two, three, four rum and Cokes, maybe more. I was in way over my head.

———

Stories about movie gaffes began popping up. The film location had been shifted to a tiny northern New Mexico mountain town, Truchas, not far from Chimayó and an hour south of Taos. A resident from Truchas walked into the Taos Bookshop telling a clerk the movie crew had planted telephone poles in his front field, destroying the view, insulting him *and* the point of the *Milagro* novel, too. A neighbor of mine, hired to be a liaison between the moviemakers and the citizens of Truchas, was fired for getting pissed at the film crew's insensitivity toward the locals. Promised jobs in Truchas had fallen through due to "union rules." Another friend, the original art director, David Nichols, was fired by Redford. Who knows why? Bob revealed that he hated confrontation. When he needed to deep-six somebody, he wished he had a toy sailing ship that he could simply wind up and release; then, while the boat floated at eye level past the victim's house, it would run up a skull and cross bones "Jolly Roger" on its little flagpole.

In Sierra Sports one day three men said, "Oh, are you John Nichols, the person who wrote the book they're making into a movie?" They weren't quite overtly threatening, but cold and possibly aching for a fight. At my laundromat the owner said, not all that friendly, "I see you're getting rich." A lawyer from Universal called, worried about me cribbing from former scripts by Tracy Wynn and Leonard Gardner. I told him not to worry, for crissakes, they'd cribbed everything *they* wrote from my novel.

A production manager said they were frantically growing beans as summer waned. First snows often hit Truchas in August! When I asked how everything was shaping up, he replied, "We're four weeks away from shooting, without a cast and without a script, but other than that everything is great."

49

WHEN I FINISHED my rewrite of the screenplay I overnighted it to Redford and Sarah Black in LA. In return I heard nothing. My wife came home from the Taos gallery where she worked, mumbling, "A little while ago I was so proud to say, 'He's my husband.' Now I'm terrified to mention your name or admit my connection."

American Film Magazine offered me two thousand dollars for two thousand words about the movie. What in blazes could I *say* about the movie? "So far it's taking shape as an unmitigated disaster?" Sarah Black acknowledged that Bob had received my script and then fled to Big Sur, anxiously incommunicado, "sorting things out." She's flying to Santa Fe, bringing scripts mentioned above and queries from Universal lawyers.

And anyway, I'm back on the Pancho Villa case and putting the final grim touches on *American Blood* and *A Fragile Beauty*, hence as far as I was concerned *American Film Magazine* could walk the plank without wearing water wings or a snorkel.

I went to hear my writer pal Jim Sagel give a speech at a local museum and sat down near a friend who quickly stood up and walked off to locate himself elsewhere. A fellow scrivener from the Santa Fe suburb of Nambe bitched in the daily *New Mexican* that Hollywood rips off and offends everyone. He had friends who were promised work but never hired.

———

Redford returned to Santa Fe unenthusiastic about my script. He's got two other writers working on it. I meet with him and Sarah, taking notes. Bob seems confused. What should be in the script, what should be out? He hates the ending but has to shoot it first in case it snows in Truchas. He demands new scenes from me to run through with actors in three days. Problem is, *he's got no actors*! A Screen Actors Guild strike threatens.

After the meeting, Sarah Black is frantic. She just wants to go home to LA.

Redford can't seem to focus. "He needs to have his cake and eat it too," Sarah complains. "He's afraid to make decisions." Has too many scripts in his head. Can't shoot it all then work it out in editing. "That'd be absurdly expensive."

A day later Sarah calls me to report that "Bob is going nuts." Somebody got electrocuted at the construction site in Truchas. Lightning struck a tin roof he was standing on. His heart stopped in the ambulance. Bob freaked out and went to take a hot tub. Just gonna soak and smoke. But he couldn't find an ashtray and wound up with his alarm clock as an ashtray in the jacuzzi. "Today he has tryouts for the pig." He hates it already. Bob groans, "I had no idea this film would be so difficult." He wishes there *would* be a SAG strike. Bob never seems to know what he'll do. So many people around him constantly tugging and pushing. Too much input. According to Sarah, "There'll probably never be a script of this movie." She's deeply frustrated. "I love the man dearly, but I'm just tired of going around in circles."

———

Filming finally started in Truchas. Redford had multiple scripts on hand and only a few actors under contract. What followed was disorganized and hilariously (though not for yours truly) controversial. Much loose talk criticizes how Bob works. He shoots a page and a half a day. The process is total chaos. People are never sure from one day to the next what they'll be doing. Bob redoes the set at a moment's notice. Tells you one thing one minute, then changes his mind the next.

My friend Victoria Plata is in charge of extras. "Bob is a bit dizzy to work with. On a sudden whim he'll have us going around grabbing people in off the streets. He wants old people. And uses them even before they're signed up. Has them speak lines before they're even under contract to do that. You just never know what's going to happen."

Sonia Braga is livid because she has many scenes with the lawyer, Charley Bloom, who *doesn't get cast until a quarter of the way through shooting*. Sonia can't speak English, mispronounces every word, and ultimately fires her speech coach. Moctesuma Esparza takes over that task. Lucky him.

Redford blows his cork at somebody and shouts, "Fuck you! Fuck you! Fuck you!" Sarah Black tells me Bob is "the master of the indecisive decision." There's a scandal in the newspaper about the film crew using County Backhoes for free.

When the governor is asked to straighten that out he won't touch it with a thirty-foot pole. Chuck Myers, the first assistant director, and a really good one—a big, tough motorcycle rider I truly like—tells me angrily, "Movies should be easy to make, but this fucking production is bananas!"

Just weeks into the schedule everybody involved wants it to be over. Their theme song for the production is a line taken from the movie: "Nobody told me, maybe somebody told somebody, but nobody told me."

And toward the end graffiti began to appear in Santa Fe: "FREE THE MILAGRO 100!"

50

ROBERT REDFORD'S FAME brought the national media into my life, from the *New York Times* to *People Magazine*. With new raw meat to devour, the press was eager to topple Bob off his *Ordinary People* pedestal. In almost every edition, the *Santa Fe New Mexican* and the *Albuquerque Journal* printed front-page stories above the fold on Redford and the *Beanfield*. New Mexico was still an impoverished, backwater, small-town state at the bottom of the US economic system. Bob was a Big Deal. The coverage usually mentioned the film was of "John Nichols' *Milagro Beanfield War* novel."

By osmosis I absorbed the blame. The attachment to Redford's coattails was "my fifteen minutes of fame." It nearly destroyed the life in New Mexico I'd been crafting for seventeen years. Some friends became obsequious, congratulating me on my good fortune. They knew the filmmaking must be the crowning glory of my life. And how wonderful it must feel now to be a millionaire. Other good neighbors and organizations asked me outright for money since they assumed I'd become wealthy. Many movement comrades, with whom I'd worked on rejecting the Taos conservancy district and Indian Camp Dam, bitched at me for selling out to Hollywood, growing filthy rich by exploiting Chicano culture.

No one believed I could be connected to Robert Redford, probably the most famous (and likely wealthiest) actor in America, without banking hoards of gelt for myself. There wasn't a drain big enough to swallow the dissolution of my reputation down it. Fame is always a two-edged sword.

A few of my Taos friends were hired to work on the movie, and they had fun. Other locals Redford employed as extras also enjoyed their roles. Yet the main actors were Sonia Braga, a Brazilian; Chick Vennera, an Italian from New York; Julie Carmen, a Puerto Rican from New York; Rubén Blades, a Panamanian salsa musician; Freddy Fender, the Tex-Mex singer; and Carlos Riquelme, a (wonderful!) Mexican character actor. Dave Grusin won a *Milagro* Oscar for Best Original Score, but he wasn't Al Hurricane, Cipriano Vigil, or Roberto

Mondragón. Citizens of New Mexico were incensed that no local actors had leading roles and bent my ear about that. They thought (*very* wrongly) that I had creative control over the film. Thus all its omissions were my fault.

Every now and then I remembered Alan Pakula, when I asked, "Why not film *Mockingbird* in Alabama?" throwing up his hands and exclaiming, "Are you fucking *kidding* me?"

51

THIS TRULY AWFUL experience I'll recount. When Rini Templeton died in June 1986 there was a memorial at her cabin on Pilar Hill ten miles south of Taos. Many of her political activist friends and admirers from New Mexico, California, and Mexico attended the event. I was de facto the master of ceremonies. We had plenty of food and booze, and many people I loved, respected, and had worked with gave their poignant eulogies. Among them were Betita and Tessa Martínez, Enriqueta Vásquez, Lee Piefer, Eduardo Cepeda, Cecilio García-Camarillo, Morty Simon, Roger McNew, and Cori Field (Rini's niece). Just before I was slated to speak, a radical Latina, I think from Los Angeles, stood up and began crapping on the upcoming racist filming of *The Milagro Beanfield War* in Truchas that Rini would have abhorred. She said, "Hurray for Chimayó!" and hoped Truchas would also send Redford packing. She dumped all over my racist novel, interspersing her enraged comments with soliloquies on how much Rini would have detested the book, its capitalist author, and the exploitational filmmakers.

I guess she had no idea I was the guy who'd written the book that was dedicated to Rini among others. Or that Rini had read each chapter and commented during its creation. Or that she had illustrated *Milagro* part headings and designed the cover.

For six or seven minutes the woman carried on until another Chicana said, "Okay, enough, *compañera*." The woman quit and left our circle. As the next speaker in line, I rose to give my brief eulogy, simply reading the words I had written. It was difficult to maintain composure because I was crying.

The following speakers, most of whom knew me, said nothing about the woman's diatribe. It was ignored. Yet her words remained in the air throughout our ceremony. And of course they broke my heart. None of my activist friends in attendance ever mentioned that moment to me. One and all pretended it never happened.

Two hours later, after we'd all spoken with much emotion and beauty, we joined hands and each person in turn shouted, "Rini Templeton—*Presente*! Rini

Templeton—*Presente!*" Then I was asked to sing a song for Rini, and I sang "Joe Hill" in honor of her and of Joe Hill's final words: "Don't mourn, organize."

Afterward we mingled, laughing and remembering Rini. At one point I walked into her cabin, and the woman who'd spoken so bitterly was there with her friend, each of them pretty drunk. I approached, seeking reconciliation. The woman snarled, "Don't you touch me, you racist scumbag," and poured out venom. Her friend joined in, calling me "a racist exploiter of the people." Both of them berated me, shitting on the memorial, swearing that Rini would have hated it. I fled.

In my journal I wrote, "I don't know, regarding my work, if I ever confronted so much hatred. No, never, not even remotely."

———

Soon a group of us traipsed west across the mesa. I separated a little because I couldn't stop crying. At the edge of the Río Grande Gorge we sang the old Italian partisan song "Bella Ciao," which has been translated into many languages. It means "Goodbye, Beautiful." A slain partisan is buried up on a mountain beneath a beautiful flower. The last verse says:

> This is the flower, of a fighter,
> Goodbye, beautiful, goodbye beautiful, goodbye, bye, bye.
> This is the flower, of a fighter,
> Who died for liberty

Then we spread out and sat down where it was peaceful and quite beautiful. We were thoughtful, reminiscing. Swallows darted above us and below our feet in the canyon. The sky cleared after a brief rain burst. In a while I passed around a sack of Rini's ashes and people took handfuls, scattering them over the cliff edge—puffs in the wind. I walked off a ways and buried my handful under a piñon tree. "Then sat there and cried some more," says my journal, "just couldn't seem to stop crying for a while."

Ambling back slowly, we recalled adventures with Rini. And zigzagged through a blooming cactus field and a prairie-dog village. At Rini's cabin most people had left. We cleaned up, taking benches and chairs over to my truck and other vehicles. Those two angry women, still drinking, were the last ones around. As we loaded chairs and benches into the truck beds, they shouted, "Why don't you get a Mexican to do it?"

52

WHILE I'M EXCAVATING old corpses maybe I shouldn't omit this *calavera*. Not long after *Milagro* began shooting in 1986 it was sued by Reies López Tijerina, Larry Cano (a film producer), and Frank Zuniga (a director). Together they were developing a movie, *King Tiger*, based on Tijerina's radical land-grant activism in New Mexico. During the 1960s Reies had formed the *Alianza Federal de Mercedes*, which protested Anglo thefts of communally held Hispano land grants in violation of the 1848 Treaty of Guadalupe Hidalgo ending the Mexican-American War. A charismatic leader, Tijerina's battles had culminated in the June 5, 1967, Tierra Amarilla courthouse raid, in which Alianza members tried to make a citizen's arrest of District Attorney Alfonso Sánchez for his harassment of Alianza members. Guns were fired, and several participants wounded. Tijerina and others escaped. National Guard troops sent by the governor occupied Tierra Amarilla. That action drew national and international attention.

The film *King Tiger* was to be funded by Columbia Pictures, who canceled its production shortly after Redford began shooting in Truchas. Cano, Zuniga, and Tijerina claimed *Milagro* was based on Tijerina's life, thus Reies was suffering invasion of privacy, defamation, unfair competition, and loss of income thanks to the *Milagro* film causing Columbia's cancellation of *King Tiger*.

The *Milagro* part of the claim was absurd. Nobody had ever made it during the twelve years since my novel's publication. When you smell Redford, though, you smell money. Curiously, the entities named in the lawsuit were Universal Pictures; Redford and his Wildwood Production Company; the other screenwriter, David Ward; and the producer, Moctesuma Esparza. But not me.

An article published in the *Los Angeles Times* on October 23, 1986, quoted "a 'Milagro' spokesman" who'd told the paper that "[David] Ward did not write an original screenplay. He wrote a script based on John Nichols' novel. And if you've read the script and the novel, you can see that everything in the script is in the novel. If anything, they should be suing John Nichols." The same article quoted "Attorney Michael Schillaci, representing Cano and fellow plaintiffs,"

The scariest newspaper story I ever read, published in the *Albuquerque Journal* on October 23, 1986. Courtesy of John Nichols.

saying, "We also feel the book [by John Nichols] is in reality based on Tijerina's life," and, "Nichols may be named later as a defendant."

I peed my pants. (Yet was never named a defendant.)

Although my imagination had conjured many reasons to fear Robert Redford making a movie of *Milagro* in New Mexico, this scenario exponentially exceeded my paranoid nightmares. Redford was the most famous actor in America. Reies Tijerina was one of the four most famous activists representing the Chicano Movement. I was among thousands of the least famous American writers. No matter, there was my headshot right beside Redford's and Tijerina's across a page of the *Albuquerque Journal* with a bold headline above: **"TIJERINA SUES TO STOP 'MILAGRO' FILMING."**

———

Naturally, my phone rang with newspapers calling. I politely had no comment because I was not gonna pour gasoline onto the flames. There's a Spanish dicho I've often repeated: "*En boca cerrada no entran moscas*" (Keep your mouth shut and flies won't enter). Redford and Esparza kept filming. And after the initial *petite* flurry of interest, no journalist contacted me about the lawsuit again.

Yet things kept unraveling anyway.

———

For example, toward the end of shooting in 1986 Melanie Griffith asked me if I thought she was right for the part. Me? She's asking *me*? We were at a Santa Fe gathering to watch *Milagro Beanfield* rushes. Robert Redford strolled by me in a huff and said, "Oh, John Nichols—are you slumming in Hollywood again?" It wasn't a joke. He was pissed because I had rarely showed up on the *Milagro* set that summer. Why not? Because I lived an hour away and had explained, before the shooting folderol began, that I'd just gotten remarried, I was working on a six-hour miniseries for CBS about Pancho Villa and the Mexican revolution, and I was preparing a novel, *American Blood*, and a nonfiction photo-essay book, *A Fragile Beauty*, for publication the following year. I was *overloaded* with obligations. And nobody had asked me to be on set. No one had suggested I be a consultant, tweaking dialogue or entire scenes as problems arose. So I figured it was Bob's movie, don't intrude, leave him alone. What director wants the book's author looking over his or her shoulder on every take, commenting on their work?

We kissed and made up. Welcome to my world. Often I reminded myself, "Forget it, bubalu—it's only Chinatown."

———

When the film wrapped in November, most everyone involved departed New Mexico because they lived elsewhere. Bye-bye, Johnny. The minute Redford skipped town residents of Truchas torched the set he'd constructed. A year later some cast and crew had to return, rebuild the set, and shoot more footage to "save" the floundering movie. When that was accomplished, local folks dismantled the set again.

I was left holding the bag while everyone else moved on. The movie would be a financial and artistic disaster. Critics could praise or condemn it in the same breath by declaring it a "charming" movie. Because I never saw the picture before it was released, I spent three years reacting to national and local news organizations asking my opinion of the film when I had no clue if it would be racist, patronizing, or a positive experience. Painfully, I waffled, striving to be upbeat even as I wished to cover my ass if disaster struck. I well understood that if the movie was outright patronizing or racist I was a dead man.

The review aggregator *Rotten Tomatoes* tagged *Milagro* as "arguably Robert Redford's most inchoate work." As for me? The saga still wasn't over, but for the moment I'd ignominiously exit stage left quoting Kurt Vonnegut again: "*Poo-tee-weet?*"

JOHN NICHOLS
AUTHOR OF THE MILAGRO BEANFIELD WAR

AMERICAN BLOOD

FIRST BRITISH PUBLICATION

'ULTRA- DISTURBING ...
A NARRATIVE EXPLICIT ABOUT SEX AND VIOLENCE .
AN IMPORTANT WORK OF LITERATURE'
LIBRARY JOURNAL

Cover of the English paperback edition of *American Blood*, published by Paladin Grafton Books in 1990. Cover illustration by Richard Parent. Courtesy of John Nichols.

PART IX

53

OKAY, NOW IT'S spring, 1987, *American Blood* has been published, and reviews are pouring in like scalding water spilled from a stove saucepan splashing onto an overcurious toddler's head. Excited by my prospects, Holt sends me on another book tour. As we sow, so shall we reap. My wife is curious, hence I take her along on my own bank account. Definitely a decision made by a feeble mind.

If any of you wannabe writers out there are reading this memoir, I should advise you that book tours are logistical nightmares involving daily airplane flights to different cities, lost luggage, media escorts who don't show up, 3:00 a.m. fire alarms in big hotels, TV appearances at 6:45 a.m., newspaper interviews with bored journalists who've never heard of you, readings scheduled at bookstores who forgot you were coming, fans who hand you drafts of their own manuscripts to read (and blurb), and occasionally women who propose to take you home and haul your exhausted ashes. This is not the sort of helter-skelter crazed experience that your wife will enjoy, especially if you have to repeatedly ask her to "hurry up, forget the makeup and the lip gloss, we're late already!" If your wife is an edgy person quick to chastise an unrepentant male chauvinist pig, you will become a resident of Hell Times Infinity every hour of every obscenely rushed and confusing day.

My advice? *Go alone.*

Either she outright hated me for not giving her enough attention or she wanted to shop while I was running for a cab. When I caught my breath I blurted, "I'm sorry, but this tour isn't about you, it's about *me*." Her reply? "Every fucking thing is *always* about you. I'm *sick* of it!"

We did have fun with Studs Terkel in Chicago; photographed ourselves bedecked with floppy strands of kelp on a Santa Barbara beach; and enjoyed great sex in Aspen, Colorado. Then we hit an emotional speed bump in Seattle that sent me barreling (thank God, *alone*!) to make my reading date barely on time at the Elliot Bay Bookstore while my wife stewed back at the hotel and wouldn't converse with me for two days because I'd called her "a wart on the asshole of progress" for blow-drying her hair, painting her fingernails, and curling her eyelashes while a taxi waited downstairs with the meter running.

And, of course, I need hardly explain that reviews of my new novel did not read like the hagiographies for *On The Mesa*.

You can't say I didn't have it coming. So just take your medicine, Johnny, and be sure to wear a Kevlar vest.

Ergo:

> I wish I hadn't read the book, since those images are now, in some way, mine too. Yes, that's his point but, like Vietnam itself, the book suffers from overkill.
>
> —The *Arkansas Gazette*

> *American Blood* is less a novel than an exorcising, grim evidence of the growing despair of a promising young writer.
>
> —The *Observer*

> This is a book that is violent, pornographic, sexist, racist. It is a mirror in the funhouse that reflects a grotesque view of ourselves. The danger in reading it is that you just might turn to your 'normal' mirror and see that same grotesque image. That's exactly what Nichols wants you to do.
>
> —*Santa Barbara News-Press*

> I'm sorry that Nichols wrote *American Blood* and sorrier still that Holt let it out.
>
> —The *Nation*

> . . . as prurient a piece of fiction imaginable this side of sado-masochistic pornography.
>
> —The *Seattle Weekly*

> The first 10 pages of this acrid novel are among the harshest I've read. The rest don't get much easier. From start to finish, the book burns with violence and hatred. Pages brim with death and mutilation. It is written in a loose, profane style that borders on pornography. For readers who can put up with it, *American Blood* is gut-punch powerful.
>
> —*Eugene* (Oregon) *Register-Guard*

John Nichols' *American Blood* is distinctive, to be sure: not because it's about Vietnam, but because it portrays human brutality so lucidly that even Jerzy Kosinski might cringe.

—*Fort Lauderdale News-Sentinel*

Ultimately, the real point of all the book's blood and guts is Nichols' belief in the power of love. The repetition of defilement is Nichols way of purging his protagonist of a total paralysis of the human spirit. By extension, the book reads like an off-color morality play, with Nichols directing us to wake up to the crimes our indifference creates.

—*Fort Collins Coloradan*

After the first shocking chapters of *American Blood*—the section where the novel's protagonist, Michael Smith, is witnessing the gory, Goyaesque horrors of the Vietnam war—readers may drop John Nichols' newest novel and question the author's state of mind. [Still, although the review ends after calling the novel my "most difficult book to date," it admits *American Blood* is] certainly a bitter but appropriate parable of the times.

—The *Portland Oregonian*

The first 30 pages of John Nichols Vietnam war novel *American Blood* are packed with more savagery and mayhem—much of it visited on civilians—than a week of prime-time television. The movie *Platoon* looks like a romp in the countryside by comparison.

—*Austin American Statesman*

American Blood is a profoundly disturbing book. Nichols has chosen to mute his engaging sense of humor in favor of the direct hit to the veins. The America he describes, the nation bathed in blood, the people who keep a loaded gun by their pillows, are more real here than in the news.

—*San Francisco Examiner-Chronicle*

Although John Nichols means well, he oversimplifies a very complex subject. Those readers who survive the initial assault will be stunned into disbelief by the end. Nichols as exorcist does not manage the fine line between being a sadist and a savior.

—The *Seattle Times*

A grotesque sentimentalism seems to underlie it, as if it were an episode of *M*A*S*H* written and directed by the Marquis de Sade. There is something gratuitously nasty about this book ... And Michael Smith is one of the most whining, self-pitying characters I've ever encountered. His passivity makes him an accomplice and deprives him of any moral resonance. Maybe I just no longer have the stomach for this sort of thing. Those who like coarse sex and slasher movies may want to check it out.

—The *Fort-Worth Star Telegram*

54

SOMETIMES IT AMAZES me that a happy-go-lucky novel like *American Blood* has been on film options for almost half as many years as was *The Milagro Beanfield War*. All those options have been held by one person, my friend Laray Mayfield, a Nashville native gone Hollywood casting director who is probably alone on earth thinking *American Blood* actually has redeeming humane qualities. Her belief in my love story, despite the violence of multiple tragedies that frame it, gives Laray my vote for Most Hopeful Person in the Universe.

She is still a schoolgirl, two decades younger than me. On the first day after she moved from Nashville to Hollywood in 1986 she met, and became friends with, the director David Fincher. And for the last three decades she has grown up casting his videos and films, among them "Fight Club," "Gone Girl," "Zodiac," "Panic Room," "The Girl with the Dragon Tattoo," "The Curious Case of Benjamin Button," "The Social Network," and, most recently, "Mank."

1991 is when she first visited me in Taos. We became friends. She optioned *American Blood* in 1994, hiring me to write a first-draft screenplay, which I accomplished *very* unsuccessfully. Later, in 2004 when Laray had a production company with the country singer (and actor) Dwight Yoakam, she renewed the option for several years. This time around I chickened out of writing a script because I couldn't deal with the violence. No matter; Laray and I remained good buddies. And she kept trying to obtain backing for another shot at the book. That happened in 2017 when she signed up once more, entering a relationship with the production company of actor and producer Jessica Biel. And, as I write this (in April 2021), the option continues being renewed, and Laray is still my lone, and utterly faithful, Hollywood pal.

We began our friendship when I was fifty-one. A couple of months from now—knock on wood—I'll be eighty-one. If Laray ever realizes *American Blood* as the powerful film it could be, I will rain kisses down on her from heaven. To me, whatever happens, her loving friendship and her blind faith in my novel have been a miracle.

55

IT MAKES SENSE that *A Fragile Beauty* was the exact opposite of *American Blood* (although their publication dates roughly coincided). Yet there's always an unexpected devil in the details. Peregrine Smith Books had planned to release *A Fragile Beauty* simultaneously with a 1987 benefit opening for the *Milagro Beanfield* film. However, part of the struggling movie had to be redone in Truchas that year and wouldn't be released until March 1988, months later than planned.

A Fragile Beauty did not take a bath, however. It sold okay. A glitch was that Gibbs Smith stiffed me for about fifteen thousand in royalties by claiming his press had a "liquidity crunch." I don't remember the exact sum because I'm rewriting this book during the 2020–2021 Covid-19 lockdown and have no access to my archival papers at the University of New Mexico's library in Albuquerque.

I protested to Gibbs by myself and also through my agent, Perry Knowlton. No dice. Perry suggested I sue, but I've never sued anybody in my life. Lawyers have always terrified me, and I'd rather eat the loss than go through the agony of the American legal process. I've seen *Primal Fear*, *12 Angry Men*, *To Kill a Mockingbird*, and *Inherit the Wind*. What I did do, though, after *Milagro* was released and Peregrine Smith prepared to remainder *A Fragile Beauty*, was demand many boxes of my book in payment for money owed. They were happy to oblige. After I rented a Taos storage locker, a Red Ball Express 18-wheeler arrived with more boxes of *A Fragile Beauty* than I could count. Each cardboard container weighed a ton because the volume *was* beautifully produced, with shiny photo-friendly pages and a lovely cloth cover.

For about five years I gave away the books as gifts, party favors, or "advertising fliers" to anybody who wanted one. As selling is not my strong point, I never approached bookstores about taking *A Fragile Beauty* on consignment. Listen to this, though.

In 1995, Mary Powell, owner of Ancient City Press in Santa Fe, published a paperback reprint of *On The Mesa*. When I mentioned *A Fragile Beauty* to her, she said, "I'd be happy to have my Colorado distributor take it on for you." Mary offered me 50 percent of royalties—a great deal. She drove her truck up to Taos, and we spent an afternoon removing the cellophane wrappers from every book so that I could sign each copy, making it more salable. Those cartons filled her truck bed and half of mine, and back to Santa Fe we drove. All those remainders were shipped to Johnson Books in Boulder, Colorado. Mary advertised them in her Ancient City catalogue.

Every year Mary Powell paid me the royalties she'd promised until all the stock was sold. I'd earned back the money Gibbs Smith had stiffed me for. People liked my glossy photo-essay. It received nice reviews summed up by this comment in *USA Today*: "Words and color photographs by John Nichols, author of *The Sterile Cuckoo*, chronicle his 20 years of living near Taos, New Mexico. His superb photographs of the countryside make this book something special."

56

WHILE I'M MEETING with New York CBS brass sometime in 1987 about the Pancho Villa project I called *Born to Attack*, I became woozy, sick, and frightened on the rush-hour subway. I almost passed out. Oh dear—trouble in River City. A Manhattan doctor hired by CBS said my EKG read like that of a man who'd had several heart attacks. Too bad; I cannot stop the momentum driving me toward a bad end. Life with the new extended family is so convoluted and debilitating. Arguing, bitching about money and kids, jealousy, ecstasy, confusion, too much drinking, too much celebrating, too much dramatic emotional chaos. I'm like a Flying Wallenda, drunk and teetering on the high wire without a balance pole while being attacked by angry birds from a Hitchcock movie two hundred feet above the pavement. I have thick journals from those days that read like a man committing suicide. How did I find time to scribble them? The clown keeps juggling all these balls, all these balls. "IIIIIIIIIIIIITTTTTSSSSSS . . . *showtime!*" How does the clown do it? *Why* does the clown do it? How, in the midst of all that confusion and family turmoil, can the clown still sit down every night at midnight and type on his projects until dawn?

It must be time to relax on an eight-week European vacation, right? As Gary Gilmore once said, "Let's do it." So my impetuous new wife and I purchased the tickets, climbed aboard a 747, ordered four two-ounce minis of bourbon and two glasses of ice cubes, leaned back our seats, and, in unison, began reciting the Lord's Prayer.

Over in autumnal (1987) Europe we went to Holland, Amsterdam, the Hague, and Nootdorp, and had a big fight in Harlingen, after which we lay angrily abed as an oversexed couple banged their headboard loudly against the wall, indulging in night-long erotic acrobatics that tortured (and infuriated) my wife and I steaming beside each other next door.

Then we commandeered a train for Paris, facing backward and choking on cigarette smoke all the way. In Paris my wife got a urinary tract infection, causing us to tramp for hours seeking a doctor who would treat her for most of the American Express travelers checks left in my backpack. In Port-Blanc, Brittany, visiting my French aunt and cousins, we couldn't flush a toilet at night without waking the entire household. And if we tried to make love the bed squeaked like howler monkeys after dark in Brazil.

That's when she and I decided to chill out with a blitzkrieg tour of the picturesque Loire River Valley châteaux. Let a few excerpts from my diary explain:

Woke up, as usual feeling 800 years old, mouth full of rocks, sweating like a stuck pig, teeth aching, heavy duty headache.

On the way back both my feet started *killing* me. My walk became increasingly painful. Then limped to the room in agony. My toe on the right foot feels like it's *broken*!

My stomach at night is Vesuvius erupting. She and I lie side-by-side with gas and chemicals going nuts in our bellies, keeping each other awake.

6pm we headed south. I felt sicker, fevered in the guts from constipation. It got dark, no rooms. Felt real sick. Guts hurting . . .

I get lost in every town. We toured the château, took lots of pictures, had more shitting adventures afterward. I went into public toilets, stall next to an old lady, and just shit my brains out—GRATEFULLY!—who cares anymore? There is no dignity!

St. Sulpice had a lovely château. Heading back, I wanted to shit. Went into the forest but got scared someone would come along, and couldn't. I'm going to write a book about Europe called "SHITTING SCARED!"

I was clenched up tight. The last hour searching for a hotel was pretty hairy. Strain taking its toll. Gave myself an enema before bed, then went to the loo. New kind of toilet, with an arm to push back beneath an 'oxygen cylinder' above the toilet. It EXPLODED with a noise I swear could be heard for 100 kilometers!

I'm just exhausted from tension of driving around. We don't seem to cover that much ground, but 10 a.m. to 5 p.m. leaves me a babbling idiot! It's raining all the fucking time.

Then, at last, the Château of Chambord. A really big, really intimidating, really obnoxious palatial manse surrounded by trees and lawns and gardens and hills and many more trees, which apparently used to be full of stags, hares, and wild boars that royalty slaughtered with their flintlock blunderbusses while back home their servant maids were balling their fat, greasy chefs.

My final European words?

I go to the WC, shit a little, and just say "Thank you, God!" She and I shriek at the indignities of constipation. I recall Luke, how much I envied his 10-year-old's turds when he forgot to flush the toilet. They were like logs shat by Paul Bunyon, twice as big as the kid himself!

Oh, to be young again.

And, by the way: *Fuck you, Europe, and the horse you rode in on.*

57

AT THE END of October we returned to America so shell-shocked we couldn't poop for a month. Still, we continued talking and joking and snuggling and eating together and drinking and watching movies and discussing books and politics. We raged at how crazy everything is, and we discussed our children's problems, or our own intellectual interests, or the bollixed-up politics of our country. We hiked together on this trail or that one, or proceeded up in the high mountains or across the mesas or down in the Río Grande gorge. We listened to each other's life histories and watched ball games on TV and drank too much while rooting.

One memorable December week was spent in Bristol, Vermont, gritting our teeth as Jenny Bowen tried to direct *The Wizard of Loneliness*, which starred Lea Thompson, Lukas Haas, John Randolph, Dylan Baker, Anne Pitoniak, and Lance Guest, fine actors all. Big problem: The director had only 1.5 million from Sundance and PBS's *American Playhouse* to make the picture. All the crew were working for scale, or for free, or for a piece of the net on the back end, which is always a fat chunk of nothing. Jenny had a terrible cold. The producer, Thom Tyson, asked me to forgo the forty thousand dollars I was owed when cameras started rolling, and I did. What the hell. Another gold star on my forehead.

Jenny was attempting to film Bristol winter scenes in December, although that December no snow fell on Vermont. They had to manufacture fake snow using rolls of white, cottony fibers. Her cinematographer husband, Richard, hadn't enough money to properly cover scenes, film reaction shots, or reshoot bad acting. I recall a half-dozen of us arranged on the Bristol green tossing dime-store rubber bats up in the air to create an autumn twilight ambiance. Rushes showed they were obviously rubber bats.

Approximately halfway through the picture their financial shoestring broke. The unsuccessful finished product had plenty of heart but no legs. According to the critic Leonard Maltin, "Top-notch acting (especially by precocious young star Haas) fails to save a haphazardly constructed adaptation of John Nichols' novel."

Night filming of *The Wizard of Loneliness* in Bristol, Vermont, December 1987. Photo by John Nichols.

Jenny swore she'd never direct another movie without an adequate budget to make it. When they released *Wizard* in 1988 I watched it with a handful of friends in Taos's otherwise-empty Plaza Theater. No news reporters or local reviewers on hand. Then *Wizard* disappeared like a faint wisp of smoke, minus even a whimper.

58

AS FOR MY "other movie?" On March 18, 1988, there took place, at Santa Fe's Lensic Theater, the Worldwide Gala Benefit Opening for *The Milagro Beanfield War*. I had yet to see a rough cut and didn't know whether the movie was good, bad, or horribly patronizing. I did hear the film had gone way over budget (costing twenty million dollars!). The Grand Opening had been delayed almost a year because of reshooting and editing problems. Apparently, Bob and company were frantically recutting forty hours before doors opened at the Lensic. Every magazine and scandal sheet (and TV show) from *People*, *Variety*, and the *Los Angeles Times* to *Entertainment Tonight* (and even the *National Enquirer*) had pegged *Milagro* as "Redford's Folly" or speculated about sex scandals involving Bob and Sonia Braga, the third assistant AD, the continuity person, the clapper loader, three gaffers, a prop master, and two stunt women.

I felt trapped inside *The Shining* or *Rosemary's Baby* come to life. Given the state of my heart, such vexations were certain to be fatal. On several occasions, while out walking our big Chow, Mangus, on Los Córdovas Mesa near Taos, I suffered atrial tachycardia attacks that dropped me to the ground, almost passing out. I performed the Valsalva maneuver while Mangus cocked his head, staring at me bewildered. This happened once only twenty yards from the truck, yet each time I stood up the tachycardia whacked me again. Almost fifteen minutes passed before I could reach the steering wheel. Understand, atrial tachycardia shouldn't kill you, because if you totally faint your heart usually returns to sinus rhythm.

Emphasis on *usually*.

I was smoking, drinking too much, consuming coffee and Diet Cokes (caffeine kills!). Made anxious to the max by all the chaos, posturing, *demands*. I slept only four hours a night.

Siskel and Ebert were coming to Santa Fe. My children, Luke and Tania, were coming to Santa Fe. My current wife's two boys, Dylan and Colin, were coming to Santa Fe. My current wife's stepdaughter and stepson, Heather and Lance (from a previous marriage, the one just before me), were coming to Santa Fe. One big happy family, *qué no*? The physical and emotional logistics were bonkers.

Film critic Roger Ebert and my daughter, Tania, giving the "two thumbs up" sign after the benefit opening in Santa Fe of the *Milagro* film on March 18, 1988. Photo by John Nichols.

The official opening was at 1:00 or 2:00 p.m. But Redford had arranged a special free showing at 10:00 a.m. for 650 local folk he'd bussed down from Truchas, Trampas, Chamisal, and Córdova, small towns up north, many of whose citizens had personal or family connections to the film.

Redford and Esparza ordered me to attend *that* event. I figured there'd be an author lynching afterward. Never have I entered a public venue harboring such apprehension. Everyone who recognized me shook my hand vigorously, gave me *abrazos*, and thanked me for the movie. *What* movie? None of us had even *seen* it yet.

The lights dim, the film starts, and every opening credit receives a standing ovation. When the music begins, *it* scores a standing ovation. The first background mountain triggers a standing ovation. Then a corral and an adobe house garner similar accolades. When a kid on a bicycle appears, the crowd roars even louder. An initial shot of Amarante Córdova's pig elicits resoundingly joyful pandemonium. You couldn't dampen the enthusiasm of these people with a water cannon from Selma, Alabama, turned on full blast!

Thirteen seconds into reel #1 I realized that my life would probably be spared. At least I wasn't gonna be stoned to death on the Santa Fe Plaza.

The official afternoon opening is a nightmare. It's for rich people who paid big bucks to get in. They all know each other and are a friendly, chipper audience. Bob gives them a hokey spiel before the projectors begin humming. I can't say there was out-of-control applause for every scene, but folks laughed and enjoyed themselves, afterward mingling among the paparazzi posing for the morning editions.

When the press beleaguers me for my comments I'm so flustered all I can reply is that yesterday American soldiers had landed in Honduras to train contra troops on how to murder Nicaraguans. If reporters asked me what I thought of the *movie*, I said US troops should get the hell *out* of Honduras and Ronald Reagan was a reactionary scumbag for sending them there in the first place. That's called evading the question by blowing off the fourth estate.

I took a picture of my extended family with Roger Ebert among them holding up one thumb. Siskel never showed. Ebert's formal review was kind to parts of the movie while also stating that it waffled too much, was indecisive, and didn't work.

According to Vincent Canby's *New York Times* sarcastic rave, "The narrative is a veritable fiesta of anti-climaxes, from the time the sun sets at the beginning of the film until it sets, yet again, behind the closing credits."

Then I gave impromptu addresses to the press, the fans, the politicos, and the nonprofit organizations slated as beneficiaries of the Gala Opening. One such group gifted me a lamb to hold while I spoke, and it pissed on me. By then my heart was galloping toward the River Styx, and, utilizing superhuman effort, I willed myself not to drop dead.

Next, we sped uphill to a millionaire's mansion torture chamber for a five-hundred-dollar-a-plate dinner to raise more cash with that bash. For their monster donations diners got to mingle with Redford, Esparza, me, the mayor of Santa Fe, some other influential bosses, and several of *Milagro's* actors. Santa Fe big shots brutally squeezed my hand while thanking me profusely for all the money and attention Redford had brought to the town and the state. I felt nauseated, crazed, dizzy, and overwhelmed at glad-handing well-wishers and basking in their bloviating congratulations. Attendees had no clue regarding my misery.

I'm not sure how we finally escaped and managed the return drive of seventy miles back to Taos at midnight or 1:00 a.m. My last words to my helpmate before conking out were, "Thank the fucking good moron in heaven that *that's* over."

59

GUESS AGAIN.

Despite my desperate protests, the lone Taos theater insisted on having *their* bloody benefit toot also. I threatened to boycott, but they shamed me into supporting the celebration. Because, after all, Taos's struggles, culture, people, and history had inspired my book. If I didn't support the event I would no doubt become the most hated person in Taos County.

I was obligated to purchase tickets for *all* of my Taos friends at maybe twenty-five bucks a pop. I don't remember the price, but if I forgot to buy complimentary passes for just one person there was hell to pay: jealousy, hurt feelings, resentment, or even death threats. The organizers blackmailed me into paying for the comestibles and refreshments as well. "You're rich now, Mr. Nichols, so don't be a miser." My guess is that *that* friggin' hoopla cost two and a half grand. Some proceeds went to a couple of Taos outfits involved in water battles. But I suspect that after all was said and done, the theater manager and his coconspirators pocketed most of the loot.

———

Then, before *Milagro* engendered a large benefit opening in Denver, Chicano Movement friends up there demanded I send them a telegram disassociating myself from the movie because Coors Beer, under boycott by Chicano activists for its racist hiring policies, had contributed money to the benefit occasion. I sent the telegram, and my friends boycotted the movie, not by parading in front of the theater waving placards condemning Coors Beer and *The Milagro Beanfield War* but rather by giving my comments (and theirs) to the local press, which luxuriated in the kerfuffle *those* opinions elicited.

I'm not saying a cross was burned in my front field, nor that 30–06 slugs twanged off my propane tank. However, I did receive a small load of hate mail that called me a hypocrite, a racist, and, believe it or not, "a cigar-smoking capitalist pig."

Sooner or later, in this vale of tears, our chickens come home to roost.

AFTER ROBERT REDFORD, the actors, and the movie crew departed New Mexico for good, and after the hoopla of the 1988 Santa Fe, Taos, and Denver benefit openings faded away, and after I had been pilloried by a number of activists I'd once worked with harmoniously . . . after all that, in January 1989 I was still attempting to educate Diana Simon, a lawyer for Universal Pictures, as to why Reies Tijerina had nothing to do with *The Milagro Beanfield War*, novel or movie. Understand, although I was not being sued, I *was* an expert witness for Universal, Redford, Esparza, and the rest of them. A typewritten, single-spaced, seven-page letter I posted to Diana on January 5, 1989, was accompanied by Xeroxes of six articles I'd contributed to the *New Mexico Review* (from 1970 to 1972). Also included were a sixteen-page in-depth position paper on the Taos conservancy district proposal I'd written; a long article by Carl Shirley about my life and works taken from the *Dictionary of Literary Biography Yearbook*; and a thirty-eight-page Amicus Curiae brief I had submitted to a conservancy District Court hearing on May 22, 1972, attempting to halt the district and sabotage construction of the Indian Camp Dam.

Those exhibits proved that I had been deeply involved in local Taos struggles, culture, and politics unrelated to Reies Tijerina's land-grant escapades.

Diana interviewed me for my "declaration" to the court, mailing me a first draft on March 8, 1989. I sent her back a ten-page letter, then a seven-page letter, then a couple more rewrites explaining stuff she ought to remove or add to my declaration. It required days to formulate these explanations crammed with nitpicking details. Diana returned a final copy of my revised declaration of twenty-one pages, the one submitted—along with Diana's thirty-one-page brief asking for a summary judgment against Tijerina and company—to a District Court in central California on March 24, 1989, for a hearing to be held April 17.

It was held, a summary judgment granted, and Tijerina's case was thrown out. The endless fifteen-year *Milagro Beanfield War* movie debacle had finally ended.

Meanwhile, my wife and I were floundering. Some relationships can only take so much garble and theatricality before they implode. Always up, always down, always sideways. We wrote long letters to each other late at night even when both of us were in residence. Sometimes we bawled each other out, or commiserated with our respective sorrows. Accusations flew between us like bats returning to the cave each morning. Then we would made love because all the time we were aching for release. And that release kept us enraptured by our mutual joyride through the manic insomnia caused by the vicissitudes and anxieties of the past few years.

In *The Dying Animal* Philip Roth says, "It's the chaos of Eros we're talking about, the radical destabilization that is its excitement. You're back in the woods with sex. You're back in the bog."

To escape the destabilization of that "bog" I opted for divorce. (Again.)

And rented a small, two-room apartment in which to lick my wounds. At least I quit smoking, thank Christ.

———

Coincidentally, my relationship with CBS was ended by a 1988 Writers Guild strike that lasted five months, from March 7 to August 7. That strike helped cause my other personal disasters to manifest themselves. When the Guild and the studios finally signed a contract, CBS wanted me to punch a time clock again on Pancho Villa. Stretched to the max and buffaloed by attempting to understand the medium of TV, I professed myself unable to continue. Frankly, the last couple of years had ripped me new assholes all over my body, my psyche, and my creative talents. And none of us involved with the Pancho Villa project were on the same page anyway. Especially yours truly, who had finally come to realize, atop everything else, that I had no idea how to script a Marxist-Leninist miniseries for a TV channel more enchanted by the fact that "Pancho Villa purportedly had 23 wives."

I apologized, forfeiting a fair amount of cash, then heaved a sigh of relief, got divorced, started a new (impossible) BIG novel I'll talk about later, and blew out the candles on my fiftieth birthday cake on July 23, 1990, asking myself, *After how many screwups in life can you keep inventing another resurrection?*

W. W. Norton's edition of *The Sky's the Limit*, published in 1990.
Courtesy of John Nichols.

PART X

61

DESPITE MY DETERIORATING health (which would eventually lead to open-heart surgery), during the first half of the 1990s I published some "little" books. *The Sky's the Limit* (1990), *An Elegy for September* (1992), *Keep it Simple* (1993), and *Conjugal Bliss* (1994). I labored on several other novels and screenplays, a long essay/memoir, and many speeches. I wrote on airplanes, in hotel rooms, in cafés, on the toilet, in my sleep—whenever and wherever. I always had literary projects going along with a few feature-film screenplays, which I considered an aside to my "serious" writing career. I willfully ignored my heart going down the tubes. Tachycardia? Atrial fib? The Valsalva maneuver usually jump-started me back into sinus rhythm. A Coumadin medical ID bracelet jangled on my wrist. Digitalis, Verapamil, and Quinaglute kept everything else copacetic. My INR (international normalized ratio) was tested weekly by blood withdrawals at Holy Cross Hospital. No, I never stopped drinking, but tried to bag caffeine. That proved difficult. Coffee was a great laxative. It produced an edge that made writing easier, more alive, more *inventive*. Lack of caffeine was like being castrated.

The Sky's the Limit is a photo-essay I developed with my close buddy, Bill Rusin, the head of trade sales at W. W. Norton in New York. The dysfunctional Bobbsey Twins produce a book together! It contains sixty-five landscape photographs of skies and mesas around Taos, accompanied by my environmental essay on how we're destroying the planet. My *Inconvenient Truth*. The essay's first paragraph explains:

> Today it is generally feared (if not universally acknowledged) that the Greenhouse Effect has begun. The six hottest years in the past century have been 1989, 1988, 1987, 1983, 1981, and 1980. The earth is beginning to overheat; the atmosphere is polluted; acid rain threatens our rivers, lakes, and oceans. Various holes in the ozone are widening. Population continues to expand around the globe, and starvation is a fact of life in the Sahel, Bangladesh, Haiti, and Bolivia. Garbage scows from large

United States cities ply the high seas, searching for Third World countries willing to absorb their toxic wastes, which, though fabricated in North America, cannot legally be disposed of here. In the summer of 1988 East Coast beaches were temporarily closed because of pollutants, which included syringes of human blood infected by AIDS.

———

Nobody listened to my descriptions of advancing devastation. Today, thirty years later, I could stick thumbs in my ears and waggle my fingers at the world: "Ha ha, I told you so!" I read (or see on television) daily reports that the ten hottest years in history have been from 2010 until this year, 2020, when I'm writing as the coronavirus is predicted to kill over five hundred thousand Americans by March 1, 2021. Though every decade is hotter, in my judgment we'd already passed "fail-safe" by 1990 when *The Sky's the Limit* reached (a few) bookstores. These days, yearning for solutions, we're simply gazing into the rearview mirror at what might have been.

Norton scheduled an extensive tour for me because the essay had caused a minor stir. I'm not sure *where*. But Bill Rusin was my benevolent handler, and he knew the score. We're still best friends thirty years later. I would travel around New Mexico, Colorado, Arizona, Texas and also do signings in Portland, Seattle, California, and Chicago.

For starters, New Mexico and Chicago were easy as pie. And I'd conquered most of Colorado until my final stop, Fort Collins, where I locked into atrial fibrillation impossible to escape. Of a sudden your legs ache so much you cannot walk, and breathing is akin to swimming underwater without scuba gear. Driving my own car I barely made it home to Taos, proceeding south on I-25 at twenty miles an hour after canceling the rest of that 1990 tour.

I was anesthetized at Presbyterian Hospital in Albuquerque, then cardioverted with electric paddles. The doctors snowed me with more pills to keep the heart in sinus rhythm. Predictably, I sank into a weighty funk, scarcely functioning outside my little apartment. My old house had been swallowed by the sinkhole of divorce. According to Chuck Berry, "'C'est la vie,' say the old folks, 'just goes to show you never can tell.'"

62

EVER THE CREATIVE masochist, I sustained hyper work hours on my next book, *An Elegy for September*. Life is a marathon, and I'd developed the critical habit of plodding onward no matter what. My thanks, and a tip of the hat to Hamilton College's track and cross-country coach, Gene Long. I lettered in varsity cross-country my junior and senior years. Coach Long told us runners that we were all in equally perfect physical shape to prevail, *but it's the mind that runs the race*. That's by far the most valuable thing I learned in college.

Keeping to myself, I rarely exercised, and stewed inside my two-room apartment possessing scant energy for communicating with family or other humans. Probably the only period in life when I was genuinely "depressed." I've always been one of those chipper nerds with a big smile, rosy cheeks, and out-of-control cheerfulness, like singers on *The Lawrence Welk Show*. I'd never before turned off my bubble machine. But now I flipped that switch for about six months.

Yet what I do, no matter the situation, is write every day. It's the promise I made to myself on graduating from Hamilton. The vow I followed on how to earn a living. Like a postman or -woman, come deluge or drought I would always deliver the mail.

An Elegy for September is very short, hardly even a novella, about a May/September romance between a young girl and an aging writer. 1992 is when it reached bookstores. As usual I had worked on several failed versions earlier. *Elegy* was an offspring of *Satan was an Angel*. That novel featured a guy whose life was crowded with many affairs. He winds up with a girlfriend who has a daughter from a previous relationship. Together they raise the young daughter, who, as a manipulative teenager, falls in love with her mother's lover, and he responds to the girl.

My Holt editor, Marian Wood, admitted that *Satan was an Angel* might sell okay, but she herself would never publish such a cynical book.

So I abandoned the novel, turning my attention to a nonfiction project detailing the month of September, my favorite time of year. From 1985 on I had dedicated those thirty days to grouse hunting southeast of Taos on the Río Chiquito, Pot Creek, and the Little Río Grande, small trout streams running through mountain foothill watersheds. Though I've described the areas in other works, here's a short reminder:

There were high country meadows, thimbleberry plants and larkspur, enormous groves of golden aspens, harebell flowers and elderberry bushes, red squirrels, porcupines, long-abandoned and overgrown logging roads, many game trails through Gambel oak thickets, spruce and Douglas fir stands, and ponderosa pines. Multiple springs fed elk wallows. Tiny rivulets cascaded down steep hillsides. Willow stands and mountain alders crowded boggy areas. Deer and black bear were present, along with hawks, red squirrels, and blue grouse. Reedy juvenile aspen trunks were cracked and bent over at a height of five or more feet by bull elk preparing for their rut.

After 1985, for at least fifteen years I had the discipline to keep my September calendar void of obligations. I often hunted for twenty-five of the month's thirty days. Having worked all night, I crashed at dawn. Waking around 1:00 p.m. I fashioned ham and Swiss cheese sandwiches garnished with lettuce, tomatoes, and gobs of mayonnaise and mustard, iced a few beers in the cooler, then jumped into my 1980 Dodge pickup and ignited the afterburners.

I always parked on a dirt road alongside one of the three small rivers at 7,500 feet, then bushwhacked straight up to 9,000 feet where the grouse were. The hiking, the weather, the spruce trees and aspen groves, and all other plants and wildlife were the point. I covered wide amounts of ground, keeping notes on envelopes on everything I saw. My imperative was to *always keep moving*. Just before nightfall I descended steep inclines to my truck and sat on the tailgate gazing at the creek, eating a sandwich and drinking beer as the moon rose and stars appeared. Perhaps I watched trout dimpling in a beaver pond. I was exhilarated and very happy.

My first versions of *September* didn't come alive. Gee, what a surprise. Too much like a guide book, I guess. Idyllic and maudlin. Bottom line: I needed a plot and some intrigue. Though September is beautiful, it's also about dying. The weather hagiography before winter can torment you with ecstasy *and* sadness. Pardon the cliché. I decided to make my story a novel set in the early autumn. Borrowing a few traits from the teenage girl who'd dominated *Satan Was an Angel*, I tossed in an aging writer like myself and gave them a short love affair during September.

The vibrant, intelligent girl wants to love the old guy. *Old?* He's a year shy of fifty! That's not "old" to me anymore. Still, he's afraid to commit. His ex-wife bitterly resents their recent divorce. The girl is nineteen and fucks him with combative affection then ridicules his lack of honest passion. They make love in aspen groves and subalpine meadows. Close by elk are bugling. They go fishing among large boulders on the Río Grande and spend twilights at small stock ponds on the sagebrush mesa west of town as bats, swallows, and nighthawks fly over the water catching insects being born.

She insults his timidity, his "old age." He's baffled by her angry youth, yet desperately *wants* her. She mocks his fear of dying. Their sex is gentle, loving, then cruel. Nasty. The affair was interesting to write, and I think touching. Elegiac, I suppose. Erotic. It excited me to publish a novel that was so brief. Was it an "almost perfect" little book? Who cares? Suddenly I felt happy again.

After I paid the *Los Angeles Times* hundreds of dollars in vigorish, here's what they gave me in return: "One of the finest things Nichols has ever written. Maybe this book is a masterpiece. The writing is stripped, simple, and beautiful, the feel of things is palpable. And that is all that matters."

Cosmopolitan magazine wrote, "As spare as a poem, here is a book for everyone who has let a promise pass by. It's beautiful."

"It's a Japanese watercolor of a novel instead of a sprawling mural," said *Booklist*. "Like the [New Mexico] trilogy, though, it's a powerful work by a gifted writer whose confrontations with life illuminate it for the rest of us."

That's about the width of public adoration. Hardly anyone else reviewed it.

(Please don't start rubbing your thumb and index finger together like the world's tiniest violin. If I couldn't've stood the heat I *never* would have entered the kitchen. You wanna write novels, self-pity is not an option. Just put on your cleats, grab a mitt, and play the game understanding that the ump *always* beats his wife.)

63

HEY, THEY HAD accepted my book, I was back in the game, and what better way to celebrate than jump on a plane in June, 1991, fly to Jackson Hole, Wyoming, and spend a weekend at the chic Crescent H Ranch with fifty other Western American writers at a literary clusterfuck called the "Dinner Party" put together by Chris Merrill and Terry Tempest Williams, an event with no agenda, no speeches, no public allowed and with nothing to do except eat, schmooze, scamper between bedrooms at night, and mostly just get to *know* each other. The most relaxed existential meeting of literary egos ever held in this nation. Nobody died or inadvertently got pregnant. It was fun, and I was ready to have fun again.

Back home I sent everyone involved a long letter. Here's an abridged, "brief" part of it:

> I thought the weekend in Jackson was fabulous, and I thank you for put-ting it together: a once in a lifetime thrill, for sure, kinda discombob-ulated in certain respects, maybe, but real sweet, full of good energy, a lot of laughs, interesting bullshitting, and, most importantly, *connections*. It all held together in a wonderful anarchical way for me, and I had a ball. The incongruity of the whole thing was a kick in the butt. I think the room assignments were the work of genius: who thought to put a crypto commie grouse killer like me in the same room with Daniel Kemmis, the mayor of Missoula? Whoever did, thank you. I actually discovered that Dan doesn't have fangs and is truly a quasi-decent compassionate human being. Unlike others like Dan Gerber and Jim Harrison, of course, who seemed profli-gate in the extreme, yet with the redeeming value of being quite cultured in certain odd maniacal ways which were interesting when not being por-nographic in the extreme. It seemed like the whole weekend was full of these nice, electric little moments, and some of the nicest for me were jousting (using my mega-wit and fertile imagination) with Jeff and Patty Limerick; listening to Dan Gerber explain the torque-relationships involved in setting de-acceleration records in a racing car; just simply admiring (and ogling)

Gretel Ehrlich in her angelic white suit; being told to "Shut up" by Barry Lopez; laughing a lot with Denise Chávez, Alberto Rios, Pattiann Rogers, Carolyn See, Charles Wilkinson (and probably many others, among them Cort Conley); just meeting Marilynne Robinson (HOUSEKEEPING is one of my favorite novels!); stuffing my gut royally while seated between Ron Carlson and David Kranes; and urinating in tandem with Doug Peacock on some sort of evergreen tree underneath a full moon (I don't think Peacock knew I was there, not by that time of night). It is always good to see Dave Petersen, of course, though he seemed a trifle sane throughout the weekend. And I wanted to hug Simon Ortiz when he came up to me and said he once made a pilgrimage to visit socialist poet Walter Lowenfels in Peekskill, New York. I was a little disappointed not to get shitfaced with Bill Kittredge and Annick Smith and sing "Little Joe the Wrangler" into the wee small hours like we did at Sundance, but still it was great to see them again and get in a couple of minutes of shitting on Hollywood. Actually, for a gathering of so many writers, I was kind of dismayed not to get into even one bull session where everybody just talked about screen deals and movie points and flights on the Concorde to Paris (though Gretel and I did manage to get in a few obligatory shots at Bob Redford [poor baby!]). And I think I did hear Jim Harrison mutter rather cantankerously that the Writers Guild hit him up for 37 Gs in dues last year. I've been trying to compute what that totals out to in Actual Gross Income (AGI), but my brain can't compute that high. I found it sheer joy to listen to Terry Williams speak, also W. S. Merwin, Patty Limerick, and Charles Wilkinson. Of course, my solution to all environmental problems is to simply take the top 14 families, put 'em up against the wall, and mow 'em down. Frankly, I thought there were too many men and not enuff women at the party, so there was a bit of a macho pall to things. But as I moved along that incredible groaning board on the final night heaping high my platter, I thought that a nice touch at the end of the table, after the wild boar, the ducks, the quail, and the venison cooked by Harrison and Peacock, would have been a platter upon which sat a small Iraqi soldier, nicely braised in organic barbecue sauce, with an edible American flag (made of glacee'd chanterelle mushroom sauce) planted in the belly button.

People have always accused me of being adept at sophomoric humor, and obviously this letter is no exception.

It went on for five more pages.

64

SO THERE I was one day, feeling cocky even though *Elegy for September* had nosedived into obscurity, when the phone rang, I answered, and soon eagerly jumped through another flaming hoop.

A manic voice asked, "Is this John Nichols?"

"No, I'm sorry, you've reached Suicide Prevention," I replied.

The voice said, "Cut the shit, I got this number from your agent in New York."

"Okay, okay," I said and fessed up.

The voice belonged to Danny Sheehan, a lawyer who was head of the Christic Institute. He and the actor John Cusack wanted me to help them pitch a movie to Mike Medavoy, the chairman of TriStar Pictures. That was in late 1992, although I forget the month they called. John and Danny hoped to make a movie about the aftermath of Karen Silkwood's death involving a conspiracy by the US government to smuggle plutonium from the Kerr-McGee nuclear facility just north of Oklahoma City (where Karen had worked) in order to help Israel build their atomic bomb. The FBI, CIA, National Intelligence Agency, Justice Department, and Atomic Energy Commission were involved. That conspiracy was not mentioned in Mike Nichols' 1983 film starring Meryl Streep, Cher, and Kurt Russell. Perhaps Karen's knowledge of the smuggling had gotten her killed. When Cusack and Sheehan first approached Medavoy at TriStar, he'd advised them to attach a writer "like John Nichols" to their project in order to develop the "human side" of the movie (the actors' relationships, personalities, and connections with each other), then come back to him for another try.

Who the hell was John Nichols?

They are mensch. They located my phone number. We talked. They sent me two books about Karen's life and death and the conspiracy to smuggle plutonium. *Who Killed Karen Silkwood?* by Howard Kohn and *The Killing of Karen Silkwood* by Richard Rashke. I read them. Danny and the colorful Wyoming lawbooks, Gerry Spence, had represented the Silkwood family seeking reparations after Karen's death. But the trial judge disallowed mention of plutonium smuggling on the grounds of National Security. The Silkwoods did receive over a million dollars in reparations for lax safety measures at Kerr McKee that had exposed Karen to harmful radiation.

Case closed.

I schmoozed a lot with Cusack and Sheehan over the phone. Our movie would be called *The Fool's Crusade*. Or *The Glass Mountain*, I forget. Between June 12 and 14, 1993, Danny and John prepped me for the pitch during three hilarious days at the Marina Pacific Hotel in Venice. Danny only wanted to rehash the "facts" and the "structure" of the conspiracy to illegally steal plutonium. However, my job was to bring alive the characters working on the case—their quirks, their affairs with each other, their *human* qualities. Whenever Danny began describing how the CIA and Israeli Mossad abetted the smuggling operation, I yelled, "Stop! Forget the CIA! Screw the conspiracy! Tell me about the *people*. Who on your team were *boning* each other? Describe the fights and scandals among the Silkwood defense team. Who fell in love then out again because the other person cheated on them? Who was a brilliant nerd, or a stupid jock? Did an FBI informer infiltrate your group? Was anybody on the case a Vietnam veteran? An alcoholic? A cocaine freak? I need an *arc*, an intimate story about the *people* involved. What was your childhood like, Danny? Did you love or hate your mom and dad?"

Nice try, and I blew it completely. When Medavoy and his assistant sat down at the conference table, Mike stuck a foot-long Cohiba in his mouth and lit it. He was wearing a silk suit and a pair of those tasseled Italian loafers that probably cost three thousand dollars. Once settled, he turned to me and said, "John, my assistant here wasn't present at the first pitch, so tell us again all the facts about the conspiracy so we can bring Joe [or Jack, or Melvin] here up to speed."

I glared at John, Danny, and Steve Pink (John's assistant at their New Crime Productions company) seated across the conference table from me. They grinned like chimpanzees caught with their hands in a cookie jar and shrugged. *Who could've predicted?* The upshot is I addressed Medavoy and his sidekick for forty-five minutes, admitting beforehand, "I don't really know squat about the conspiracy but I'm willing to give it a shot."

Afterward, Cusack was ecstatic. He said, "You shit on Medavoy, you shit on TriStar, you shit on me and Danny, you even shit on yourself—that negative sell *just might work!*"

Not in a million years. TriStar never offered us a penny of development bread. Medavoy could detect the bullshit of an amateur ingenue the second I opened my mouth and didn't even have the guts to complain of his fucking cigar smoke, which almost gave me an asthma attack.

However, life now turned upside down once more. I was awake again and ready to rock and roll. Around the time I returned from the Sheehan-Cusack fiasco, a friend from far away went off the wagon on a trip to Taos for a weekend debauch after seven years of sobriety, and she called me for help from a local motel. I hadn't even known she was in town. When I fetched her at the motel she was bruised, battered, and dirty, and had been gang raped. She resembled a person who'd barely survived a car accident. I brought her home, cleaned her up, and gave her some food and a sleeping bag on the futon. When she conked out my phone rang, and it was a young woman whom I barely knew. She said, "I want you to know that my feelings for you are not just platonic."

Bingo! A few months later I married that youngster and life went head over heels, thrilling and almost killing me again. Why is it so alluring to break all the rules? It's scary, but also somehow wonderful, to be a junkie for the euphoric turbulence of that emotional chaos.

65

OH YEAH? I always seemed to forget that a chaotic life has *consequences.* It's January 1994 and I'm in Holy Cross Hospital dying of endocarditis (the same thing that killed my mother, Monique, when I was two, except that hers was "staph" and mine is "strep"). In a private room, hooked up to penicillin and gentamicin IV's, I'm typing clean a script for the director Ridley Scott (*Alien, Thelma and Louise, Gladiator*), which is due next week. When you sign the contract with a delivery date, Hollywood doesn't mean a week *after* that, it means exactly *on* the due date. Or, if possible, earlier. That's because every contract emphasizes that "time is of the essence." It's why they pay you the big bucks. For me, compared to publishing books, Writers Guild minimum wage *is* big bucks.

Why am I working for Ridley Scott? Apparently because John Cusack suggested to him last year that I might be a decent choice to rewrite the screenplay of one of his current movie projects.

I'm typing on my old Olympia portable. It replaced my last Hermes Rocket eighteen years ago. I have no health insurance. My soon-to-be third wife sleeps on a cot in my room at night. That year my endocarditis would lead to congestive heart failure, which would result in open-heart surgery, which would cause a serious reduction of my activities . . . for a spell. While I was in congestive-heart-failure mode (before heart surgery, but *after* getting remarried!), Henry Holt sent me on a twelve-city book tour for my novel *Conjugal Bliss*, a satirical send-up of my specialty: marital dysfunction. Why *not* do a tour? I was still alive, wasn't I? There's a little more blood in this stone.

———

I probably know exactly how my mother felt as she lay dying of a staph endocarditis infection in Miami Beach during late July and the first week of August, 1942. For both strep and staph endocarditis my *Merck Manual* says, "Without treatment, IE [infectious endocarditis] is always fatal."

I kept a diary of my illness, describing how I dealt with November 1993 through April 1994. I was fifty-three years old. My joints ached, I ran a fever of 101, I was dizzy, I had a sore throat and surged in and out of hot and cold sweats, shivering. I woke up at night with my hair drenched, my T-shirt soggy. At first it resembled the flu, so I didn't call a doctor. In my journal I wrote, "I'm feeling as dead as a person can be and still be alive!" Two weeks into the disease I wrote, "I still feel dizzy all the time, constant headache—when I cough it kills me. I ache and ache and ache." My head ached, my neck ached, my kidneys ached, my whole body ached. My hair and shirts were soaked in sweat, and my hands kept going numb. My heart felt squeezed, uncomfortable, wacko irregular. I had spates of vertigo. My ears buzzed with loud tinnitus. "I am dead inside," I wrote.

After three weeks I saw my doctor, but for a couple more weeks he couldn't diagnose the problem. When he figured it out on December 30, 1993, I hied myself to the hospital, had a heparin lock cut into my throat, and absorbed three days of IV antibiotics (a stay that cost around $8,000 I paid off in two big chunks and then at $150 a month for several years, during which I almost drowned in hospital bills and demands for payment.) Then I went home and for the following ten days gave myself six IVs a day of penicillin and gentamicin through the lock in my throat with a feed line directly into the heart. After each use I had to inject the lock with a needle full of heparin flush so it wouldn't get blocked by coagulated blood. An alarm clock awakened me every four hours and I almost died from lack of sleep. I wrote, "The cure is killing me!" Although antibiotics finally stopped the infection, by then it had destroyed my mitral valve. I entered *serious* congestive heart failure.

That's when my new lover and I got married. Good choice, kids!

Then, feeling super rickety, I flew to Los Angeles.

———

I forget where I stayed when working for Ridley Scott. No doubt at a hotel near the offices of his film company, then called Percy Main Productions. What I remember most, in a story conference, is how instantly Ridley, Sue Williams, and Mimi Polk Gitlin reacted to a faint aftershock from the 6.7 magnitude Northridge earthquake, which had happened on January 17, 1994, a few days after I finished slugging my heart with antibiotics in Taos.

Ridley jumped up to call his girlfriend. Mimi immediately dialed her

My "marriage calavera" from an etchings suite of calaveras that I did in 1976. Courtesy of John Nichols.

husband. And Sue sat there paralyzed because her apartment had already been trashed by the quake. The kick is that I never *felt* the aftershock tremor. Those people were tuned in. Me, I was likely preoccupied with my congestive heart failure problems only moments after surviving endocarditis. Difficult to concentrate on other disasters. My mitral valve (see above) was non compos mentis, regurgitating about two-thirds of its flow.

However, I maintained a stiff upper lip and cracked jokes until I was out of sight because I *needed* the job in order to qualify for Writers Guild insurance to pay for open-heart surgery on the near horizon. I believe there was a three-month gap between signing a film contract and Writers Guild health insurance activating, and I'd slipped in just under the wire. Pretending to feel good when you're on death's door is a bankable talent.

Ridley's movie, *Amazonia*, concerned Kayapo Indians on the Xingu River in the Amazon basin fighting to halt a dam, funded by the World Bank, from being constructed on their reserve. In a nutshell? *The Milagro Beanfield War* goes to Brazil.

When we met almost the first words out of Ridley's mouth were, "Do you like science-fiction movies?" My reply? Without thinking I said, "No, I hate them." I must have been brain dead to say that to the director of *Blade Runner* and *Alien*. I was hired anyway, enjoyed the work, and, of course, the film went into turnaround and disappeared. Sad, granted, until you consider that I *did* qualify for the Guild insurance to pay for open-heart surgery.

These days Jair Bolsonaro is president of Brazil, the Amazon is burning at alarming rates, and the Kayapo—and their region—have been trashed and destabilized. Sometimes I feel that I'm watching the world cutting its own throat. Actually, I *am* watching the world cutting its own throat.

———

After I returned from LA, the heart failure grew worse throughout February, March, and April 1994. My new wife was appalled. My journal recorded, "I feel basically suicidal, really sick. I survive totally wiped out all the time with my heart like this. My heart thumps and thumps, no way I can get to sleep. I feel close to the edge of dying. My heart is in and out of paroxysmal atrial fib. It pounds. My neck aches. My ears hurt." My ankles swelled from water retention. I began taking a diuretic, Lasix, along with my other pills. I had "real trouble breathing. Can't walk 10 steps without huffing and puffing ..."

66

THIS SECTION ISN'T an abrupt turn leftward for no logical reason. It's still part of my heart-failure story. Bear with me. The final book I published in the 1990s was *Conjugal Bliss*. When I left my second marriage in 1989 I had rented that two-room apartment attached to a big house in downtown Taos. The bathroom worked, and a kitchen wood stove kept me warm. A sleeping mattress occupied half the other room. Though waylaid by depression and increasing heart problems, I was relieved to be alone. The landlady, who lived on the other side of my eastern wall, was an ex-girlfriend from long ago. No matter. We were cordial until, during my 1991–1992 literary/Hollywood resurrection, I brought a woman back to my pad and the landlady sent me packing.

I found a small, cheap, sketchy house to buy. Needing a cash down payment, I accepted a 1992 spring semester job at the University of New Mexico (in Albuquerque) teaching a graduate creative-writing seminar and another course I invented, *The Writer and Society*, which attracted sixty mixed grads and under-grads. My teacher evaluations for the second course ran a gamut: "The best class I ever had, with the most freedom." "Professor Nichols dresses like a bum, but he's very interesting." "This course was an excellent Marxist-Leninist group grope."

Assessments of my writing seminar were mostly negative. I'm paraphrasing: "Professor Nichols spent the whole semester forcing us to do line-by-line edits." "Honestly, I was bored to death." "This wasn't a 'creative' class, it was like working on a chain gang." "Frankly, I didn't learn a damn thing."

Here's the good news from that ordeal. Around mid-April I was soaking in a hot bath when the first line of a new novel popped into my head: "The fight started this way." Jumping out of the tub I dried off, grabbed a notebook, and began scribbling. *Conjugal Bliss* is the fastest book I ever wrote and then actually sold. It's an over-the-top send-up of marriage. My take on Tolstoy's *Kreutzer Sonata* as written by the Marx Brothers. I had more fun creating it than kids on a loop-the-loop roller coaster at Disney Land.

Another of my ubiquitous calaveras, which is either an alternative take on the "Angel of Death" or simply an "Angel of Celebration." You choose. Courtesy of John Nichols.

After five drafts over a year and change it was "done." Twelve months later (February 1994) Holt published *Conjugal Bliss* and sent me around America on a tour shortly after I'd survived strep endocarditis, gotten remarried, and scored a job with Ridley Scott. What I remember about the tour is that I couldn't breathe trudging the hills of San Francisco, and had the same problem in Portland, Tucson, Denver, Chicago. No spells of heart fatigue ever laid me lower. My response was to raid hotel mini-fridges for bourbon shooters as I followed the Stanley Cup hockey playoffs on TV. When I phoned her, my new wife sobbed because you didn't have to be a rocket scientist to know where I was headed.

The *Chicago Tribune* called my book "a hilarious, raucous, painfully graphic portrait of The Marriage from Hell." The *Philadelphia Inquirer* said, "The ribaldry is on a par with Henry Miller at his best." Even *Publishers Weekly* enjoyed my "lively, personable narrative and a myriad of piercing insights on the politics of marriage [that] spice this piquant, entertaining domestic comedy." The *Detroit Free Press* thought it "a nonstop comedy of errors." Believe it or not, the *New York Times* pocketed their venom machine in order to dub the novel "an enjoyable pell-mell narrative." *Newsday* praised its "breezy, irreverent style that conveys great bolts of emotion." And what did the *Los Angeles Times* say?

"*Conjugal Bliss* is a larger-than-life anti-romance, antic and full of low-jinks. Imagine *Othello* by the writers of *I Love Lucy*."

No doubt after reading that I called my Albuquerque cardiologist, Dr. Leuker, arranging an open-heart surgery appointment for May 3, 1994. My readings in Palo Alto, Berkeley, Colorado Springs, and Boulder were bizarre attempts at acting healthy, say like Stephen Hawking blinking his eyelashes at a computer in order to sing "Blue Suede Shoes." Booksellers must have wondered, *Why is this crippled person on the road promoting his stupid book?*

———

On May 3, 1994, an Albuquerque surgeon named Carl Lagerstrom cut me open, attached my heart to bypass, sewed an annuloplasty ring into the mitral valve, readjusted the heart correctly in my chest cavity, and stapled me back up. So far, that operation has given me an extra twenty-six years of life. Without antibiotics in 1942, and without open-heart surgery, Monique's staph endocarditis infection killed her in two weeks. She never had a chance.

67

A BRIEF HITCH followed Lagerstrom's operation. I went to ICU recovery after surgery. My daughter, Tania, says I was blue and swollen when they wheeled me from the operating room. That's because they pack you in ice. She and my wife ran away, crying. In the dark nighttime ICU I was intubated. The pain was excruciating, and I couldn't breathe. Nor could I talk. Heart monitors kept ticking and beeping away. Because my wrists were tied down I couldn't pull free the respirator tube. Whenever I started to pass out I felt like a pillow was suffocating me. Frantically, I kicked my heels against the foot of my bed to call a nurse. Irritated, she told me the heart monitor indicated I was doing fine. I made a writing motion with my constrained right hand. She brought a pad and pencil and positioned the pad at my hand while I wrote: *Remove tube, call doctor.* She refused, telling me I was okay. It was 3:00 a.m. More morphine entered the drip, and I suffocated again, kicking my heels for attention. The nurse was pissed at my antics. Once more I scribbled on the pad: *Can't breathe, call doctor.* She demurred because the heart monitor indicated I was in top-notch condition. Additional morphine entered the drip. When I began to drowse I suffocated once more and hysterically tattooed my heels for help. This time when the nurse approached, the heart monitor had gone berserk. I was locked in hellish atrial fibrillation, and everything else was awry. The nurse yelled for a doctor who rushed in and removed the tube from my throat, allowing me to breathe again. I couldn't talk, but he untied my wrists. And saved my life. Nobody drove me to Los Alamos in a hearse.

That nurse then kept her distance. A different one brought me slivers of ice to suck on and stroked my hair because she was an angel. Apparently I was going to live. Surviving that night has puzzled me ever since.

———

Still and all, recovery after open-heart surgery is slow. The operation is painful.

You spend two months hugging a pillow against your chest demanding that nobody tell a joke making you laugh or you'll kill them. The day after surgery they have you walking ten feet down the hallway and back to your bed. Seated in a corner, my wife is studying for her final exams before graduating from the University of New Mexico. Next day it's twenty feet down the hallway and back. She keeps studying. By the end of a week you're shuffling to the end of the corridor and back. There's no rest for the weary. They release you from the hospital with orders to walk a little further each day, and eat plenty of Jello, drink coffee. You (or your recently activated—thank God!—Writers Guild health insurance) just coughed up around thirty-two thousand dollars (that's sixty thousand in today's dollars!) for heart surgery, and you're supposed to eat Jello and drink coffee? "Earth to the American Health Care Galaxy, come in, please."

I walked thirty feet from our Albuquerque apartment front door to the sidewalk and back. My wife is grumpy because I'd promised we would live it up in Spain after she graduated. Obviously, that's not in the cards. Next, I did thirty feet again and proceeded north on the sidewalk for thirty feet more and back. Then fifty feet and back, sixty feet, seventy feet, and so forth. At week's end I reached the next street north and returned to the apartment. My wife kissed the tip of her finger, touched it to the tip of my nose, and said, "Congratulations." I only showered once a week, scared to death of slipping in the tub. And required five minutes to lower myself in bed for the night, groaning every inch of that painful descent to a prone position. I was terrified of falling or bumping into something or somebody. If my wife had tickled my chest with a feather it would have knocked me over backward, shrieking.

———

Time passed. She graduated from the university and home to Taos we drove. I walked up Valverde Street twenty yards and back, then thirty yards, then forty yards. Two canes gave me assistance. Soon I climbed the little hill on La Lomita, turning north at La Loma. Sometimes my wife tagged along. By reaching the Enos García Grammar School I'd progressed a third of a mile from home. There I often sat on a bench for ten minutes catching my breath. Already it was late June. Would I ever be able to manage half a mile? Though chest pain had receded, I remained fragile. One false move and I was dead meat. Don't even blow dandelion seeds at my face . . . *please.*

Holy Cross Hospital in Taos kept bugging me to pay off my entire debt to them. On August 21 I wrote,

> I find the massive and repeated billings totally incoherent and often completely non-specific. There's no way I'm gonna pay your remaining $2693.05 in a lump. My insurance company has paid out over thirty thousand dollars I believe this year; they have also done an audit on charges, found that there is a lot of over-billing among various practitioners or institutions, and refused to pay the difference. It's all Greek to me, and obviously very stressful; sometimes it seems that the cure is worse than the disease, given the stress level of endless confusing billing procedures, and the necessity to keep trying to recover my health and earn a living while going deeper in debt trying to stay alive long enough to earn a living and pay the debts. But no doubt you've heard it all, and aren't in business to respond to anybody's sob stories about how costly it is to try and stay alive.

Yet on September 1, 1994, 116 days after open-heart surgery, I hiked Fowler Trail from the Little Río Grande river up to a deserted logging road at nine thousand feet on the first day of grouse season—with a knapsack on my back and a .16-gauge shotgun in hand. No grouse were flushed. I spooked a couple of deer, saw a red-tailed hawk and two ravens, and watched Steller's jays and chickadees sporting among the spruce and aspen branches. I have never been so grateful to be alive.

Chronicle Books' 2001 front cover of my novel *The Voice of the Butterfly*. Artwork by Melinda Beck. Courtesy of John Nichols.

PART XI

68

TWO MONTHS INTO 1995 I underwent a double hernia operation that crippled me for several weeks. It entailed learning how to walk *again*. After the pain left I noticed an increased disequilibrium. Not from Menière's Disease; no dizziness or nausea was involved. I'd be ambling along and abruptly lose my balance a little. When I fished the Río Grande gorge I feared the boulders and avoided hopping from rock to rock. Previously, I'd been a mountain goat. Occasionally, for no reason at all, I bumped into a shelf at the supermarket dislodging a tuna-fish can or mayonnaise jar. When I progressed forward the landscape bounced a trifle as if I was a handheld movie camera. The condition is called "oscillopsia."

That fall my young wife flew to Spain without me. I remained Taos bound, finishing another draft of the *Amazonia* script for Ridley Scott (and rewriting a short "civil-rights" novel called *Great Feelings of Love* that Marian Wood rejected in a New York minute because it was an awkward piece of polemic shit). For years I'd played ice hockey in over-thirty men's leagues. So when the local rink froze I suited up for a game. That was a shocker. At the first miniscule body check I spun around, thudding onto the ice. Up quickly, I was bumped again with the same result. From then on the slightest faint collision sent me sprawling. I had lost all coordination.

An hour of punishment sufficed. I barely navigated the sideboards and collapsed on the bench in confusion. How could I have become so clumsy? Though I didn't know it then, I'd never play hockey again. As for tennis games? Say goodbye to those, too. During a few months of queries and research I learned that gentamicin therapy for endocarditis was to blame. A side effect of the antibiotic is ototoxicity, a loss of vestibular reflex in your inner ears. My balance now came mostly from eyesight, which is but half of what makes us stable. I'm being simplistic here because although I've read much about the condition, it's difficult for me to understand the complex scientific lingo.

I could not proceed comfortably through the dark anymore. Night driving became a challenge because headlights coming at me jiggled. Gentamicin patients are called "wobblers." Soon I couldn't ride my bike without painfully dumping it, so that recreation ended. On crowded sidewalks I was scared of bumping into other pedestrians.

A year earlier I'd been more coordinated than a trapeze artist in *Cirque de Soleil*. But now I was a bumbling spastic case. Around mid-February 1996 I joined my wife in Spain. We had fun together, but knew the adventure was over. Returning home we divorced in July, writing the agreement ourselves. I filed our papers with the Taos County Clerk. My friend Judge Joe Caldwell signed the document after barely scanning it. A classical guitar virtuoso, he handed over a CD of his latest recital, shook my hand, and said, "On to the next one." As a "free man" again I thought, *Maybe I shouldn't do this anymore.* Our eventful two years followed by the split had been jaunty and effervescent, but also sad. I'd spent too many of our days and months together fighting for my life. After promising her the moon I had toppled our house of cards with persistent crises and recuperations coupled with nonstop work obligations.

Legitimate deal breakers as far as she was concerned. And I agreed. So we wept, then kissed each other goodbye.

69

IN LATE 1995 I'd begun a second project with Ridley Scott, a sequel to the 1978 film *Midnight Express* that details American Billy Hayes' five-year stay in a Turkish prison for attempting to smuggle hash out of the country. A successful movie directed by Alan Parker and scripted by Oliver Stone, it made Billy Hayes famous while projecting a completely negative view of Turks and their country as racist, stupid, and sadistically violent. Billy Hayes himself protested that image, to no avail. The picture has been hated by Turkey ever since.

Oliver Stone received an Oscar for his gratuitously vicious screenplay; Giorgio Moroder won for his score; director Parker was nominated for directing; and David Puttnam earned a producing nomination. I didn't like the movie. Yet after conferring with Ridley, his co-producer Mimi Polk Gitlin, and Billy Hayes, I decided the sequel could be a whole different ball of wax.

Hypocrisy is the handmaiden of survival.

Like, I needed to keep up my Guild health insurance because no private companies would cover anything related to my previous health conditions. Plus, let's face it: between 1995 and 2001, when I tortured myself hoping to solve badly crafted novels, I earned close to zero royalties from other books still in print. And my most recent divorce had cost an arm, a leg, and my left ear. Divorce and open-heart surgery are often referred to as the "Bankruptcy Twins."

Behind my back I heard people whispering, "Look, he's like a tiny little Norman Mailer!"

The *Midnight Express* sequel involved Billy's escape from a Sea of Marmara island prison during a fierce storm, then his harebrained travels through Asia Minor, Istanbul, and Thrace to reach Greek freedom. We called it *Midnight Return*. Not long after commencing work, Ridley and his co-producer, Mimi Polk, parted ways, and Mimi took the movie with her. Gone was Ridley's collaborator on *Thelma and Louise*.

I worked with Mimi and Billy Hayes on a script from the end of 1995 through 1996. After that Mimi bailed, and the project was picked up by Peter Davis and Bill Panzer, producers best known for their *Highlander* movie franchise and TV series. I switched to collaborating with them and Billy Hayes on a screenplay.

Midnight Return is the sole project I worked on not progressive or politically left. I envisioned it as a classy thriller like *The Fugitive*, the Harrison Ford / Tommy Lee Jones film. A buddy movie I believed could be entertaining, tense, often funny, and infrequently violent. Studio "coverage" of initial drafts were promising. You don't believe me? Read this:

> An excellent, tightly written script with great characters, excellent dialogue and superb pacing. The story begins with intense action, plunging us directly into the nightmare of Billy Hayes's final moments in Sagmalcilar prison, then the equally perilous prospect of "freedom" in a hostile country. Once you're out, what do you do? The action has several well-placed pauses throughout, and measured crosscutting to the excellent ancillary characters, all of whom are well drawn and interesting in their own right. The dialogue is also superb, always natural and to the point, never clumsy or over the top. Harvey in particular has some great lines, making him a welcome, believable comic foil to the almost unbearable tension that's created in this hair-raising odyssey. While the story sometimes seems to go out of its way to paint Billy as heroic—something that's perhaps difficult under his circumstances—the actual escape is quite credible, and his determination and intelligence are certainly impressive. I can't wait to see this film.

But Davis-Panzer couldn't raise the money. When financing was offered by Tunisia, they asked me to set the escape there instead of in Turkey. No problem. I bought Tunisia guidebooks, read a couple of political tracts, and had at it again until 2000, when Tunisian backing evaporated. Eventually, Middle Eastern politics freaked Davis-Panzer so much they switched the locale to Latin America.

Piece of cake. I mean, I speak *Spanish* (after a fashion). However, their suggestions for script additions and subtractions went downhill rapidly. When the producers and a potential director, Walter Hill, asked me to cross a red line of cruelty I couldn't stomach, I bowed out with no regrets. They hired David

Abramowitz, who'd worked on *Highlander* movies and TV shows, to produce a new script and sent me a copy. I deemed it a cartoon disaster and heard nothing further.

Next, on a 2007 vacation in Idaho, Bill Panzer went skating with his family, fell to the ice and bumped his head, and died.

I'm sure that would have ended the project for Davis-Panzer. In any case, the film was never made.

Yet hear this. A 2016 documentary was titled *Midnight Return: The Story of Billy Hayes and Turkey*. Directed by Sally Sussman Morina, it tells how Billy Hayes returned to Turkey thirty years after the *Midnight Express* film in order to speak with some Turkish cops who wanted to bury the hatchet. Billy, director Alan Parker, Oliver Stone, Giorgio Moroder, and producer Puttnam are in the documentary, which Google tells me is fascinating. I haven't seen it.

Frankly, the first I knew of the documentary was a few days ago when doing research about what happened to the Davis-Panzer version of *Midnight Return*. I've never had the internet—no Facebook, email, Snapchat, Google, or the rest of it. Then halfway through the 2020 Covid lockdown, my daughter, Tania, and her husband, Marco, gave me an Apple tablet attached to data on Tania's Verizon smartphone. Suddenly I can Google stuff I'm writing about and get some of my facts straight.

At last I possess my very own magic "fire stick."

———

Not many characters in my circles know this, but Ridley Scott has a son named Jake who also makes music videos and movies. A film he hoped to direct in 1994 was *Fear and Loathing in Las Vegas*. Although Hunter S. Thompson's drugged-out journey through hell is not in my wheelhouse, it was weird enough to catch my interest. The only drugs I've taken are booze, cigarettes, and fifteen joints. I thought *Fear and Loathing* might be hilarious if written by a geek who'd never ingested mescaline, quaaludes, ecstasy, cocaine, heroin, uppers, downers, diethyl ether, ketamine, GHB, adrenochrome, amyl nitrite, or a sheet of sunshine acid. My Marxist friends would've tarred and feathered me and carried me out of town tied upside down to a pole.

But after you justify your initial sellout, the rest are easy.

Jake Scott showed me a first-draft screenplay by he and the eventual producer, Laila Nabulsi. It did not sparkle. I reread *Fear and Loathing* and a few other Thompson books, then mailed Jake a critique of his manuscript attached to twelve pages of suggestions for a different approach. No doubt my ideas were so irrelevant that Jake and Laila must have wondered what drugs *I* was taking. After sharing two long conference calls with Jake (and Sue Williams, whom I'd worked with on *Amazonia*), we never proceeded. Memory tells me that Percy Main Productions could not obtain the rights.

A film directed by Terry Gilliam was released in 1998. It starred Johnny Depp and Benicio Del Toro. I like Gilliam, who directed *Brazil* and two outrageous Monty Python movies. He acted in a third (*Monty Python and the Holy Grail*). But Leonard Maltin called *Fear and Loathing* a "BOMB." I can't weigh in because I never saw it.

70

SPEAKING OF MONTY Python, Terry Gilliam, *Fear and Loathing*, and *Brazil*, back in 1988 I had decided to write a large, obscene, slapstick novel about environmental doomsday. It would target the Reagan-era S&L scandals and resultant financial collapses, city hall corruption, the greed and venality guiding our so-called democratic elections, planned obsolescence and conspicuous consumption, environmental collapse, yada yada. An absurd Keystone Kops / Batman movie-cartoon-action-thriller driven by ludicrous pratfalls yet dead serious about our disintegrating planet. Excuse me for flattering myself again, but think *Catch-22* meets *Das Capital* in Alice's *Wonderland*.

Its first title? *Democracy in Action*. The name of my town was Suicide City. My plans were to promote no nuance at all in the novel. Like most of American pop culture it would be in your face, up your butt, the opposite of subtle. A derisive Rodney Dangerfield on stage with the Three Stooges. "Buy this iPhone, drive that Lexus, order My Pillow right now and get a second one free!" It would be a reincarnation of the bawdy scatological genius of Chaucer, Boccaccio, Rabelais, Swift, and William Burroughs. Outta control, no money down, un-PC from guggle to zatch. A salad made from *Gulliver*, *A Modest Proposal*, *The Decameron*, *The Miller's Tale*, *Gargantua and Pantagruel*, and *Naked Lunch*. Why not?

The initial manuscript ran to 1,300 pages. Four drafts later I changed my title to *The Voice of the Butterfly*. The plot hinged on a small pod of bumbling activists organizing to defeat Proposition X, an electoral attempt to construct, with taxpayer funds, a highway "bypass" going directly *through* Suicide City (instead of around it), a project of the town's greedy S&L bankers, criminal realtors, and cutthroat developers planning to create tax-free enterprise zones on the bypass using upstreamed loans based on "future equity," zombie thrifts, rigging scandals, worthless junk bonds, "sewergate," and other psycho capitalist ventures made famous during the Reagan administration that John Kenneth Galbraith called "the costliest venture in public malfeasance and larceny of all time." Passage of Prop X, creating the non-bypass "bypass," would drive a tiny endangered butterfly, the Phistic Copper, extinct while forcing the FSLIC to go broke using countless billions of taxpayer dollars to bail out the deregulated S&Ls.

Beginning *Democracy/Butterfly* in the third person, I later switched to a first-person narrator, Chelsey McFarland. Her husband was Charley. They were the clumsy ringleaders of an inept half-dozen revolutionary misfits out of *Dumb and Dumber* or *The Gang that Couldn't Shoot Straight*. About the first draft I sent her, my Holt editor Marian Wood hissed:

> What's wrong with *Democracy in Action*? After 800-some pages, I had to conclude just about everything. It's got no center and the result is it has no real plot. The scams don't work. The motivations are glossed over. The characters are paper thin. The effect is part harangue, part maudlin commentary, and large part, tedium. This is a big monster of an oil spill, flowing every which way, meaning very little. It has no heart, only speechified good intentions. In any case, for the book to work, the deals and scams have to be made real, not just thrown in to set the mood.

She continued for three pages. Max Wylie redux. I scurried back to the drawing board. Over the next handful of years Marian Wood rejected my rewrites with the same despairing accuracy. She hated the novel like cats hate baths.

———

But you already know unreasonable persistence is my survival code. "If at first you don't succeed, fail better next time." I wanted to create a readable draft of the *Butterfly* book and *publish* it. (When I was thirteen I also wanted to fuck Marilyn Monroe!) So I continued slogging away on the *Butterfly* remodel like Sisyphus rolling a gigantic snowball across Death Valley in July. Marian Wood gave me her opinion when I submitted other drafts, though never her approval. She felt I was running in place, repeatedly defecating into my literary diapers, and we finally let go of our professional relationship after twenty-six years together. That was traumatic. I owe my career to Marian. I owe her everything. She was another remarkably valuable gift I received at age thirty-three, and it has lasted the rest of my life. Marian tolerated my idiosyncrasies and helped me to write better than I ever could have imagined.

Around the same date Marian and I broke ranks circa 1998, Perry Knowlton retired from Curtis Brown after thirty-three years as my agent. Whoever replaced him had no desire to represent my belligerent *Butterfly*.

A double whammy. I was gobsmacked.

71

BUT NOT FOR long. Ages ago I mentioned that in the mid-1960s I wrote three drafts of a novella called *The Empanada Brotherhood*, then put them in a trunk for decades. Remember? Well, in 1997, shortly after the divorce from my third wife and my haphazard rewrites of the *Butterfly*, I removed the novella copies from their trunk and, ignoring the smell of mildew, began using *Empanada* as tranquilizer-pill therapy after I'd painted myself into another corner with the elusive *Butterfly*.

Over the next ten years (1997–2007) I concocted forty drafts of the *Empanada* manuscript. Don't ask me why. All my life desperate times have called for desperate measures. I hadn't kept a New York diary, and my original novellas held scant information on which to elaborate. When in doubt, invent. However, my memories were shot. Pumping life into the story fell flat. I had no plot; characters were thin; I needed to "flesh things out."

Sound familiar?

Brainstorm! Let's make *Empanada* believable by adding early 1960s politics to the manuscript. Say, President Kennedy's assassination. Or the Juan Perón scandals infuriating my Argentine amigos. After months perusing *New York Times* microfilm, I sabotaged my book with enough political/historical research to stop a charging water buffalo—or even Robert Caro—in their tracks.

Okay, bad idea. Axing the politics, I worked harder to develop believable characters. *And* to install a plot. That process would take place between 1999 and 2001. The novel, a first-person narrative, was told by a young aspiring writer like myself at age twenty-two, the only Anglo mingling with Argentines and other Latins frequenting the kiosk. This narrator was pathologically shy. He observed, though rarely interpreted or explained. The only person on board who's never named. The Argentines call him "blondie."

It required months to create a gang of Latin strangers brought together by a small open-fronted cubicle in early 1960s Greenwich Village, where they momentarily became friends, almost family, until the booth's *dueño* closed shop and everyone dispersed. Admittedly, not much to hang a hat on. In fact, it came across like a shaggy-dog story where nothing really happens at the end.

Interchanging my work nights between *Empanada Brotherhood* and *The Voice of the Butterfly*, I was chewing gum while rubbing my stomach and patting the top of my head. There were more characters, plots and subplots, hyperbole, twists, turns, shouting, exclamation points, climaxes, and bombs exploding in *Butterfly* than in a Marvel Comics superhero digital celluloid adventure extravaganza in 3-D, Cinemascope, and Technicolor, whereas *The Empanada Brotherhood* was mostly a gentle, understated story as quiet as a mouse. Although I retained and dated all drafts of each book, eventually sending them to my archives at the University of New Mexico's library, keeping track here of my back and forth on both novels (one night the invasion of Normandy, next night a scene from *The Old Man and the Sea*) would be insane, so I'm not gonna do that.

———

Figuring I lived too far from New York to record accurately the city of long ago, I switched a few Argentine characters from *The Empanada Brotherhood* out west to my hometown of Taos, where my Anglo narrator fell in love with a young Chicana flamenco dancer. Because he was too restrained to openly court her, my "plot" became the agony of his unrequited love. For a handful more drafts I held to the first-person narrator. Until, eager to murder my project, I switched to the third person—a decision akin to marching the novel outside at dawn, placing it up against a wall, and ordering my literary execution squad to "Fire!"

The title changed from *The Empanada Brotherhood* to *Duende*. Welcome to the monkey house. At that point I gave up, switching all my ground troops to the battle with *Voice of the Butterfly*. Until, still needing to scratch the itch, I exhumed *Empanada* from its grave, retitling it *Danny and the Dancer*. I might as well have retitled it *Eat Shit, Loser*. Who can explain why all my life I've been so driven despite the paucity of my success rate?

———

Inevitably, the *Empanada* story limped back to New York, lugging with it the revivified first-person Anglo narrator and the sorrowful account of his unrequited love with a teenage Argentine flamenco dancer in Manhattan. To repeat: my anonymous narrator was naive and did not analyze or explain what he witnessed. Everything was understated. He rarely gave his opinion. I wanted the reader herself to comprehend "the underside of his iceberg," so to speak. The narrator's powerful true emotions, unrecorded in print during his observations, drove the force of my story.

Striving to write more simply than I had previously was difficult given my inclination toward adolescent humor, sarcasm, and spasms of "clever" hyperbole. *Empanada* and *Butterfly* were exact opposites. Think Steinbeck's *The Pearl* versus *Gravity's Rainbow* by Thomas Pynchon. For three more years I typed another fifteen drafts of *Empanada*, developing my characters and the plot, but this time around I had helping me a wonderful editor, Jay Schaefer, from Chronicle Books in San Francisco. Jay had enormous patience, a right-on critical eye, and a gentle manner that sternly rejected schlock without making me feel like a numbskull. Due largely to his perceptive critiques and encouragement, a thousand miles down the road, when I turned sixty-seven (in 2007), *The Empanada Brotherhood* was published by Chronicle. Though it disappeared without a trace, I care for that book more than for most of my other creations.

Scarcely any news media reviewed the novel. Kirkus slammed it per usual: "The human energy swirling around the empanada stand is full of sound and fury but signifies very little."

However, some reviews by ordinary people on the internet touched me deeply. One man said, "I loved every word and memory evoked by this authentic and beautiful story." A woman wrote, "This book reminded me so much of home. So much of home I could cry. I loved *nene*, he described those around him with love, respect and awe." A guy named James called it "an interesting and very sweet story." Reid thought it "a wonderful, warm, and very short novel." Florence touted *Empanada* as "charming, wistful, and very true in all its cultural diversity. Highly recommended." And Mayra described it as "a memoir of time lost, of friends so dear and close but lost forever, of places so clear in one's memory like they were walked just yesterday, of youth, innocence and ambition, of a world in another life and in one's dreams and made immortal by a writer with a heart."

72

DROPPING BACK TO 1998: The big question after Marian Wood and Perry Knowlton said goodbye was, What to do with my faltering career now that those two had abandoned me to the vultures? First off, I needed another agent. And, despite my total lack of networking with New York publishing for the past thirty years, I actually found one pretty quickly who thought *The Voice of the Butterfly* was "brilliant." She could sell it in a heartbeat if I simply fixed one problem.

Okay, cool. What was the problem? Well, my female narrator, Chelsey McFarland, did not even remotely have the persona, language, emotions, or resonance of a woman. Therefore, I must rewrite the novel from scratch using a male point-of-view if I wished to make it viable.

Yikes! I could have responded in a negative fashion except for one thing. Despite all the scatterbrained gibberish cluttering my melodramatic days, deep down I actually possess a useful talent. It's called "a semiprofessional instinct for survival."

This new agent was the first voice emerging from the Big Apple's publishing world *friendly* to the epic satire I'd been creating since 1988. Ten bloody years. Therefore, with barely a whimper I set to work rewriting the novel from scratch featuring a male narrator, Charley McFarland. The rewrite highlighted his ex-wife, Kelly, the true hero, a hopeless yet brilliant dipsomaniac who was the fucked-up brains of the operation leading their pitiful crew to a desperate victory at the heart of her own dismaying plummet toward suicide.

Kelly McFarland is the saddest, craziest, most intelligent, hilarious, interesting, messed-up, and tragic character I ever created. I often think of her as representing all of remarkable humanity in our headlong rush toward extinction.

———

Speaking of suicide.

At the University of New Mexico, Los Alamos branch, I was supposed to address my friend Jim Sagel's literature class. Jim and I would have dinner afterward. The class met at 5:00 p.m. on April 6, 1998. But Jim didn't arrive, and his office was locked. Eventually the school's director, Carlos Ramírez, found me and explained that he'd just learned Jim had hung himself down south in a wildlife refuge near Socorro. Instead of my planned riffing, I had five minutes to prepare a eulogy for Jim's class. When I started it most everyone began crying. Jim was a resourceful, clever, humorous, and dedicated bilingual writer, a great teacher, and only fifty when he killed himself. I had never realized he was bipolar.

That week I eulogized Jim again in Los Alamos and gave another remembrance of him in Taos. I was driven to Crested Butte, Colorado, where I delivered an absurd ramble about development, terracide, doomsday ecology, art, slapstick, and the *Voice of the Butterfly* novel I was rewriting. Returning home, I produced a forty-minute discourse for the Barbara Waters Healing Conference in Taos. Simultaneously, I published a eulogy for my dear friend Mike Kimmel in *Fly Rod & Reel* magazine. Eight months earlier he'd died at age fifty-seven of a sudden heart attack. I also wrote an introduction to a photography book on the Bisti Badlands by a guy I didn't know and had never met, and I typed another article on climbing Devisadero Trail east of Taos for *New Mexico Magazine*. Soon as that was posted, I prepared a speech, "What is to be Done?" for a June conference in Breckenridge, Colorado, followed by another talk, "My Sentimental Education," for the Rocky Mountain Association of Collegiate Registrar and Admission Officers annual meeting. Too, I was putting together a collection of my essays called *Landscapes of the Universe*. When published by the University of New Mexico Press in 2000, the title had changed to *Dancing on the Stones*.

You'd think, given Jim's suicide, that I might have slowed down to avoid killing myself. But I didn't. Tragedy strikes, yet life goes on. The world barely flinches. I said it before: everybody wants to "live fast, die young, and have a good-looking corpse."

73

THE NEXT YEAR, 1999, I slogged forward daily on *Voice of the Butterfly* revisions. For money I obtained a green light to invent an original screenplay about Che Guevara and Fidel Castro—with no interference from the producers, a studio, or a director. I had free reign to let my imagination loose, and they'd pay me twenty-five thousand dollars. I plunged in like Franco Harris of the Pittsburgh Steelers heading for a touchdown, reading Jon Lee Anderson's biography of Che, Fidel's letters from prison, Hugh Thomas on the history of Cuba, and Che's *Motorcycle Diaries*. Twenty other books and several film documentaries joined the research parade. It was great fun assessing Che and Fidel's friendship and conflicting ideologies related, in particular, to Fidel's collaboration with the Soviet Union after America had blockaded his insurgent island. Though sympathetic to their politics, I found much humor in Che's revolutionary purity compared to Fidel's long-winded socialist pragmatism. Somewhat-inebriated producers might have called my vision a "thought-provoking Marxist comic opera."

I fancied my initial script of *Che and Fidel* was as entertaining as *The Producers*, the Mel Brooks farce starring Gene Wilder and Zero Mostel about creating a deliberately unsuccessful Broadway show called *Springtime for Hitler* that becomes a huge hit raking in billions despite its hapless producers' desperate need for a total flop's tax breaks.

My producers thought otherwise. They urged me to continue, but hammered the screenplay for its anti-imperialist and communist sympathies. What had they expected from Che and Fidel? *Jonathan Livingston Seagull?* Not at all. They preferred instead a movie that presented Che as an apolitical, bearded, counter-cultural hippie icon who could sell millions of Che T-shirts, coffee mugs, and *Qué Viva!* tin lapel buttons across the world.

Sheepishly, I bowed out because "integrity" had slipped another Mickey Finn into my literary cocktail. That's the last script I ever produced. Back I returned full-time to *The Voice of the Butterfly*. No question, that overloaded, off-the-charts, hysterical bombardment of maniac capitalist annihilation was betting against "the house," and "the house" always wins. Yet occasionally, when one of the monied thugs like Steve Mnuchin, Donald Trump, Jeff Bezos, or Deutsche Bank is asleep at the wheel, "the house" forgets to correctly rig its machine, and you might even win a jackpot.

74

WHEN, FOR MY archives at the University of New Mexico in Albuquerque, I typed a computer inventory of *The Voice of the Butterfly*'s progress from 1988 until 2001, I counted eighty different compositions of the satire, many mere sections with corrections. But still.

My new agent Xeroxed thirty copies of the reimagined final product, sending them simultaneously to thirty New York editors who returned twenty-three rejections over six weeks. One- or two-sentence rejections with no additional commentary. *Yup, John Nichols is a good writer. Nope, we don't want this book.* I yelled at the agent to give me back my masterpiece before she completely ruined my reputation. She ordered me to back off because I didn't know squat about the industry. So just let her do her job and keep my filthy paws to myself.

"*Give me my fucking novel!*" I bleated louder. Okay, calm down. Whatever. Reluctantly, she sealed the manuscript in bubble wrap and trusted it to the United States Postal Service.

I figured no reader could stand my off-the-wall cartoon diatribe for five hundred pages. Hence I cut half of them and returned the battered remains to New York. No arms, no legs, and bleeding from a ruptured appendix. But my new agent soon found a publisher in San Francisco: Chronicle Books. That's when I met Jay Schaefer, and for about a year he expertly helped me "clean up" the deliberately atrocious *Butterfly* manuscript so that his publisher would spring for serious bucks to launch my insanity. 2001 is when the doomsday environmental comedy hit bookstores, and five minutes later found itself on the corner of Market Street and Geary rattling a tin cup full of pencils, begging for dimes.

Jay Schaefer not only didn't get fired, but he also insisted that he was proud to work with me. He became a valuable and supportive friend, who, as I've already explained, helped me enormously, a few years later, to solve *The Empanada Brotherhood.*

———

What's the bottom line here? *I had published the Butterfly book!* And reviews came from newspapers and magazines all over America. So I'm going to hit you with the Full Monty (again!).

A syndicated critic named Chauncey Mabe appeared in newspapers from Fredricksburg, Virginia, and Tallahassee to St. Petersburg, Florida, and Honolulu. He said, "The brains of the outfit is not Charley, who is its engine and moral compass, but his derelict wife, Kelly, a marvelous creation who is drinking herself to death because she has lost hope in the fate of the Earth." Mabe continues: "Using vulgarity to combat vulgarity would be paradoxical were it not so clearly intentional. Nichols wants to explode through our complacency by means of gross excess. Misguided, but admirable." And finally, "'The Voice of the Butterfly' is at once charming and disgusting, clever and overdone, entertaining and infuriating, and in the end, as if by sleight of hand, almost spiritually moving."

From the *Philadelphia Inquirer*: "Nichols remains as high-spirited as ever. His genius stuffs sentences with relentless brilliance, which may be fun to write, in fact may act like a morphine drip into his arm. Farce screwed this tight, each syllable clamped to the next, doubtless lends strength of purpose and keeps Nichols' faith in his project high. But for readers it calls for a fat memory for scattershot detail."

Conclusion? "I enjoyed the book only in stretches and in many of its riffs, but often had to strain to tab facts in an orderly way. Let's let Nichols review himself: 'You overload the brain you know what happens? It empties completely. The core problem of modern times: We can't evolve fast enough to incorporate all the meaningless information that clutters up our skulls.'"

Tim Aydelott plugged it in *Flagstaff Live*: "The book's epigraph poses a simple question: 'How can we save ourselves before we self-destruct?' Nichols' sarcastic venom as he depicts this mess, which sometimes becomes downright gross, may not be to every reader's liking, but universal appeal is not this writer's goal. Instead, he is genuinely interested in answering the question in his epigraph, and, by the book's wildly implausible ending, he has given us at least a couple of possible solutions: we have to hope, and we have to participate."

High Country News dubbed the novel "a hyperactive meditation on transformation in our post-modern, über-consumption world. Full of gritty slapstick zen, Nichols' morality play pulls no punches. For Nichols fans, the ensuing brawl is worth the price of admission."

Toronto Canada's *Now Weekly* was cheerful enough: "Nichols unravels a rip-roaring highly original yarn laden with hyperbole and purposefully ludicrous metaphors, dripping with sarcastic invective, all delivered via a rambling run-on style that bursts with energy."

The *Washington Post* declared, "It's hard to describe the vitriol that boils through these pages, colorful and crude. It's mostly Kelly's actions that drive Nichols's zany plot; the effect is of a malevolent Warner Brothers cartoon. Readers will have to decide for themselves if Charley is an obsessive alarmist or the heroic oracle of our planet's impending doom."

During their review, the *San Antonio Express-News* said of my *Butterfly*: "This is why one insightful critic called Nichols the 'Fellini of prose.'"

Even *Publisher's Weekly* was sort of kind. "Nichols plumbs a familiar, wacky vein in this completely over-the-top sendup of the mindless ambitions of our shallow, materialistic, upwardly mobile modern-day society. Silly, tasteless, wild, profane and often laugh-out-loud funny, this book will put off many readers, but will hit the spot for those with entrenched grudges against recent societal developments and a curmudgeonly taste in comedy."

The *San Francisco Chronicle* expressed sadness that I wrote such a shitty tome. "This [my novel] would be heartbreaking, if only Nichols' hostility to development didn't extend to that of his characters. Most of the dialogue— between friends as well as enemies—degenerates quickly into insult humor, sapping the book of much emotion besides moral outrage and an inversion layer of recurring bathos."

The *Colorado Springs Gazette* ended their piece: "Nichols' message starts off as a recurring, annoying snooze alarm before it rapidly evolves into a full-fledged siren wake-up call. Just let the lessons of protecting the planet mingle with the humor and far-fetched characters for one outrageous carnival experience. It's hard to ignore."

Booklist didn't exactly cream in its pants over *Butterfly*. "Nichols' latest novel is so over-the-top that at times it's hard to care about the characters or the cause they represent. Their enemies are nothing but cardboard characters with absurd names. Still, there are some truly humorous moments, and fans of Nichols and those who enjoy zany satire will probably be curious."

Bacon's Magazine accused me of patterning the work after Hunter S. Thompson and concluded, "So heavy is the farce laid on that when tragedy does strike the Butterfly Coalition it elicits confusion rather than sympathy.

Still, it's an amusing satire that, in its own way, manages to rebuke today's political realities."

And *The Seattle Times* thought, "Nichols creates a huge cast of deliciously flawed characters, whose slapstick antics often fly way over the top. Comedy can be an effective vehicle for a serious message, of course, and while much of the book is great fun, several events begin to stretch credibility too far. Nevertheless, many fine ideas thrive in the novel's goofy goings-on, where Suicide City resembles Lake Woebegone on peyote."

75

MY EXTENSIVE 2001 book tour for *The Voice of the Butterfly* and *An American Child Supreme* pretty much ended my life as a bit player in the commercial publishing world. You already know enough about my endless rewrites of the *Butterfly*. *American Child* is a novella-sized essay I produced for the Milkweed Editions *Credo* series published by Emilie Buchwald and edited by Scott Slovic. Milkweed described the series as offering "contemporary American writers whose work emphasizes the natural world and the human community the opportunity to discuss their essential goals, concerns, and practices."

My essay used the old title from my tormented 1960s "political" novel that I'd finally abandoned in 1971. Yet I was talking about the same subject matter thirty years later, albeit looking back with far more equanimity.

Here's the first paragraph:

> It's a mystery to me how anybody among us develops a social conscience. We are raised in a so-called democracy whose Declaration of Independence informs us that all men are created equal. But our economic system is predicated on ruthless competition that trains most everybody, including writers, to be relatively heartless predators. A majority of us blithely accepts the inequalities that define the system, even though, in our more reflective moments, we understand that our attitudes and our lifestyles are driving the system toward an environmental apocalypse increasingly ordained as all the elements of our consumptive folly merge into a single overriding catastrophe. When I say "environmental" I mean human community as well as everything else. *All* life on earth is natural, no exceptions.

That extended tour at age sixty-one convinced me that I was *begging* for another heart operation. Between reading and selling gigs in Colorado, New Mexico, Arizona, California, Oregon, Seattle, Texas, and Chicago, I also traveled for non-book-tour events to Telluride, Santa Fe, Albuquerque, Colorado Springs, Phoenix, Denver, and Aspen giving speeches on "100 Years of New Mexico Literature"; screenwriting for movies; hiking the high mountains; racial murders of Hispanics in a Rifle, Colorado, trailer park; drought in the west; "Killing Osama for Peace" (trashing the Afghan invasion); family histories in Belen, New Mexico (this one a humorous talk, half English, half Spanish, for the town's *Raices Del Río Abajo* celebration); and "My Not so Distant Doppelganger," a thirteen-page speech for the Frank Waters Centennial Celebration in Taos.

In the midst of all that I speed-typed three drafts of a memoir, castigating my recent travels: *My Midlist Writer, Rolling Thunder, All-American Book Tour*. Possibly the most pissed-off rant I ever vomited, and obviously never published. "It's just as difficult to write a bad book as it is to write a good one." Especially when you're working on it eighteen hours a day, with no sleep, in between jumping on airliners flying to various cities of the western United States.

You didn't ask, but I'll force you to holler "*Uncle!*" anyway. Here's a slightly abridged version of *Midlist Writer*'s hyperbolic chapter 1:

> What the hell am I doing at age sixty (in my condition) in a little green 1993 Dodge Shadow with 112,486 miles on the odometer speeding along at seventy-five miles per hour in bumper-to-bumper steaming hot July 12, 2001, traffic on I-25 heading north toward Fort Collins, Colorado, to give a reading and do a signing for my novel, *The Voice of the Butterfly* (Chronicle Books, 240 pages, $24.95 US), at the Jade Creek Bookstore, which is somewhere up ahead under a huge wide dark (almost black!) sky so fucking menacing at two p.m that I just know it's going to birth a tornado at any second, picking up my frail tin blob and hurling it end-over-end across the empty manicured prairie, ending any dream I might have harbored about surviving my American Midlist-Writer Rolling Thunder Summer Book Tour From Hell in one last frantic spasm of violent futility?
>
> I'm almost six weeks into my Book Tour From Hell, and not only terrified of abruptly veering sideways or being battered to a bloody pulp by a tornado, but I also find myself locked into A-fib (and unable to get out of it by executing the Valsalva maneuver), probably thanks to the stress caused by being trapped in such a speed-oriented congestive

"La comadre Sebastiana" calavera, my version of New Mexico's "Angel of Death." Courtesy of John Nichols.

traffic failure where one slightly wrong move on my part will project me instantly into the James Dean-Jayne Mansfield-Jackson Pollack-Albert Camus Auto-Death Hall of Fame, which is a place I really really don't want to be in, girlfriend.

Long ago I came to terms with my own mortality and pride myself on not being afraid of dying. At the end, however, I still don't want to be mangled in an airplane crash or a car wreck. Never, in my long and chaotic life, have I ever driven toward a more ominous imminent weather manifestation. The sheer width and height of the blackness is overwhelming. Only two hours ago I left Colorado Springs in bright sunshine and blue skies, happy as a little old lark after my "successful" signing the previous evening at the Chinook Bookstore.

Granted, being still alive is a triumph of some distinction, I believe. This distinction is lessened by the fact that after thirty-eight years of life as a professional writer I find myself out on the hustings scared shitless in bumper-to-bumper traffic like some kind of tanktown third-rate polyester Willy Loman sucking on nitro tablets headed toward a charming halfpint struggling tanktown independent bookstore that Stephen King and Tom Clancy wouldn't even wipe their asses on in some not-so-charming culture-starved cowtown out on the prairie surrounded by enough four-legged bovine methane gas machines to open an ozone hole directly overhead bigger than the state of Rhode Island.

No time for a whole lot more reflection, however, because just as I reach the first Fort Collins exit off the highway onto Harmony Road, something happens to the entire almost pitch-black panorama in front of me: It erupts. Serious shit happens. Rain and hail and thunder and lightning do not fall from the sky, they are not dumped from the sky, they detonate simultaneously from everywhere—above me, below me, beside me—like an enormous weather bomb going off, a sort of Hiroshima of hail hitting my wee automobile with what can only be described as a really NOISY chattering clattering bashing crashing sound, and a massive volume of water that could be described as the effluvium from a VERY BIG DAM bursting appears, instantly reducing visibility to zero for all of us, all the Toyotas, all the SUVs, all the 75-miles-per-hour semi trucks, and everybody hits their brakes because it's as if we are all of us all-at-once caught up in one of nature's extraordinary nervous breakdowns.

Immediately, I pull over zooming along the shoulder. I can't see the road, I can't see my fellow travelers, I can't see a fucking thing except thumb-nail-sized hail bouncing off my windshield herky-jerking my suddenly claustrophobic universe the way I imagine a body reacting to the electric chair. I am caught in a horrendous display of voltage, terrified to stop because then I will be crushed, banged into, knocked over, and collided against willy-nilly by hundreds of other vehicles I can't see that were speeding alongside of me and fore and aft when this natural disaster hit. Picture Mount St. Helens.

Then my Dodge Shadow seems to jump a curb, leaving pavement for a soft mulchy substance, so I brake and hunch over expecting to be rear-ended by a fossil-fuel-burning machine the size of a sperm whale. Cringe isn't the word for my actions. I am grinched up, raisin wrinkled, prunelipped, quivering in expectation of being violently crushed by other vehicles, or else the hail will blow out all my windows at once, pulping me to bloody gristle with shards of flying glass.

Even as these terrors occupy my thoughts, I am also thinking: I don't believe it. Here we fucking go again. Why me, God? How could I ever agree to do this again? What possessed me? After my previous touring disasters I didn't learn? Never again. I don't care if I never publish another book, I'll blow my puny brains out before I'll hit the road for mammon at this pathetic, despicable level of grubby groveling. You finally manage to publish a fucking book so they punish you, they torment you, they drive you to wrack and ruin, they humiliate you, they take every last shred of your dignity and shove it/you up the ass of every independent bookstore remaining in Western America. Then they terrorize you just for good measure, telling you that returns of your novel are running at sixty percent. And the press refuses to review your stupid book anyway, except for the one asshole who actually does review your book, in the *San Francisco Fucking Chronicle*, who calls you "a talented, politically engaged but slightly weary writer who might just rather be fishing."

You're damn fucking RIGHT I might just rather be fishing!

This is me in my old age, still playing "I Got Mine" on the guitar. You can't teach an old dog new tricks! Photo by Susan Crutchfield.

AFTERMATH

GUESS WHAT? DURING my sixties and seventies I continued writing books. Right up until today when I'm six months past my eightieth birthday and Donald Trump is no longer president. I'm like a zombie who keeps coming at you even though you never quit shooting me in the chest with your literary-critic .357 magnums or your NYTBR sawed-off 12-gauge shotguns while I'm imploring you to "STOP ME, BEFORE I KILL AGAIN!" But you can't. I'm too bloody indefatigable. And I have *no* shame.

One recent novel, *The Annual Big Arsenic Fishing Contest!*, began as a long short story I churned out while recuperating from my third hernia surgery on February 6, 2007. I screwed around with *Arsenic* for twenty-three drafts until 2009, when I abandoned it because I had other fish to fry, namely a book titled *On Top of Spoon Mountain* that began in the year 2000 as a 1,224-page monster, and, over seven years and seventy drafts, got whittled down to a twenty-four-page short story called "Spoon Mountain or Bust" that I sold to *Orion Magazine* for a thousand bucks.

Then I rewrote that short story as a "different novel" with the same original title—*On Top of Spoon Mountain*—which, thanks in large part to editor and friend Beth Hadas's wisdom and important suggestions, the University of New Mexico Press published in 2012, the same year I began reputtering with *The Annual Big Arsenic Fishing Contest!*, a novel I strong-armed the same press to finally release in 2016, but only after UNM's Elise McHugh asked me to tone down the misogyny. The cheerful designer Lila Sanchez went through the Looking Glass trying to realize my cover designs for that one, and my pal Maureen McCoy, a fellow novelist, made key observations that caused me to rewrite, this time with genuine compassion, the last forty-five pages of the story.

The following year, 2017, I published (again with UNM Press, poor dears) a coffee-table-sized photo-essay book, *My Heart Belongs to Nature*. That was after I'd organized, triaged, and computer inventoried *all* my 35 mm photo transparencies dating back fifty years. Two hundred hours I'd spent staring simultaneously at rows of slides on three light tables and tossing away two-thirds of them. An experience like chewing through granite. It cost a couple of grand to have scans done of 150 slides I chose as possibilities for the project. A hundred and eight made the cut. An eleven-thousand-word introductory essay began the book.

In order to publish a hardcover version, UNM Press demanded I mail them five thousand dollars. I caved in and sent it. The book looks great because the designer, Felicia Cedillos, knew exactly what she was doing. I am forever grateful.

Next, in 2019 I self-published with Ingram a little print-on-demand "memoir," *Goodbye, Monique*, about the four years my mom and dad spent married between 1938 and 1942 (when Monique died). I'd worked on that project for twenty years, envisioning an enormous family saga with Monique at its heart. Think *Anna Karenina*. It wound up almost novella-sized, like *Breakfast at Tiffany's*. The University of New Mexico's Center for Southwest Research claims *Goodbye, Monique* has 103 different drafts.

When people ask, I tell them, "I always begin with huge ambitions, and wind up just trying to salvage a book from the carnage."

My friend Kay Matthews, a skilled writer and political journalist who for years published a northern New Mexico investigative paper, *La Jicarita News*, helped me design the book and jumped through all the technical difficulties needed to place the book with Ingram Spark. Thanks in large part to her technical magic it came out lovely.

Some readers have told me *Goodbye, Monique* is a poignant story. I thank them for that. Perhaps I can say, "And now my life's work is done."

———

Yet at age eighty I still put my nose to a grindstone every night, seven days a week, fifty-two weeks a year. I mean, I'm still alive, what else should I do? Writing has been how I breathe. Otherwise, heart-failure pills make me impotent. Major deterioration afflicts the rest of my body. I used to be six feet tall and weigh 170 pounds. Ten years later I've lost four-and-a-half inches and tip the scales at 125 pounds. I can only defecate by using gobs of laxatives, which result in pandemic diarrhea. The more I eat the more weight I lose. A twisted spine from osteoporosis means I walk all bent over, and any minute I expect pedestrians will stop me to touch my humpback for good luck. I'll jab at them with my canes, saying, "Run along now, sonny, or you're liable to get poked in the ribs."

Three years ago, on Friday, March 4, 2018, I fell in my house and whacked the left side of my body. The pain was so great I feared a ruptured kidney, spleen, or liver, and drove to Holy Cross Hospital at 4:00 a.m. The doctor on duty ordered a CT Scan. It showed no organ damage, but he was concerned about my aortic root aneurism. I explained I'd already decided to forgo another open-heart surgery. Been there, done that. I refuse to be intubated again.

———

Alan Howard and I talk on the phone late at night. We've been dear friends since college days, sixty-one years and counting. He lived in New York City for much of his life, but now he and his wife, Rosa, occupy a cottage in Barnegat Light, New Jersey. Alan is the guy I visited in Guatemala the spring of 1964. He's the mentor who helped me become a politically aware person back in those days. Another precious gift that radically changed my life.

Now we are growing old together and talk often about the end-of-life experience. Alan's back is killing him; he suffers from painful sciatica. My heart is in advanced failure; the ejection fraction is only 30, and an aneurism is poised to kill me. I ignore it. Whatever will be, will be.

Alan and I banter about authors we've admired. Both of us are writing books. We discuss language, words, sentences, *literature.* The act of creation still fascinates us. Some day soon one or the other of us won't be here anymore. How can we make best use of the time remaining? Basically, we just keep typing.

———

Every other Monday I play guitars with five buddies in the back of the Brodsky Bookshop or at Sean Murphy and Tania Casselle's house. Or I did, anyway, before the Covid-19 lockdown began a year ago in March 2020. We started jamming fourteen years ago and have rarely missed a session. We gather from

7:00 p.m. to 11:00, give or take. Our players are Rick Smith (seventy-two), a former Louisiana documentary filmmaker who owns the bookshop; Sean Murphy (sixty-one), a novelist, literature teacher, short-story and nonfiction writer, and zen practitioner; Craig Smith (seventy-two), a biographer and mysteriously impeccable guy who's been everywhere and done everything but rarely talks about it; Morten Nilssen (seventy-one), our Norwegian representative who used to run a recording studio in Taos and who, during his younger days, spent seven years at the Findhorn Ecovillage in Scotland; and Chipper Thompson (fifty-four), an Alabama native, professional musician, raconteur, novelist, and artist who plays bass with us because on stage he usually rocks as the lead guitarist of several bands.

Our instruments are an accordion, harmonica, Dobro, a couple of mandolins, acoustic guitars, a Telecaster, Strat, banjitar, an electric bass, a Gibson Blues Hawk, my Francisco Barba flamenco guitar, and a kazoo. We call ourselves "Ricky and the Rewrites." We play Neil Young, Van Morrison, Wrinkle Neck Mules, Linda Rondstadt, Chuck Berry, the Nobel laureate Bob Dylan, Hank Thompson, the Staple Singers, Joni Mitchell, Emmy Lou Harris, Aretha. Once in a blue moon I sneak in a Spanish tune. And I often play "Johnny B. Goode," "Wine Spodee Odee," and the "San Francisco Bay Blues." I'm a boogie fan, but the other guys aren't, although sometimes they humor me. These days my voice is shot, but I used to be a contender.

I've really missed our sessions during the last year of quarantine. I've hardly picked up my guitar, and April 10, 2021, arrives tomorrow. Not only that, but during the quarantine Morton Nilssen's wife, Kate, died of pulmonary fibrosis, and he sold their house and moved to Connecticut. Suddenly he's *gone*. Then Craig Smith and his wife, Lynda, decided to relocate in Albuquerque. Adding insult to injury, Rick Smith had to close the Brodsky Bookshop, my beloved home away from home, on January 31, 2021. During a year of Covid-19 the store's income had dropped by 45 percent. I don't know if "Ricky and the Rewrites" will ever be born again.

Instead of practicing the guitar I've watched too much news about a divided and entirely dysfunctional America, demonstrations and looting, white supremacists, Blacks and Hispanics dying disproportionately from the coronavirus, and threats that Trump would cancel the November 2020 election and install himself as dictator for life. Our divisiveness has been demoralizing. He Made America Hate Again. Joe Biden and Kamala Harris won the election even though Trump legally challenged every Democrat's vote. The January 6, 2021, storming of the Capitol building suggests we might be heading toward a civil war.

Only occasionally do people visit me. Last summer we sat outside socially distanced and wore masks. Summer was so scorching from drought that we only met near twilight. Now it's too cold and too dark for that. In New Mexico, and nationally, Covid-19 is spiking horrendously. I fetch the mail each day and shop for food every two or three weeks. Otherwise I'm alone except for a few phone conversations. My heart appears to be sinking fast. I'm breathless a lot. Part of that is caused by tension from watching TV. Though I sleep eight or ten hours a day, I feel exhausted *all* the time.

Despite the former chaos of my whirlwind exploits, I've always been independent and self-sufficient, happy as a clam to inhabit my own little world without interruptions. I've lived alone since my last divorce in 1996. Usually I feel upbeat, yet lately the state of affairs on earth makes me sad.

And for the first time ever I feel lonely.

———

I'm writing this paragraph to report that Marian Wood, the editor and dear friend who more than anyone else gave me my writing career, died in early May 2020. Not a Covid victim, but rather from old age. I wrote her a long letter in December 2017 when her most successful and beloved author, the Alphabet Mystery writer, Sue Grafton, passed. Then Marian retired. I never heard back from her and was meaning to call and check on how she was coping with these difficult days. But I didn't pick up the phone in time.

———

I read all the time and figure I'll probably die sitting on the toilet with a book in my hand. The one I read just a few weeks ago was by a British economist, Ann Pettifor. *The Case for the Green New Deal*. Pettifor calls for the overthrow of a privatized global capitalist economic system based on infinite growth that is destroying humanity and the rest of life on our planet. I've underlined almost every page of her insightful book detailing how capitalism forges climate change and human poverty. No, I'm not really a four-foot-tall Stalinoid dwarf.

Yet I also admit that my life, my decisions, and the books I have described publishing (and the movies I've worked on) in this memoir have been all over the map. Nevertheless, please understand that everything Ann Pettifor says in her book I agree with totally. Quote:

> To protect earth's life support and to achieve such a radical transformation we must escape from capitalism's globalized, carbon-belching financial system—designed and engineered to issue trillions of dollars of unregulated credit to fund supposedly limitless consumption, and in turn to furiously fuel toxic emissions. It is an economic system that over a relatively short period of human history has wrecked earth's natural systems. And thanks to capitalism's dependence on a system enriched by imperialism, racism and sexism, it has bound all human societies to a form of slavery. And yet, some have made historically unprecedented capital gains from this system. They are the 1 percent.

———

So every night I read, I write, I read and write, I write and read. I go to bed at 6:00 or 7:00 a.m., setting the alarm for 2:30 p.m. My telephone rings at 3:00 a.m. "I can't sleep," the caller says, "and you're the only person I know who's awake at this hour."

Often I sit here at 4:00 a.m. staring at the mess surrounding me in my little house. Eight hundred square feet. Papers and letters and books and manuscript boxes and newspapers (*The Guardian Weekly*, which I call *Armageddon Weekly*) and magazines (the *New Yorker* and AARP's version of *People*) are stacked all over the pigpen. Clutter clutter everywhere, nor any drop to drink. It resembles my first New York crib at 438 West Broadway when I was twenty-three. File folders on top of a table, piled on counters, across desks, on the floor by the bed, or in the bathroom. Nothing but clutter. A less polite phrase would be, "I'm a scary hoarder." It's a disorderly shitheap, but I mostly know where everything is, except that nowadays I have many senior moments, brain farts, and memory losses. A big jumble of research crap defines my house. File cabinets, fold-up tables covered by a used toner kit, drum and developer containers, every available surface a shambles of books, discarded Post-Its, unanswered letters, manila file folders, tissue boxes. Uh-oh, am I repeating myself again? (My eighty-year-old nose is always running! Kleenex dispensers ahoy!)

Floor-to-ceiling bookcases dominate the kitchen, living room, bedroom, even the bathroom. I haven't vacuumed for two years. My chairs are plastic garden chairs from Ace Hardware. Films of dirt cover my heaters, my thirteen-inch TV screen. Dust bunnies are taking over. There's nothing of value in the house except my guitars. Go ahead and rob me. This computer is so old its gray beard almost touches the floor.

At midnight I eat pickled beets and bean sprouts and Swiss cheese with mayonnaise, pepper, and a glass of wine. I surf the fifty-nine-dollar Emerson TV that I probably bought in 1987. It must weigh two-hundred pounds! Or I listen to snow ticking against the stove pipes. Opening my kitchen door at 4:00 a.m., I watch snow falling on the small twisted apple tree in front of me. I hear my father saying he has to "clean off his desk" before he dies. That would never happen. These days I myself don't have much time left to "clean off my desk."

When asleep I breathe oxygen from a concentrator machine enclosed in my bathroom with the door shut so the noise doesn't keep me awake. Last winter, on February 5, 2021, at midnight, the temperature was one degree below zero and sinking. I had been really cold since winter began in November 2020. It snowed a lot. My friend Eric Flores never fails to blade the driveway and clear a path to my kitchen door. The driveway is only forty feet from a paved street, but at an uphill slant gets quickly covered by ice. Even using two canes it's a difficult trek twenty feet from my door to my vehicle. I'm terrified of slipping and crashing. Sometimes my wheels can't reach the road because of the ice.

I've always loved winter and prayed for snow, but that love affair has died. I'm afraid of winter now because it could easily kill me. However, we desperately need the snow and the moisture it provides in our mountains and fields stricken by climate change, global warming, and drought. Philosophically (and intellectually, pragmatically), therefore, this winter I prayed for snow and ice to continue. I remember how much I enjoyed snowshoeing in the high mountains from October until June every year.

P.S.: Rewriting this page on April 10, 2021, I continue self-quarantining because of the Covid-19 virus. I'm actually not afraid winter's cold will snuff me anymore. There's a new sheriff in town.

Why is this man laughing? Because he's publishing books, working on movies, and just about to catch a bunch of lunker trout fly-fishing on the Rio Grande. Photo by Michael Kamins.

EPILOGUE
A WRITING LIFE

THE PROPER THING to do now is a summing up, isn't it? I think back to my anguish in New York, about either being on the barricades or writing books. That quote I gave from Camus, and my letter from Bernard Malamud. The anti-war movement, the march on the Pentagon. Becoming a father, raising kids, moving to Taos, New Mexico. I did produce books like *Milagro*, *The Magic Journey*, and even *The Voice of the Butterfly*. I wonder if *American Blood* belongs in that line up? I certainly gave many speeches and participated in hundreds of rallies and demonstrations. I'm proud of *Missing* and most other films I worked on that "never saw the light of day" nor "appeared on the Silver Screen." No, I'm *not* proud that I type one cliché after another, glorifying in their usage. What was it with me and clichés that I always felt gave me cachet because I was thumbing my nose at the Canon, at all the Eliot Fremont-Smiths of the world and especially other high mucky-mucks at the sacred *New York Times*? I couldn't stop myself from writing *The Nirvana Blues* and *Conjugal Bliss*. Perhaps if I hadn't been such a clown I would've gotten a Medal of Freedom from Donald Trump. Me and Rush Limbaugh, together again. If that doesn't prove awards are meaningless I don't know what does.

Whatever the case, what's done is done. I have to say I had a lot of fun. I hope that's evident from the preceding pages. Any indications to the contrary, writing was never agonizing, no matter how difficult (*and* agonizing!) it was. Trying to piece together the Chinese puzzle was always a fascinating endeavor and a great way to accelerate from zero to eighty. Did I have a dramatically *interesting* existence? You tell me. Yes, I enjoyed much time outdoors, and my heart really *did* belong to nature. You can read about that in some of my other books.

During the last ten years I've grown physically weaker by each successive birthday and now find myself, nine months after my eightieth birthday, in a fragile condition. My friend Charley Reynolds used to say, "Hell ain't that far away when you're perched on the brink of eternity." We always laughed. He had it pegged.

Obviously, the main effort of my journey, its core experience, has been writing. In notebooks and letters, on typewriters, at a computer, across the backs of envelopes. That's not exactly an action-packed, exciting metier. Add that I'm obviously not the greatest author on earth. Though god knows I tried, I've never been able to "grow up." Echoes of Damon Runyon kept sabotaging my left-wing sincerity. When I was in the throes of creation, attempting to write like Bernard Malamud or Toni Morrison, I was often interrupted by inspiration from Max Shulman's *Rally Round the Flag, Boys!* and *Barefoot Boy With Cheek*, or turgid sex scenes compliments of Henry Miller and Erica Jong. I'm not a famous revolutionary, nor pregnant with philosophical wisdom. Most people connect me to *The Milagro Beanfield War*, and they didn't read the book, only saw the "inchoate" movie.

Years ago the publishing industry dubbed me a "midlist writer," a mediocre joker who never sells more than ten thousand copies. That was then—my "salad days"—and this is now. My last ten published efforts probably averaged sales of a thousand copies apiece, or less. Given my attitudes about money and fame, that makes sense to me. I thought it would be a political act *not* to become "successful" in the American definition of that word.

Understand, I'm not looking down at the ground and humbly shuffling my feet in the dust while mumbling, "Aw shucks," like a two-bit con artist trying to generate sympathy for my excruciating "lack of arrogance." If you are any kind of professional writer, at my level or above or below it, you have to be an amoral selfish narcissist or you wouldn't last five minutes on the literary hustings. My favorite quote of all time I think came from the mouth of George McGovern when he was running for president against Richard Nixon in 1972. As I recall, he said, "I'm just a humble, self-effacing, egomaniac."

And that certainly rings my chimes. Granted, I may have some different borders than many other vainglorious American loudmouths, but you can't deny the devil underneath no matter how much I try to disguise the horns and the hooves. For what it's worth, that's the real me in *Milagro*, *American Blood*, and *Voice of the Butterfly*. Don't be fooled by *My Heart Belongs to Nature* or *If Mountains Die*. If you truly double-crossed me, I wouldn't think twice about cutting out *your* heart and eating it while it was still beating.

And don't you ever suspect I was given a raw deal. The truth is I got what I wanted. And I also got what I had coming to me (double entendre intended). The irony is that despite myself I *was* sort of "successful." I earned a living writing books and movies. I own my beater house and my two beater vehicles free and clear, I have no credit card debt, and I bank a generous Social Security and Guild Pension Plan check every month. I *embody* the American dream. That's what socialism can do for all you wacko capitalist evangelicals out there if you'd only wake up and fly right.

Yet happily my work that's still in print, or wallowing obscurely on publishers' internet accounts as e-books, returns piddling royalties each year. No exaggeration. For the last three years every royalty statement from W. W. Norton has been for $0.00. Why do they enjoy so much rubbing my nose in shit?

Because they know I love it! You see, I was *born* to "lose." That's how you win the game.

I frame those royalty statements and hang them on my walls next to a poster of Che Guevara the same way I used to display publisher's rejection letters and Marian Wood's crucifixions of my novels in progress. It was so much fun to be stomped on and disemboweled, then to jump up and yell at your tormentors, "COME ON, YOU BASTARDS, GIVE ME EVERYTHING YOU'VE GOT, THAT WAS JUST MOSQUITO BITES!"

Or can you remember way back to my snarky little daughter Tania saying, "*That* didn't hurt?"

I rest my case.